THIS SIDE OF THE DREAM:

A Memoir

Also by Stefani Milan

Non Fiction:

Oh, the Stories You Will Write

Fiction:Children's:

I Liked You Much Better When You Were Outside

I Think I Like You, Cat

Fiction: Adult

The Secret of Kolney Hatch (under pen name R.A. Milan)

Kolney Hatch: Green with Envy (under pen name R. A. Milan)

THIS SIDE OF THE DREAM:

A Memoir

STEFANI MILAN

Starseed Universe Press

To request permission, contact the publisher at stefanimilanauthor@gmail.com.

Hardcover: 9780999125144
First paperback edition December 2020

Cover art by Melanie Cassie Photography
Layout by Stefani Milan

Printed by Amazon.

Genres: Coping with Grief | Personal Growth | Family and Relationships

This book is dedicated to my mother. I love you. I love you. I love you. And one day, I know I will see you again.

Table of Contents

ACKNOWLEDGMENTS ix

PREFACE xi

INTRODUCTION xiii

PART ONE: THE DESCENT

ONE: LIFE IN SURVIVAL MODE 1

TWO: IN MEDIAS RES 3

THREE: THE FIRST SIGN 6

FOUR: A LONELY DECEMBER 10

FIVE: THE FIRST DEATH SENTENCE 15

SIX: MESSAGE IN THE WATER 18

SEVEN: TWO MINDS, ONE HEART 21

EIGHT: THE SECOND DEATH SENTENCE 25

NINE: THE BABY AIN'T BROKE 28

TEN: MY FIRST BREAKDOWN 32

ELEVEN: PRAYERS TO THE AIR 34

TWELVE: BAGS OF ICE AND BACK RUBS 40

THIRTEEN: FIRE DRILLS, FIRE DRILLS, AND MORE FIRE DRILLS 42

FOURTEEN: THE SUN 44

FIFTEEN: MOM'S ADVICE 47

SIXTEEN: THE THIRD DEATH SENTENCE 50

SEVENTEEN: THE FOURTH DEATH SENTENCE 53

EIGHTEEN: HELL-BENT ON A STENT 56

NINETEEN: MOM'S BIRTHDAY 59

TWENTY: OBSERVATIONS IN THE ATRIUM 61

TWENTY-ONE: GARGOYLES AND OTHER DIMENSIONS 65

TWENTY-TWO: THE PHONE TONE FROM HELL 70

TWENTY-THREE: THE LAST TIME I WOULD EVER SEE HER 72

TWENTY-FOUR: MOM IS LISTENING 75

PART TWO: WALKING IN-BETWEEN WORLDS

ONE: THE EULOGY 81

TWO: DEATH, A NEW CONCLUSION 84

THREE: THE IN-BETWEEN WORLD 88

FOUR: DARK THOUGHTS OF MY INNER WORLD 90

FIVE: CELEBRATION OF LIFE 93

SIX: A GLASS OF ICE WATER 96

SEVEN: WONDERFUL THINGS ARE HAPPENING 99

EIGHT: THE BLUE DAWN: A POEM 102

NINE: KALEIDOSCOPE DREAM 104

TEN: CAROL AND STEVE 108

ELEVEN: A SONG TO MY MOM 111

TWELVE: ONE MORNING WHEN I WAKE 114

THIRTEEN: JUMPING IN THE RIVER 117

FOURTEEN: MUSIC FOR MY WEARY SOUL 120

FIFTEEN: ANOTHER DREAM: BE READY 122

SIXTEEN: FEAR OF THE FAMILIAR 126

SEVENTEEN: WAKING UP IN SEPTEMBER 130

EIGHTEEN: FOLLOWED BY FEAR 133

NINETEEN: REACHING A MILESTONE 136

TWENTY: THE DAY BEFORE SEDONA 138

TWENTY-ONE: SEDONA: DAY ONE 140

TWENTY-TWO: SEDONA: DAY TWO 144

TWENTY-THREE: THE FIRST VORTEX 151

TWENTY-FOUR: THE SECOND VORTEX 155

TWENTY-FIVE: KEEPING MEANING IN THE JOURNEY 162

TWENTY-SIX: THE BUTT-CRACK OF CATHEDRAL ROCK 168

TWENTY-SEVEN: THE UNFINISHED ROOM 179

TWENTY-EIGHT: A NEW BABY ARRIVES 182

TWENTY-NINE: THE FIRST MEDIUM 184

THIRTY: THE SECOND MEDIUM 191

PART THREE: BRAVING THIS NEW WORLD

ONE: CARRYING ON TRADITION 205

TWO: THE ANNUAL COOKIE EXCHANGE 207

THREE: ROSANNA ON THE RADIO 210

FOUR: DROWN OR SWIM 212

FIVE: WELCOME TO EARTH SCHOOL 217

SIX: A NEW VIEW ON DOCTORS... 220

SEVEN: SHIFTING TIDES IN MARCH 226

EIGHT: THE BEST DREAM I EVER HAD 228

NINE: ONE YEAR ANNIVERSARY... 231

TEN: MAY IN MUSIC CITY 234

ELEVEN: THOUGHTS IN A DRESSING ROOM 238

TWELVE: THE THORNY PATH 240

THIRTEEN: ON THE LAST DAY IN MAY 2019......................... 244

FOURTEEN: ONE MONTH UNTIL THE WEDDING 248

FIFTEEN: TWO CATS AND A FLY 252

SIXTEEN: A SIGN FROM CATHERINE, DAISY, AND MOM 255

SEVENTEEN: TIM MCGRAW ON THE RADIO......................... 259

EIGHTEEN: THE DEATH OF A DREAM.................................. 263

NINETEEN: GRIEF IF MIGHTY FLIGHTY 266

TWENTY: THE WEDDING 269

PART FOUR: THIS SIDE OF THE DREAM

ONE: INSIGHTS FROM ITALY 275

TWO: A WALK IN THE CITY 278

THREE: THE CHURCH OF SANTA CROCE 284

FOUR: THE LAST NIGHT IN FLORENCE................................. 287

FIVE: THE AMALFI COAST 294

SIX: THERE'S MAGIC IN RAVELLO 298

SEVEN: SORRENTO 301

EIGHT: JUST ONE NIGHT IN DUBLIN 305

NINE: THE CROSSROADS OF LIFE 308

TEN: RELEASING TRAPPED EMOTIONS................................ 312

ELEVEN: THE POWER OF MEDITATION 315

TWELVE: TWO STEPS FORWARD, THREE STEPS BACK............. 318

THIRTEEN: A MESSAGE FOR A NEW YEAR 321

FOURTEEN: A QUICK GETAWAY.. 325

FIFTEEN: FEAR, THE REAL DEVIL 329

SIXTEEN: THE FLOWER SHOW 333

SEVENTEEN: LIFE IN QUARANTINE 335

EIGHTEEN: ON A QUEST TO FIND MOM 339

Nineteen: Like Water Flows, Life Changes 344
Twenty: Reflections on Time 346
Twenty-One: Is Life Just a Dream? 349

ADVICE FROM THE HEART 353

SYMBOLISM OF DRAGONFLIES 359

REFERENCES 363

ABOUT THE AUTHOR 365

Acknowledgments

I'd like to acknowledge the many people who have been on this journey with me through the good times and the bad. So many people helped in the making of this book.

First, thank you to my mom in Heaven. My mother will always be my number one supporter. Without her, truly, this book would not have come to be. She is the one who always encouraged me to follow my dreams, and for that I give her the biggest thanks. But most of all, I thank her for giving me life and for being my best friend in this life.

To my husband, Jon, thank you for standing by my side in the darkest of times and for encouraging me to keep going when I didn't think I could. Thank you for sharing this life with me. I love you with all my heart.

Dad, thank you for always supporting my dreams, and when I almost gave up writing, pushing me to continue with this book.

Thank you to my brother, Raymond, and to my sister-in-law, Lauren, for holding my mother's hand as she took her last breaths. As you learned from the medium, mom was so thankful to you both for being with her.

To my friend, Carol Harkavy, author of *Rosie and Me: A Memoir*, thank you for being my guardian angel, my wisdom keeper, and my writing buddy. Thank you for being the first to edit this book. You continue to stay by my side, encouraging me to keep going. And to Steve Harkavy, thank you for always giving wise advice.

To Anna Marie Hrivnak, how can I thank you? Not only were you an amazing friend to my mother, but you are to me also. You are an incredible light in my life and so many other people's lives. I wish you nothing but the very best, and I can't thank you enough.

I'd like to thank my friends and family who kept me sane during my darkest moments: Karina Verrecchio, Lindsey Wells, Theresa Hrivnak, Nicole Goncalves, and Melanie Cudnik.

Debi Nass, thank you for sharing in the writing journey with me. Our writing meetings have kept me focused on completing this work, and many of my others.

Thank you to Diana Vespe for reading this work and helping me continue working with it. Thank you for always checking in on me to make sure I was okay.

And to my original Music Biz family, Evelyn, Patty, Jim D., Jim H., Nick, Terry, Nicole, and the rest of the team for your patience and support during those dark times.

Preface

No one prepares you for how grieving affects you well after the actual loss of someone. No one prepares you for the feelings of wanting to run away and escape your life, even if it's the most perfect life you could ever have imagined.

No one prepares you for the physical symptoms that creep up on you just about two years after a loss, sometimes before, or for the dip that your immune system takes and unexplained pains where emotional trauma stores in your body.

No one prepares you for wanting to suddenly pack your things and move to an island or some exotic destination where you can be alone and away from all the pain.

While everyone else in your life has returned back to a normal life, yours has been shattered, and you cannot understand why no one else is feeling as broken as you are. Some people cannot understand how after your loss that you'd prefer to live a life of adventure instead of the same old familiar life because the familiar life is causing you the most anxiety you never knew you could experience.

No one prepares you for the desperate need to escape, which is fueled by relentless anxiety.

No one prepares you for changing your mind about wanting to have children, or about getting married, or about living with one person for the rest of your life.

No one prepares you for the apathy you feel for the things you used to love to do and for contemplating giving up your dreams.

No one prepares you for the neediness you may feel, the constant need to communicate what's on your mind, or for the times you shut everyone out because they simply cannot understand how you feel.

No one prepares you for what it's like to suddenly be on a completely different mental and emotional page as your partner, when previously you were on the same page.

But those are the things that can come along with grief, maybe not in the same exact way for everyone, but in some form. And if you are wise, if you've spent a lot of your time studying higher consciousness and have a lot of awareness, then you know that your anxiety, stress, and trapped emotions can destroy you if you let them. You realize you don't have to run away from your life and the people in it, but you do have to face your new reality and *accept* it. You understand that sometimes the only thing you can do to get by is let anxiety wash over you, release trapped anger and pain, and make a choice to find inner joy and happiness.

This book is for all the people who want to understand what the process of rebuilding oneself after tragedy is like. It's for all the people who have suffered in some way and who are trying to put the pieces of their lives back together. It's for all those who want to run away from their current situations because they feel hopeless. It is for everyone because it is everyone's story at some point or another.

-Stefani

Introduction

I grew up in a loving family in the suburbs of Cherry Hill, New Jersey, in a neighborhood full of manicured lawns and tall Oak trees that shaded smooth, black-paved streets. In the summer, the smell of honey-suckles overpowered a quaint park tucked at the back of the neighborhood—a haven for children, away from any cars or busy roads.

I was a lucky child—in fact, I have no complaints. My father did quite well for himself and our family. He used to tell us stories about how, when he was young growing up in South Camden, there were times when money was scarce. His father was a carpenter. Along with being a feast and famine trade, the job did not pay well. One time my grandmother went to a deli and only had enough money for one hotdog. She split it three ways for her, my dad, and my aunt. Despite their money issues, he always talked about how his parents raised his sister and him with a lot of love, which was most important.

When he was eighteen, he started working in a warehouse for a new music company called Warner, Elektra, Atlantic. For the next seventeen years, W.E.A promoted him to several positions within the company. He established his way to becoming the Northeast Regional VP of Sales and was a key music executive for fifteen years.

On the other hand, my mother came from wealthier surroundings, not rich, per se, but comfortable. Her grandfather's family owned the South Jersey Bottling Company, which expanded to Atlantic City Bottling Company before the family sold it in 1981. I was the product of the union of these two families, raised in middle-class wealth, but with a humbleness that my father reminded me of when I received anything new as a child.

My mother was an accounting music business executive (she met my dad in the business) who gave that life up to be a stay-at-home mother. She was the only accountant I knew who was fiercely creative but also very organized. She handled being a stay at home mom like a CEO—always the PTA mother, always on time, always fighting for what was right. She never let people walk all over her and stood up for her children's education, like no other parent.

She was hard on me as a child, especially when it came to school. I resented her for many years until I understood the real reason why she pushed me so hard. She didn't want me to be the underdog. She knew how well I could do, and she wanted me to show the world my capabilities. She wanted me to prove to everyone else that girls could do anything. Girls could rise to the top. She was a strong, passionate Aries, but I was a stubborn Taurus, a bull who did my own thing when I wanted. So, in high school, I rebelled against her. I stopped getting my straight A's and went to a mostly A, B, and occasional C student. It wasn't because I couldn't do the work. I absolutely could. I just didn't *want* to.

It was only in college that I realized I loved learning and school. I graduated with high honors and a prestigious English Department Award. I had thrived on every challenge and soaked up every learning opportunity. And I haven't stopped reading, studying, and learning since.

I was one of those fledglings that never quite left the nest. Looking back on it, I know exactly why. In my twenties, my mother and I became best friends. I suspect we always were, but sometimes our age difference made it hard to enjoy the same interests. You know, when I was playing with barbies, I'm pretty sure my mother didn't want to. And even though we hung out every day in my teens, I'm pretty sure she wasn't into NSYNC like I was. But as I grew older, we started to enjoy our time together. On our days off from work, we would go on lunch dates, walk at the park, take yoga classes, and shop for new clothes. Other times we went on road trips (to Virginia, South Carolina, or Florida), museum trips, or took a ride to the Jersey shore to get a nice summer tan and grab a slice of pizza from the Ocean City boardwalk. We were fiercely loyal as friends, the bull and the ram, and even if we butted heads or argued, five minutes later, we were laughing again.

Our adventures alone could fill an entire book.

I spent countless hours seeking her advice about relationships, to which she would always reply, "You don't need anyone to be happy." When I would ask her about my jobs and what to do, she would never answer, "You need to make money," but instead would say, "You need to follow your dreams."

I pursued an acting career, and my mother would drive to New York with me for an audition or a shoot, no matter how small. She was always eager to help me pursue anything artistic. When I first started writing, she didn't look at me with a quizzical look like my other family members did—one eyebrow cocked and a "Are you sure you want to throw your life away?" look. Instead, she pushed me to write. She helped me research elements for my book, read every page, and gave me constructive criticism.

She could visualize details better than anyone I knew and express the picture she saw in her mind. My mother was an artist herself, extraordinary in drawing and painting, and exceptionally gifted in design. I remember thinking she was some kind of high priestess or white Goddess—the embodiment of feminine creativity.

Her insecurities to pursue her own artistic career are what I believe made her so encouraging of my brother and me. When my brother said he wanted to be a musician, she let him practice for hours on end at our house with his band. When other mothers would complain of noise and be in bed by eight or complain to their girlfriends that their son needed a "real job," my mother was up late, listening to my brother play and working on whatever creative project she was in the middle of at the moment.

For my mom, when "mom-duty" ended, she thought she would be able to pursue her own talents. But financial hardship did not skip our house. It nearly demolished our family. Our family's financial troubles weighed heavily on all our minds, and our relationships with each other broke down piece by piece.

To get out of our hopelessness, my mother and I studied many books about enlightenment and obtaining higher consciousness. In addition, my mother was fascinated by gemstones—their beauty and their ability to interact with our energy fields. She had also been a lover of butterflies her entire life and brought them into everything she did (I still have butterflies she preserved as a child).

After two years of studying almost every day and changing our mindsets, we started to pull ourselves out of the wreckage of our financial decline. We tried every day to transform the negativity avalanche that had been hurtling down the mountainside of our lives. I returned the encouragement my mother gave me to pursue my artistic talents by helping her set up a gemstone jewelry business called *Rosanna Gemstone Creations*. I worked with her closely over the years. She loved helping people through her gemstone creations. My mother was never in it for the money—possibly to her detriment. She was the type of person who, when she knew you needed help, she would give you the stone or bracelet you needed.

She also wanted peace in her mind. For some reason, she didn't have it. But she tried to find it, and we worked on bettering ourselves every day. To do this, we spent a lot of time in nature. Because of our studies, our walks at the park transformed from "getting in shape" to spending time breathing fresh air, calming the mind, and taking in the beautiful scenery around us. My mother loved the beach because of all the elements coming together in one place: the sand as the earth, the breeze as the air, the ocean as the water, and the heat of the sun as fire.

"The beach grounds me. It centers me. I am at complete peace when I'm there," is what my mom would say to me or anyone who asked her.

Our annual "girls' retreat trips" were always to the beach. It was a way for us to ground and center ourselves before returning to the normalcies of life. My mother and I spent time with friends who loved us, and we traveled everywhere as a team: to my friends' or her friends' houses, to dinners, on our trips, everywhere.

Then, one day, she got sick. And just a few months later, she was dead. I was devastated, to say the least. My worst fear had happened to me. I not only lost my mother, whom I would always need, but I lost my best friend.

Upon reading this book's title, one might think it's merely about my mother's death. But it isn't. *This Side of the Dream* is a personal growth book detailing the choices I had to make following my mother's death. It is the detailed story of my healing path to peace.

What happens when a story wants to be told so badly, it nags at you every day? You *must* let it out; you *must* write it. I knew that writing this book would be difficult. We humans have the extraordinary capability of not only accessing our memories but for the emotionally charged ones, reliving them through every sense as though they were happening to us all over again. What do I mean by this? Think of your most powerfully charged memory: the first time you made love, the heartbreak that stills stings, the friend who never spoke to you again, the time you won the lottery (lucky you), the day you welcomed your first child into the world, the time you got a scary diagnosis or the time you lost your friend, parent, sibling or child. If you think about that event, you may suddenly find yourself immersed in the experience as though it's happening all over again. You remember the sounds (what was on the television when it happened); the tastes (you may remember that delicious piece of tiramisu you were eating); the smells (antiseptic); or the sights (dim lighting in a hospital room).

The fact that our brains can access these memories and be all-consumed in them once more is as miraculous as it is dangerous. It is miraculous because it's almost like a superpower to time travel to another time that isn't happening at the moment but that we are experiencing as though it is. It is dangerous for the same reasons. Reliving an unpleasant trauma or experience can be bad for us psychologically and physically. And it's one of the reasons why I've had such a difficult time writing this book. You see, when I found out my mother was ill, I decided to keep a live journal of her journey. I mostly did it because I thought she would recover—I thought I would be sharing her incredible success story with the world.

I honestly did not believe that she would die, suffering tremendously from pancreatic cancer.

The detailed journals I kept are the real-time thoughts of a desperate daughter. I try my best to be as descriptive as possible. Sometimes in my journals, I may seem irrational, or one can feel the rage brimming inside me. My thoughts change about different subjects like doctors and God. Dreams are an essential part of the healing process for me, and so is art.

In those journals, I reveal all my raw emotions of my experience watching my mother die. I knew I had to share this raw emotion with the world, but I was terrified of revisiting these memories. Every time I did, I was in that memory again. I found myself at a crossroads—I had to share my story, but how would I share my story with the world without being stuck in another time in my life, one I wanted to forget?

Eventually, I could no longer put off the call to share my story, which burned like a wildfire in my bones. This experience was mine. No one else could tell this story but me. And yet, there was a whole mess of people out there who would probably read my words and say, "Yes, I know that feeling. I've been in that place too." Or, "I am there right now."

I had many troublesome thoughts in writing this book; namely, why would someone even want to read it? Eventually, I realized that millions of other people had experienced similar suffering like me, and long after this book would be published, millions more would suffer too. I reasoned that if this book reached even one struggling person stuck in the in-between that often follows tragedy, it was worth writing.

What's Inside this book?

Part One focuses on my tragic experience of losing my mother. It is a raw, vulnerable piece of me that shows how humans sometimes hold on to hope until the very last second. It is the most moving part of this book as I try to hold on to a life that changes too rapidly for me to process. At the same time, I am walking in the death realms with my mother, and I experience incredible insights and messages from a higher plane of existence.

Part Two focuses on the time after my mother's death. In the "in-between," I am partly in my old life and partly in my new one, trying to find my footing. I experience vivid, life-altering dreams, signs from my mother, and I consult with mediums and travel to Sedona in a desperate attempt to connect to my mom on the other side.

In **Part Three**, I begin to plant a firm foot in the new world I am in, using dreams and creativity to guide me on my journey. I realize how our adversities present us with a choice to rise to our highest potential in life.

Part Four is partly introspective, focusing on what I have learned on my journey so far. It also incorporates my travels to Italy as well as other eye-opening experiences.

We all cope with tragedies differently. I want people to know that if they are going through even remotely similar pain to what I went through, there is a way out of that pain. They can overcome.

Part One
The Descent

"The only way to escape the abyss is to look at it, gauge it, sound it out and descend into it".

Cesare Pavese

one

March 2018

Imagine crouching in a luscious green jungle and leaning against a tree with a deadly poisonous spider climbing toward you. Despite the imminent threat from above, you dare not move. A hungry male lion, who is slowly walking around just feet from where you are, may have noticed you were wandering through the jungle. Your heart is pounding; panic courses through you. What is your next move? What is the lion's next step? Or the spider's? You can't think straight—but you force every bit of concentration into what you're doing. Are you going to die in this jungle? Or is there a way out?

The scenario above is an example of survival mode. And survival mode is the place I find myself in every day. It's a place I imagine our earliest ancestors felt each time they went on a hunt or a walk. It's a feeling anyone undergoing any trauma, intense fear, or tragedy has felt—a familiar, universal feeling in humans and animals, which triggers our fight or flight response.

When an imminent threat triggers our sympathetic nervous system and turns on chemical processes in our bodies, we have to decide to flee or fight.

This is me. I don't know where to turn next. I don't know whether to flee or fight. I cannot shut my mind off from fear. Everyone is a threat to me. Everything is a danger.

two

IN MEDIAS RES...

Sometime in March 2018

I imagine everyone thinks about writing a book like this one. At least thinks about it, anyway, and then quickly dismisses it. To write a book like this one, the worst has to happen to you. I don't think writing any book is worth that-- not even to become a best-seller. I just want to be clear on that.

It is the worst of times, the absolute worst of times, as in, it couldn't get any worse of times. I imagine Dickens shaking his head from the heavens saying, "What has the world come to?" At least *his* worst of times was also the best. Not mine. Not now. Sinatra would say, "that's life," but I haven't even made it to April, and my "life" car has violently steered off course and off a metaphorical cliff. That has been happening since December. There is no riding high, just a bunch of twists and turns out of my control. I am not even driving the car anymore. I am bouncing around in the backseat hoping the car will hit a tree and just fucking stop already.

I am sitting on the beige rug of my mother's sitting room. Cold, winter sunlight pours through the windows and reflects off the peach-colored walls. My back hurts from hunching over as I type, but I want to be close to my mother.

My mother coughs.

Is it the cancer? Or is it the pulmonary embolisms? Or, is it just that she hasn't been walking around?

Five minutes later, she's crying. I get up and sit with her.

"I'm so sad. I'm so, so sad," she says.

"Me too." Now, I'm crying. We cry together. I was doing a lot of that these days. Every day, my mom and I sit and cry together.

I sit next to her and hug her tight. I could do that all day.

My mom, my best friend, who spent most of her life reading *Prevention* magazines, eating organically, never smoking, never drinking, never abusing her body in any capacity, is dying of pancreatic cancer. The news hit me like an unexpected flash of lightning—one of those bright strikes that lights up an entire room and sizzles after and is almost indefinitely followed by an ear-deafening boom. Immediately, I was thrown into survival mode. And now, my mom and I are at war.

Maybe I am in denial, but I find it hard to believe, as does everyone else. Not *my* mom. She has always been strong: physically, mentally, and emotionally. Now I am watching her crumble in front of my eyes, like a building being demolished floor by floor, but I refuse to believe defeat will be her fate.

Anyway, this book can go two ways.
She lives, or she dies.

three

Thanksgiving 2017 is fantastic. My mom and I have spent the last two months decorating the house and preparing for our favorite event of the year. My mom has prepared this year, and for the last thirty-four years that I know of, the very best Thanksgiving parties. This year is just as extravagant, and one of the best.

That morning I wake to smell the turkey is in the oven. Downstairs in the family room, two eight-foot tables are dressed with gold-vined table cloths, my mom's fine china, and gold silverware. I shower as quickly as I can and am downstairs shortly after (with my hair wrapped in a towel) to help my mom. I peel potatoes, fill deviled eggs with sweet relish egg filling, and turn on some festive holiday music (Sounds of the Seasons to be exact).

Thanksgiving in our house is zero percent about the historical bloodbath and all about the Holiday season. It's our precursor celebration to Christmas. Every year we buy little Christmas gifts for each guest, start up the Christmas music, and have the house fully decorated with Christmas décor. This tradition may seem strange to other people, but to us, it's a small slice of Heaven—like the cocktail hour before a wedding.

On this day, my mother and I get ready and take our annual pictures by the dining room table, which is adorned with angels, cherubs, and greenery. My mother looks beautiful as always; her blonde hair is curled, and she's dressed in a beautiful black short-sleeved shirt with pretty rhinestones on it.

All our guests eagerly arrive at two in the afternoon; my grandparents, aunt, uncle, cousins, brother, and sister-in-law.

We eat our appetizer course (always the hit of the party) and then begin on our first course, my mother's amazing home-made cavatelli and gravy. She and I always take one day, a week or so before Thanksgiving, and make homemade cavatelli and Italian Gravy (it's gravy, not sauce in our house). Then we flash-freeze this "Thanksgiving gravy," which is known to anyone who eats it as "liquid gold."

This year, at around four, when the turkey is ready to be carved, my mother comes to me.

"I picked up the turkey and pulled my back out," she says.

"Then take it easy, mom," I say. "You shouldn't be doing this all yourself anyway. Just let me know what you need help with, and I'll do it."

"Everyone wants to come over," my brother interrupts. "Is it okay?"

He's referring to his friends who used to come over after our big Thanksgiving meal for the Thanksgiving after-party. We had not had one in years, but this year everyone is insistent on coming.

"Yes," my mom says.

I help my mom with the last course, more than usual.

We take our annual group photo and then eat yet another course of yummy mashed and sweet potatoes, peas, corn, Brussel sprouts, cranberry sauce, stuffing, and turkey.

By the time my brother's friends arrive, we are full—as in, better put your sweats on because those jeans are going to pop, full. For the first time in years, the house is so packed with people; it's like a mini-wedding. As sappy as it sounds, I can't help but have a tear in my eye. Having my brother's friends here, plus all of my mother's side of the family, reminds me of my childhood.

One of my brother's friends brings his new baby. His wife, also a friend, asks my mom if she wants to hold him.

"I would, but my back hurts. I don't even think I can hold the baby."

This statement strikes me as odd. Never in my life has my mother been in pain enough that she wouldn't put it aside to hold a baby.

Her statement makes me wonder how much pain she is actually in. But I quickly forget about it because the night is so perfect and lovely.

When the last guest is gone, my mom and I sit on the couch, exhausted but extremely gratified.

"Another one for the books," she says.

"It was amazing."

"I just wish my back felt better."

"I know. But hey, you did a lot. So, just rest up now. You have the weekend."

"Yeah, I'm sure it'll feel better in a day or so. Now, let's load the pictures."

As we do every year, my mom and I upload all the photos of our favorite "holiday" onto the computer and put them into a folder. When we're finished, we go to sleep, well-fed, happy, and full of love.

four

A LONELY DECEMBER

Every year my mother and I go Christmas shopping. We have so much fun pal-ing around town buying gifts for everyone. This year, she doesn't want to go. It bothers me.

"Why?"

"I just don't feel up to it," she says.

"Can't you just go out for a little?"

"I really can't. I'm sorry."

I feel like my mother is pulling away from me. Our traditions are so much fun; it bothers me when she says she doesn't want to go. I go by myself, but I'm not happy—in fact, I'm miserable the whole time.

"Don't worry," my mom replies. "Once this back heals, I promise we'll go shopping."

On a trip to Cancun with my boyfriend just a few days before Christmas, I am unsettled. Jon and I are in the descent of the plane when the piercing pain first hits my ear. I feel like my eardrum is going to burst. "Jon, something's wrong."

"What is it?" He asks.

"My ear. It hurts so bad. It hurts."

I lean my head on his shoulder as tears stream down my cheeks. Now I'm paranoid that my eardrum is going to burst. My head feels like it's going to explode. My heart starts to race, and the last eleven minutes of the flight go by painfully slow. Once we get off the plane, I am disoriented.

"Are you okay?" Jon asks.

I have to be okay. We are in Mexico, and I don't want to go to a hospital. I'm a little dizzy, but I shake it off.

"I'm fine," I reply.

Jon and I are in Cancun for three days, and the entire trip is upsetting to me. My ear is blocked. It feels like there's water in it. At 2:00 am on the first night we are there, I wake up, shivering.

"Jon," I shake him. "Jon."

I start to cry.

Jon rolls over, half asleep.

"What's wrong?"

"My stomach is sick," I cry. "I think the food made me sick."

"You barely ate," he says. He knows I'm afraid of experiencing Montezuma's Revenge. "And anything you did eat, I ate. You're fine."

But for some reason, even though I know he's right, I still don't feel well—sweat forms on my brow, my stomach gurgles.

"I'm really afraid, Jon."

"Of what?"

"I don't know."

"Just try to get some rest," he says. "We're on vacation."

"I want to go home," I start to cry. "I just want to go home."

Now Jon sits up.

"You're okay," he says. "I promise."

But I'm not okay. For some reason, I feel strange. My stomach is sick, and my ear is blocked. I run to the bathroom and hug the porcelain god. I'm sick.

I cry as I sit on the bathroom floor.

When I finally come back to bed, Jon has fallen back asleep. I'm still shivering. Something's wrong, but I just can't put my finger on it.

I finally fall asleep at 4:30 a.m. When I wake the next morning, I feel much better, but my ear is still blocked.

The next night, I don't sleep either. Instead, I have an intense fear of a tsunami crashing on the shore and killing me. I stare at the ocean from my hotel bed all night. I stay awake for many hours.

In the morning, I call my mom.

We chat for a while, and my mom tells me everything is going to be okay.

"There are no tsunamis coming to Cancun," she laughs. "I promise." Talking to her makes me feel a little better.

"Next year, you and daddy have to come. You'd love it here. It'll just be relaxing for everyone."

"Absolutely. I'd like to go to Florida in January. Maybe after this stupid back heals, we'll go."

"I am all for it."

On Christmas Eve, we always go to my aunt's house. My mom doesn't want to go. She's been sick with a cold for a couple of weeks, and in addition to that, her back still hurts.

"You have to go," I pressure her. "What are you going to do? Sit home by yourself on Christmas Eve? You're going to be in pain whether you go or not."

It's something she's said to me a million times—something that has always pushed me to do things I didn't want to do.

My mom finally agrees. I take her to Christmas Eve dinner. She's a little upset, but she eats and has a good time.

On Christmas Day, I spend it with my mom. She couldn't go Christmas shopping with me, but she did take a day to get me presents. She tells me she pushed herself to go out because she really wanted to get me a couple of important gifts. One was a set of hair curlers. Later that day, we go to my other aunt's house. My mom doesn't go to this. I tell everyone her back is still hurting, but she wishes she could be here. My aunt sends my mom home a ton of food—eggplant parmesan, ravioli, meatballs, and salad.

In early January, at the start of 2018, I sit down to write. I'm working on a science fiction novel. I wake up on a cold, Jersey-gray winter morning and sit at my computer. Immediately, I'm dizzy, very dizzy. But it's so much more than that. Suddenly, I have this thought. I feel like I'm falling through realities. It sounds weird, even to me, but it's the best I can describe how I'm feeling.

"It feels likes each day, my reality grows darker. I don't know how to explain it except to say it's like there are all these possibilities, and I'm falling to the very bottom of them."

I start to get anxious and cry. My mom hugs me.

"Aww, why don't you lie down? Maybe you're just not recovered from the trip."

"I don't feel right," I say. I take a nap. The feeling doesn't subside. It's stuck with me. I'm falling, always falling through these realities. I feel impending doom. The feeling sticks with me for weeks.

five

THE FIRST DEATH SENTENCE

January 27th, 2018.

Jon and I return home from the movies. *Jumanji* is a funny movie. I'm wearing a white sweater and jeans, and my hair is long and dark. Jon and I spend some time making funny Snapchat videos. When I get home, I step out of the car on a cold, January night, and my dad is outside, smoking a cigarette.

"I'm taking mom over to the hospital."

"What? Why?"

"She wants to go. She doesn't feel right."

"Okay."

I run into the house and up the stairs to my mom.

She is there in her bedroom.

"Are you okay?"

"I don't know. Something's wrong."

"Okay, well, let's go to the hospital. We'll see if they can help you."

The drive over, I am a wreck. My heart is racing, and I find it difficult to breathe. Whatever is happening, it doesn't feel right.

I sit with my mom in the ER waiting room, holding her hand.

"I'm so scared," she says to me.

"It's okay. I'm sure whatever it is, the doctors can fix it."

"What if it's something really bad?"

"Mom, it's fine. There's nothing that could be that bad. You're going to be okay. You're a healthy person. You always have been."

"But this isn't right."

"I know. We'll figure it out. I'm right here with you. I'm not leaving your side, so it's fine."

I try to stay strong for my mother, but my gut-wrenching uneasiness overwhelms me.

A few hours later, when my mom is in a hospital bed, a doctor enters the room.

"We took a scan and see you have blood clots in your legs and pulmonary embolisms. But we're more concerned about the lesions on your liver and pancreas."

"What?"

My mom is horrified.

None of us know what this means. None of us understand.

My mother's psyche heads into a downward spiral. She reminds me of Professor Trelawney in Harry Potter during one of her intense visions. My mom grips my hands, her eyes wide with fear.

"Stef, I'm going to die. I'm going to die." She's hysterically upset. "I'm not going to be here for your wedding or to see your children."

The doctors give my mom drugs to calm her down. I'm freaking out, unable to contain myself. Nobody said anything about death. Nobody said anything about dying. I run outside of the hospital, crying so hard I can't breathe.

There's a moment where I'm sitting on the cold pavement, just outside the ER, watching cars ride by. I'm in my hometown, a place I've always known, and I feel like I don't know where I am or what this life is. I sit there, crying my eyes out alone, and I just know from this moment, our lives will never be the same.

six

MESSAGE IN THE WATER

January 27, 2018- Later that Night

This cannot be my life. This cannot be happening. This cannot be happening. It's wrong. It's wrong!

I'm crying out loud, screaming out loud to no one.

The house is dark, empty. I can feel a cloud of dark energy shrouding over it. It feels thick and heavy. I just want to escape, but I can't. I have to be strong for my mother.

My mother has never been in a hospital, and here she is staying the night.

I want her home. I need her home. I don't want her there.

I am emotionally drained, tired, sad, confused—every emotion I can think of. I am restless, uncentered, angry, fearful.

This isn't real, I think. *It can't be. It's not real.*

What can I do? I think. What can I do to help my mom, to get her out of this mess, to help myself right now?

Can I meditate?

My body aches all over. I am shaking uncontrollably. I need to feel at peace. Please, let me feel some peace.

The usual vibrant bright lights in the warm pink bathroom are dark, dull, and dreary. All I feel is that dark energy, which is hard to describe except that it feels like being immersed in a gray cloud.

I decide I'm going to sit in a warm bath. Our bath is also a jacuzzi, and I decide it might help me relax. I pray while I sat in the warm bubbly water. I pray and pray and pray.

Please, heal my mom. Please.

I beg, as much as a person can beg, amidst a stream of tears.

I've read *A Course in Miracles,* and now I keep it by my side. Some of the pages crinkle as my damp fingertips thumb through them. The book talks about prayer, how it must be genuine, and from the heart.

I love my mom so much. I would do anything to see her well. I would sacrifice anything, even myself. I bare my soul to God, pleading for help. At first, I cry, beg, and plead, but eventually, I stop. My mind is quiet. I am in the bubbling jacuzzi, eyes closed, meditating.

"Stef!"

I jump out of the jacuzzi and run to the door.

My mother's voice, as clear as day, calls to me. Is she home? Could it be it is all a mistake, and they released her? My heart flutters with hope and excitement. If I am delusional, if I imagined the whole ordeal, I will gladly admit myself to the nuthouse if only to find it isn't real.

I hop out of the jacuzzi, quickly wrap a towel around me and run to the bathroom door.

I fling open the door to see an empty room.

"Mom?" I call.

19

I heard her clear as day. But she isn't here. She is still in the hospital. My heart thumps out of my chest. But I had heard her so clearly. So, so clearly. Now, a new worry fills me.

What if...

"No!"

I cast the idea out of my mind like a wizard casting a powerful spell on some foe, but it creeps back in slowly. What if the voice I heard was my mom's spirit? What if my mom's spirit already crossed over and was trying to connect with me at this moment, because right now I'm the most open, the most vulnerable?

"No!" I yell out loud. My mother is going to make it. She's not going to die.

seven

TWO MINDS, ONE HEART

The next day, I arrive at the hospital early, and I sit with her. My mother's heart rate, blood pressure, and all her other levels are near perfect. Even the nurses are whispering, "We just don't understand it."

"But my mother doesn't smoke, she never drank, she only ate good foods, she exercised...why would she have anything wrong?"

The doctor, who was my age (early thirties), furrows his brow.

"We can't explain it. These things just happen."

How was this explanation good enough, I think?

Maryann, a nurse at the hospital in our hometown, has a kind, warm smile. She isn't like the doctors; she's empathetic to the situation.

"Just remember, a happy mind is a happy cell. And a happy cell is a healthy body."

I throw myself into hours of research about lesions. What I'm finding is making me sick. Liver Cancer? Pancreatic Cancer? Or even more dreaded, the vilest word a doctor can ever mention: metastasized.

I have to give my mom shots of blood thinner. Stabbing my mom in the abdomen doesn't sound like fun. I am nervous, and I don't want to hurt her. It seems like a huge responsibility, but I must do it.

I have to wrap my mom's legs every day with leg wraps. My mom is upset. We all began to fight, really, really bad ones. My dad insists my mom doesn't have cancer. My mom thinks she's dying. I'm trying to help her, give her shots, wrap her legs, cook her meals.

My grandmother is telling her everything is okay. She doesn't have cancer, and her lesions are normal, no big deal. I understand why she's telling her this. Longevity runs in our family; my grandparents are in their nineties. It makes sense.

The shots of blood thinner go on for weeks. My mom's mental health begins to decline rapidly—she is crying a lot, angry, and doesn't want to go anywhere. She doesn't want to watch our favorite shows together, doesn't want to do anything. I try so hard to lift her spirits and assure her everything is going to be okay.

One day, I try to write to calm my nerves. Now, when I open up my novel, all I can think is, *I really am falling through realities. How do I stop it so I don't hit rock bottom? I know what's at the bottom. I know it. I lose everything. I lose my mom. I never thought of that as a real reality before. Ever. Except now, between my feelings and my mom going into the hospital, suddenly, things have changed.*

When I look at my cursor blinking on the 120,000 words I've written, two full novels, I think, this is my fault. I had my main character's mother die. My reality is presenting that as a possibility now. I desperately try to rewrite the book, this time with the mother living.

I don't know what I hope will happen. Maybe I think I have some unknown superpower to change the reality I think I have fallen into. I don't feel right. I'm still dizzy. My body feels off, shaky. My emotions are off—I'm extremely erratic and emotional. I just can't think straight.

In early February, my friend dies of brain cancer after a five-year battle. He's even younger than me, and I'm only 33. At his viewing, I am in a daze, my stomach is in knots, and all I can think about is my mother. *Will this be her fate one day soon,* I think, as I watch a long line of people paying respects to Dan's grieving family.

No, shut up! I think. I can't even conceive of it. I won't.

When all my friends, some of who I haven't seen in years, gather at the Phily Diner to celebrate Dan, I stop by just to say hello, but I'm still in a daze. I barely see them. I hardly recognize them, but not because they look or act differently. It's as if they're in a different world than me. It feels like I am just outside of their world in a big, cloudy fog. I feel like I'm at the entrance to the River of Styx, heading to the Underworld, and all the people in my life are shadow-remnants of a world I used to be a part of. I don't want to be in this place. I want to return to the world of light, the world of the living. I drive home, but I am not paying attention. When I arrive at my house, I don't remember how I got there.

How did I get here? I wonder, thinking about this frightening new reality I am in. My life was fine. My life was great. I liked it. I loved it. I appreciated it. How did I get here?

eight

THE SECOND DEATH SENTENCE

In March, we go to another hospital in Philadelphia. This time it's because my mom's family doctor says it's an emergency. My mother's bilirubin levels (something to do with the liver) have risen.

Emotionally worn from all the fighting, crying, and fear from this situation, I am not my best self. I am the worst version of myself. I am mean to my dad, my grandmom, and my brother.

My mom is angry, screaming in fear as we go to the hospital. She doesn't want to go. But she is always being pressured by other people. I just want to do what she wants. Her body. Her choice. But everyone has an opinion. Yes, her liver isn't doing well, but apparently, there's nothing they can do for her anyway, so what's the point of entrusting herself with the doctors?

My mom is scared.

I've never seen my mother scared in my life. She is the toughest person I know. I am the scared one. I am the one who worries about everything, who is a complete hypochondriac. That my mother is so terrified has me on edge. She doesn't want to have cancer. Anything but cancer. And especially not the worst, most hopeless cancer. She begs to get into this treatment center that supposedly offers holistic and integrative approaches. She really wants to try natural remedies.

We call them. They are perfectly nice on the phone, but they are a scam. Getting in there is like getting into an ivy league university. Good luck. First, they deny my mom because you must have a biopsy to go there. Then, because of her bilirubin level, we are forced to go to a plain old hospital. This breaks my mom's heart. I don't understand why they just don't let you in the damn place and give you the treatment when you need it. What good is the holistic natural remedy if you have a list of rules to get in the damn place? I'm infuriated.

I don't know how to make her feel better. It's like seeing some fearless warrior suddenly express she is afraid. How do you help someone like that? When she was always the one who lit the torch of bravery for you.

I know the only way I can help her now is to try to be there for her, let her know that no matter what, I am by her side like a loyal soldier—that I will fight for her until death.

At the second hospital, they convince my mom to do a biopsy. She really doesn't want one—she's afraid. My mom is an extremely intuitive person, and I get that from her. I think we both know what's happening, but we are so desperately trying to fix things. My mom just can't understand how this happened. She never smoked, never drank, ate organically, never ate processed meats. She did eat organic chickens with no antibiotics. She exercised also.

I just can't wrap my head around what's going on. I just want this to be over. I want my mom and me to go home, and I want us all to return back to normal. I want my life back.

nine

THE BABY AIN'T BROKE

Early March 2018

Bernie, one of the nurses, comes in one night laughing and giggling. She has smooth dark skin and a gleam in her eye. Honestly, I can't understand why she's so damn happy. I am sleeping at the hospital tonight. I already have my PJ's on and am laying on a pull-out chair, my journal open. Bernie takes one look at my mom's sad eyes and sits by her bedside. Cupping my mother's hands into hers, she smiles,

"Listen, Miss Roseanne, just because you sittin' here in this bed does not mean you are going to die. You want to live; you'll live."

Finally, some hope. Being in the hospital, I realize how cold and heartless the doctors can be. Some doctors, not all, are not in the profession to *heal* people. I see the very obvious flaws in our medical system, at least when it comes to cancer. One only needs to be in a cancer crisis to see how much we are failing at treating this disease, no matter what marketing schemes pharmaceutical companies try to sell everyone.

First, I notice that at all the hospitals we go to, they pride themselves on being on the same page, but observing them as a layperson, I see that they are on very different pages from one another. Here is an example.

My mother ends up getting the biopsy. They wheel her down to the room where the biopsy is to occur, but no one ever checks her records to see that she has pulmonary embolisms. They almost give her sodium bicarbonate as she is about to get the biopsy. My mom, in all the distress she is in, has to say, 'I have blood clots in my lungs.'"

The doctors' shriek.

"How come no one told us?" the doctor says indignantly to my mother.

"It's all in my charts," my mom, who should not be concerned with this, says.

Yes, the charts they never bothered to read.

Secondly, it is quite evident that no doctors are trained in nutrition, which is scary. Neither the doctors nor nurses check to see if my mother eats. They don't even know what she's eating. I would much rather be treated by a biochemist who knows vitamins, minerals, and nutrients than a doctor for this kind of disease. All doctors should extensively be trained in nutrition, vitamins, minerals, and nutrients first. Synthetic drugs should be minimal and last on the list. That just seems like common sense to me.

What bothers me most is how some doctors have lost bedside manners. They are not really trying to save the patient—it's all about the drugs they can pump into him/her. These doctors all feel like sleazy salesmen who are giving you the "Believe me if there was any other way" line in order to get you to buy their product. And should you suggest another way, they will immediately shut you down because it isn't in their sales book.

To me, after listening to two different sets of doctors at two different hospitals, it seems these doctors (from internal to oncology) can only speak one language, and it's the good old-fashioned book they learned from. They have accolades and degrees, and they take a bunch of fancy courses and memorize the big "book," and when anything goes wrong, they preach the book to you. But the truth is, they only really know about synthetic treatments to treat symptoms. And cancer is a billion-dollar business that is about making money, not saving lives. They aren't trying to cure a single soul. I think they're open about that, but why do we want people taking charge of our fates if they can't cure us?

But more importantly, let me get back to Bernie. First, here's how I feel about these nurses. Some nurses are great. Some are just doing a job, and it's quite evident. But nurses like Bernie? They are the best. They are here helping patients more than doctors and other nurses by merely instilling hope. Some of these doctors are too busy taking hope away. They could use a good dose of Bernie and a good dose of compassion.

My mom and I talk about our fears with Bernie. My mom worries she won't make it to my wedding and will never see her grandchildren.

Bernie launches into a story about her daughters.

"Listen, Miss Roseanne. When your child needs you, you tend to stick around. Look, my daughter can't even raise her own kid," she says. "I am taking care of the baby. One day she comes to me and says, 'Mom, I don't know if I'm doing a good job. I think the baby is broke.' The baby ain't broke, I tell her. The baby ain't broke. You're doing just fine."

There's a metaphor in there somewhere, and I'm trying to figure out what Bernie is saying. I don't need to.

"The point is, you ain't dead until you take your last breath, Miss Roseanne. Other than that, you're doing okay. You ain't broke 'til you dead."

Bernie makes us feel better and then leaves. I never see her again. I wonder if Bernie is a messenger from the spirit world, an angel even, but I quickly dismiss the thought.

ten

MY FIRST BREAKDOWN

That night I sleep at the hospital. I hear the beeps of the machines all night and wake several times. Clearly, there is some contest at hospitals for how many times a nurse can take a patient's blood pressure during a particular day (especially at night when their body needs sleep). Sleeping in a hospital with a loved one who is ill is the most frightening feeling. No clown movie could ever top the fear for me (and I loathe clowns). I feel like I'm in a nightmare I cannot wake up from.

Still living in the place where my higher being occasionally surfaces (and I try so hard to deny this as I'm in such emotional torment and pain, but alas, I cannot deny it), I can say this. In this hospital, while the doctors are most unhelpful, I do meet some very lovely people —most of the nurses and transports are amazing. I see them every day. One technician, John, has seen me ugly cry more times than I can count. Every day, he asks me how I feel, and even though I'm feeling the worst I ever have, I am thankful to him for asking.

The doctors tell my mom if it is what they think it is, then there's really nothing they can do. The success rate for pancreatic cancer is so low because chemotherapy doesn't work, and if it's on her bile duct, they can't do surgery on it. And the hopeless just became more hopeless. Thank you, Debbie Downers.

One night at the hospital, I completely lose it. This moment is my breaking point. I'm crying so hard and am so unable to breathe; my dad cannot console me. I feel my heart swelling. I can't even hear him anymore; I am so hysterical. I'm shaking. He gets my aunt on the phone, my mom's sister. She doesn't seem to understand the scope of what's happening. But I knew the scope of what *this* was.

I can barely breathe on the phone, and I'm crying harder than I ever have. My aunt is trying to calm me down, telling me to take deep breaths. I barely hear her.

I don't know what to do. I feel like I'm going to die, that my heart is going to give out. I don't even care. I don't care because if my mom is going to die, then who cares if I die also?

eleven

PRAYERS TO AIR

At nighttime, I pray, but I don't dare pray to God anymore. He is a letdown. Right now, to me, he does not exist. To me, he does not save anyone, and I am not naive. God isn't going to come down from Heaven dressed in white and give me some heart-warming smile and a task to be strong. At least then I would have something to hold on to. God equals disappointment in my mind. I'd sooner align with Lucifer. But he doesn't exist to me either. There is no devil, no one to blame for our shitty behaviors or lives. The only person we have to blame is ourselves.

No, no. Don't get it wrong. I am *not* an atheist. I don't believe in life and dirt. I believe in third-dimensional life and higher dimensions. Well, usually, I believe that anyway. I believe in consciousness, in spirit, in our ability to heal. I believe in our connection to source, a different kind of God that is a part of us—along with everyone and every living being, including animals, plants, and trees. I believe that there is a great spirit that runs through everything, and we are all one. We are all part of that spirit. I believe in energy and frequencies. I just don't believe in the traditional religion. Or at least, I think I have transcended that belief of religion. I *think* I believe those things about being all one. But maybe I don't. If I have, why am I so damn angry with some man in the sky? Why do I feel like he's letting me down? Maybe I think I've moved on, found something greater to hold on to, but subconsciously I'm still holding on to all those years of my Roman Catholic training. Because of that, the disappointment of not being heard, prayers unanswered, leaves me feeling betrayed, angry, and full of hate.

But I wonder, how many people have prayed to God for a miracle only to be let down?

How many have prayed and actually received that miracle?

If God granted only some miracles, then he would be the most un-just creator. Some of my family members are so Catholic; they are always trying to convert me back to what I have happily left behind. I have imaginary conversations with them in my head.

"Then why do people die?" I ask.

"Sometimes, it's time for you to come home to the Lord."

"Yes, but *why*?"

"God needs no explanation."

"What kind of cockamamie shit answer is that?" Not even sure what the true definition of cockamamie is, but I heard it once. "So, let me get this straight. Communication, connection, and love are the keys to a successful relationship, but God doesn't have to communicate to anyone unless he decides maybe he feels like it because it's Wednesday and the weather is nice? Oh, and because you've confessed and gone to church? Well, I have a news flash for you people. Christians die of the same terrible cancers as everyone else, and if you're okay with believing God abandoning you is okay, well, then I can't help you."

I'm getting awfully worked up for a conversation in my head. I need to calm down. Where are these feelings coming from? I don't even believe in this stuff in this way anymore.

The hospital discharges my mom, but we are far from relieved. I'm walking around my mother's room the next morning, picking up towels, and I cannot stop the rage inside me.

My mom can barely walk.

I'm pacing as I gather my mom's clothing and put it into a laundry basket.

To me, God doesn't grant miracles. We grant them to ourselves through our beliefs. Miracles are asked for and prayed for, but they don't always happen.

My mom and I talk after I help her shower. She can barely stand, so she uses a stool to wash. I put the stool in the shower, help her to the shower, help her wash, let her take care of her personal parts, and then help her out and back to her bed. I grab her fresh clothes and help her dress.

"We are good people," I say. "We don't deserve this suffering."

"I know," my mom begins to cry.

"I don't believe in prayer. It's not realistic."

My mom doesn't respond.

"I mean, I don't believe in praying to God or Jesus or whoever. I believe in Jesus's teachings because he teaches love and about belief, but not in praying to him to save us. Jesus always hears our prayers, but he couldn't answer them all if he wanted to. Because just praying isn't enough. Prayer, in itself, isn't effective. If it doesn't work 100% of the time, it's not technically a natural method of achieving something. And if you subscribe to the pray-to-God-and-he'll-heal-me-method, you'll probably die. If you go that route, you'll be angry and thinking *he's just letting me suffer.* Something feels wrong about that. Like maybe everyone's got it wrong. If we stop personifying God as a man, I think we'll all be much happier. We'll stop being angry. It's so easy to get angry with something when you personify it. But when you take away the fear, the sin, and the church, you just have an all-loving presence. There's no one to be angry with. Religion is based on fear but tries to sell love to hook everyone. 'You'll go to hell,'" they scream, "but love your neighbor, please!' It's all just a bunch of bullshit. A great way to control everyone."

My mom nods, but it's half-hearted. I can tell she just doesn't care about this right now.

"I also don't believe in modern medicine. Because it doesn't work." (Clearly, this infuriates me.) "Not really. If it did, it would work 100% of the time for everyone. Then it would be real, but it doesn't work like that."

She nods again.

"The only thing I believe in that works 100% of the time is belief. If you believe you're healed, whether it's through God's prayer or modern medicine, then you are. Jesus even said in the Bible about belief and healing. That's why some doctors are so dangerous to human existence. The world is dependent on them, and they're trained to deliver bad news and auto-suggest to you that your prognosis is grim. But many of them have no education in the power of the mind and belief. They condition people to believe something is incurable. That's why it's up to us to change our beliefs. The medical field is just like religion. It markets through fear but pretends to sell good health. You can only fool people for so long. People are finally waking up. Unfortunately, it takes a crisis to see what's going on. There's something else going on here. It's like we've been tricked into believing our body isn't intelligent when it is."

My mom agrees, but she is weary.

"I know what you're saying, but I don't think I can change the course now. I really don't. I've lived my entire life thinking the opposite."

"Have you really? I think you, me, all of us think we believed one thing, but actually, we are still so attached to those old beliefs. I don't want you to give up and be defeated. You are so powerful."

I need to shut my mouth. Why do I keep opening my mouth right now?

"No, I had just accepted the auto-suggestion a long time ago. You're right. My subconscious beliefs are too deep."

"Then let's dig them out."

My mom rolls her eyes. I would also. I'm annoying *myself* at this point.

I don't want to argue with her, and I feel she is getting a little angry with me. The last thing I want to do is make her upset, so I stop talking. We just sit in silence on her bed.

We've spent years studying the power of belief. I know she can heal herself. I know she can at least ease her suffering. But I don't know if she can do the work. There's a difference. Anyone can read a book, but not everyone can change their lives. I want so desperately for her to try something. Anything.

And I know she would say the same to me. My mom is the strongest person I know. I am so strong *because* of her. We don't have it in our blood to give up like this. At least, I don't think so. Now I am not so sure.

"I would take nanos at this point," my mom says. We've watched enough about the future of humanity to know what's coming next. Trans-humanism is only one step away.

"Honestly…" I nod. "Who cares at this point? We're all going to be half-robot someday."

twelve

Bags of Ice and Back Rubs

Every night, I fill bags of ice. This is for mom's back when it hurts.

"Freeze the mother-fucker," we say about the lesions.

Mom is angry. I've never seen her this angry. It's the liver qi again, acting crazy.

"Calm down, mom," I remind her. "We have to stay calm."

We know that the adrenaline and stress hormones are not going to help the situation. They will only add to her decline. But how can she find peace at this moment? How can I?

My spine is killing me for the sixth day in a row.

I can barely sleep at nighttime. It hurts so badly. My entire left side is in so much pain; it's indescribable. I am not

40

beyond connecting my physical pain with the emotional pain I'm going through.

I sleep with a heating pad.

I've lost thirty pounds.

There's a wrinkle on my forehead that is deepening each day. It's my suffering wrinkle. I should wish it away, but it's a reminder of this pain. A reminder that I'm in the trenches, fighting for my mother. I'm in survival mode. We're still at war.

My hair is much grayer, and I'm too young for that.

Thirty-three is the worst of years. Must be the threes.

Damn these bags of ice. We are up all night trying to help my mom sleep. My dad and I are continually bringing ice bags to my mom, which slightly helps her with the pain. Then he and I take turns giving her back rubs and trying to help her get out of pain. She's going through all this with no pain meds because of her liver.

We do this for weeks. I don't remember sleeping through a night from March to April.

It doesn't always help, but she gets some rest when it does, and I am so genuinely happy.

I am no longer a daughter. I am a mother, worriedly watching and caring for my child. I wonder if other daughters go through this? Not every daughter has the type of bond my mother and I have. We are genuinely best friends and family. We have a bond like the characters from *Fast and Furious*—I would die for her. My mom isn't perfect, but she is the very best friend I could ever ask for—the most loyal, the biggest dreamer, the most fun. Plus, she is my mom—the one person I know who loves me unconditionally. I need to save her. I'll do anything.

thirteen

FIRE DRILLS, FIRE DRILLS, AND MORE FIRE DRILLS

I reason either my mother will one day read this book and be like, what a god damn awful nightmare, or she'll be dead and never read it.

I am seriously hoping for the former.

Ever since my mother went to the hospital for the first time in January, we have been on what I like to call the "fire drill" schedule.

Here's how it goes.

Go to the hospital. Receive bad news. Get released. Go to the doctor. Receive bad news. Go home. Cry. Go back to the doctor. Receive bad news. Go to the hospital. Receive bad news. Go home. Go to the doctor. Receive bad news.

Our small win of getting taken off the Lovenox is crushed once more with "bad" news.

My mother's bilirubin levels are even higher now.

I think, well, she was still on the Lovenox when they took her blood.

My dad says, "We should go to the hospital."

I think we should wait, or at least ask my mother what she wants to do.

My mom doesn't want to go to the hospital on the weekend of Easter, so we decide to wait.

My ninety-one-year-old grandmother, my mom's mom, who is still alive and well (my ninety-four-year-old grandfather is also, hence why this illness makes no sense), says through Facebook messenger, "You know, they took the blood test when she was still on the Lovenox."

She and I are thinking on the same page without knowing it.

I type that to her.

Still, my mother wants to go to the hospital, just on Easter Monday, when the whole holiday business is over.

I'm still mad at Jesus for not helping, so I refuse to care about whether or not he decided to resurrect. I'm still waiting for a miracle or a sign that he's even listening, but all I hear are crickets.

fourteen

THE SUN

"I'll never see the beach again," my mom cries.

"Don't say that! Mom, let's just get in the car and go. We have nothing to lose. Let's just…"

"I love the beach so much, the sunshine, and I'll never see it again. I'll never spend another summer in the warm sun."

There is no greater gut-wrenching feeling than listening to someone you love with all your heart say something like this.

"We're going to the beach again, mom, I promise."

"No, she says," breaking into a full cry. "I just want to go somewhere beautiful and sit on the beach and relax, breathe in the fresh air."

My mom and I cry together. I don't even know how to console her at this point.

One day it is warmer than usual.

"Come on, mom, sit outside."

My mom does, surprisingly, but soon she comes back in.

"I can't do it," she says. "I know I'm dying, and it hurts too much to think I'll never see this place again."

"Stop saying you're dying. You're not dying."

My mom stares into space and doesn't answer me.

Later, we sit in silence when suddenly she gets up and pulls her wedding dress box out of the closet.

"Open this, will you?"

"Why?"

"When you get married, maybe you can still wear it. I don't know if it held up…"

We open the box to find the dress is yellowed. The irony is not lost on me. My mother kept her dress perfectly preserved, just like her body, but in the end, it yellowed anyway. I put the dress on. It's too long, and I look like I'm straight out of the Victorian period.

"Well, you can't wear it, but maybe you can use something from it."

"Yeah."

"You'll have to rely on your Aunt Diana to help you plan your wedding."

"Don't say that," I feel the tears again. "You'll be there, or I'm not getting married."

"Stef. Get it together," she says angrily. "I won't be here."

The thought is too much to bear.

"Please, mom. Please. Don't do this," I plead.

My mom, as she so often does now, sits in silence. And I am left standing in her yellowed-wedding dress, full of despair.

fifteen

Mom's Advice

My mom wakes up one morning, afraid.

"I had a terrible dream," she says. "I was dead, and I was in this strange waiting room with all these other really, really sick people. It was dark and gray and terrifying. I don't want to go there, Stef. I don't want to go there."

"Mom, don't worry about that. You're still here with me. Focus on that. Let's do something fun today. Anything," I say.

"No," she shakes her head. "There's no point."

"Mom, please? I just want it to be like us for just once."

The tears well up in her eyes again.

"It's never going to be like that again. Don't you understand? Why are you not understanding this?"

She's angry with me, and it makes me cry. All I want is for her to do one thing, smile just once. She calms down and says, "I want you to travel. I want you to see the world. Don't live small like me. I want you to live big, do you hear me?"

I don't say anything because I'm still crying.

We move into my mom's sitting room. It's another sunny day. This time my mom refuses to go outside.

"When I'm gone, Evelyn will help you." Evelyn is my co-worker. She is older than me but lives her life to the fullest. "Make sure you spend time with her. Live young, as she does. And if you need to talk to someone, talk to Anna Marie."

"Mom, please stop."

She ignores me and says, "I promise I'll come back to you as a blue butterfly."

Then my mom begins to sob and says, "I don't want to go into the hospital."

"Then don't, mom. Don't go."

"Because I'm afraid I won't come home. And I just want to spend a little more time here in this beautiful home on Easter."

I am, as every day, in uncontrollable tears.

Over the next few days, my mom distances herself from me. She doesn't talk to me. Sometimes she's even mean to me, wishing I would leave her alone. I just want to help her, and I'm running out of ways to. I feel like there's nothing I can do to save her, nothing I can do to change this.

For some reason, in an effort to make my mom feel better, my brother tells her he's having his first child. I am horrified by this otherwise jubilant moment. The timing isn't right. My mom is horrified too. I don't tell my brother, but this sends my mom into a deeper depression—knowing that she won't get to meet her grandchild is what I think sends her over the edge. She stops communicating with me or anyone and just stares.

sixteen

THE THIRD DEATH SENTENCE

After Easter, we find my mom's latest numbers come back with bilirubin that's overly high, and we know it's time to go to the hospital.

I sit with my mom in the ER, holding her hand. I dream of us leaving, going out to dinner one more time, going on a trip to the beach, or going shopping. But a part of me knows those days are not in our near future. Maybe someday, but not today.

We settle her into her hospital room and leave. I leave the iPad with her, just in case she wants to talk to me. We are only home a few minutes before my mom messages me on the iPad.

Omg! Omg! She writes. *A doctor just came in here and said I'm dying, and I only have three weeks left to live. You have to come back here, please.*

Right away, I have a pit in my stomach. We call the hospital. My dad yells at the nurses. "Who was it that came into my wife's room and told her that at midnight?"

It is the night doctor.

"Put her on the phone, now."

The doctor calls us. I yell at her.

"Who do you think you are going into someone's room like that?"

She and I get into an ugly fight.

"Where is your compassion? I say, and who are you anyway?"

"I'm an internal medicine doctor."

"And did they forget to teach you to be a *human* in doctor-school? All your degrees mean absolutely diddly squat to me. Especially if you can do nothing to help my mother, which you obviously can't. And if you have no humanity left, then you *really* mean nothing to me."

My dad separates us on the phone. I tell him I am sleeping at the hospital tonight. I pack my bag, and my dad drops me off. I arrive there at about 1 a.m. My mom's nurse is weeping. She feels terrible that this doctor came into the room and did this to my mom, and she is going to report her anonymously.

I thank the nurse. My mom keeps saying how wonderful her nurse is. How compassionate she is and how if even one doctor treated her the way this nurse did, the world would be a much better place.

"Don't worry," I tell my mother. "I'm here with you now. And I will not dare let them say a word to you."

If anyone in that hospital dares to cross her, I will be there to fight them.

seventeen

THE FOURTH DEATH SENTENCE

"Do you understand the gravity of the situation? *You're dying.* You have stage-*four* pancreatic cancer, and there's nothing we can do. Do you understand? This is a very serious issue. You are dy-ing. Do you un-der-stand? There's nothing we can do here."

My inner southern Italian blood is boiling. One of the hospital doctors keeps drilling this same speech into my mother's brain. I am like Drogo defending the mother of dragons.

"Can you stop scolding her like a little child, like she did something wrong? Like this is her fault?"

"I'm not."

"Yes, you are. You're talking to her like she's a little child, over-enunciating everything and constantly stressing the point that she's going to fucking die. Like we fucking get it! It's stage four cancer. We're fucking intelligent, and we understand what that means. And who do you think you are coming in here and constantly pointing that out?"

Dracarys, bitches.

"It's my job as a doctor to tell you what's going on."

"First of all, it's your *job* as a doctor to have compassion and be there for your patient. It's your *job* to do everything you can to save that patient's life. It is not your job to come in here and spout off you're dying, and there's nothing we can do. Don't even get me started on our medical system right now. They need a major cleanout, clean up, and rewiring. But let's focus on you and your team. You all have done nothing but caused my mom heartache since we got here, giving her absolutely no hope to live. Have you ever studied neuroscience? Do you know what you're doing by impressing upon someone in a highly negative, emotionally charged state over and over again that they're going to die? Also, please do not treat us like idiots. When you speak, you will speak with more compassion and humility, and as though you're speaking to people who are your equals, or you will get out of this room and never return. Be very careful about the next words that you utter from your mouth."

"Why don't we come back when you're settled down," the doctor says, trying not to snap at me. She knows I will go at her throat and leaves.

What I want to say to her is that one day, when we prove that what you say to people impacts them in life and death, when they realize the power of the brain and the harm they're causing by being so objectively truthful without taking that into consideration, their smug, high and mighty way of doing things will be considered a crime. The rage inside me is so great; I don't know how to contain it.

My brother and father seem mad that I reacted that way.

"Well, someone had to stand up for her since *you* two aren't!"

My brother storms out, angry at me, or maybe he is just frustrated at the situation. My dad leaves too for a smoke break.

I look at my mom.

"Don't worry, mom. Even if we go down in flames, just know I've got your back the whole way."

eighteen

HELL-BENT ON A STENT
April 3, 2018

I ask about different treatments for my mom, but every doctor, from the Oncologist to the Radiologist, has my mom dead already. If I hear that there is "nothing they can do" one more time, I'm going to freak out. I have intelligent conversations with this oncologist who is at least honest about the fact that it's the funding of research that holds up progress.

"What about these new procedures you're advertising?" I ask the radiologist. He's nice and pretty friendly, but even he shrugs.

"We don't really use it, honestly."

"But then why do you guys advertise it as the newest technology?"

He shrugs. "I don't know. We don't really have a say on what they advertise."

He doesn't have answers, and it infuriates me.

"But that's why we came here," my mom says. I can hear hope further drain from her voice. Her powerful tone becomes constricted and froggy. "Because we researched that you guys do this procedure."

"I'm sorry," he says. "I don't know what to say. It's good marketing." He throws his hands up. "We just don't have that capability yet."

When the doctors leave, I am so numb, I feel like my body could just give out right now, and I'd be okay with it.

The doctors have mostly given up, but they think putting a stent in my mother's liver may help. I feel, immediately in my gut, that this is a bad idea, and my mom isn't keen on it either. But they keep insisting, like solicitors repeatedly calling the house or religious folk stalking out your home to convert you with pamphlets.

"It should help," they say.

"Should...or will?" I say under my breath.

My dad and brother push for the stent also. I am breaking down at this point. My mom and I exchange glances. My mom is now too weak to make her own decisions, but I know she doesn't want this. I want to fight for my mom's wishes, but I can't do it alone. Caving under pressure, my mom says.

"Well, just put a plastic one in."

My mom wants to live. She wants to preserve her body in any way she can.

We agree with this decision, and they say my mom will be getting the procedure.

"We'll need to give her Vitamin K…"

They give her a dose of vitamin K. Within a half-hour, her leg swells.

"This isn't normal," I say to the nurse.

"Oh, she has swelling. I wonder what that's from."

"Well, logically, it's from the Vitamin K. They gave it to her, and about 15 minutes later, she started to swell."

"Okay, I'll tell the doctor."

The doctor doesn't come in for hours, and when she does, she says the Vitamin K did not cause the swelling. It must be something else. I am so frustrated I could bang my head against a wall. How can they not see the connection here?

My mom keeps saying she doesn't want the stent but feels confused now. I don't know what to say or how to feel. I just sit there, talking with her about what the stent might do to help.

We have to be optimistic, even though we both feel it's the *wrong* decision.

"You can always back out of it," I say. "You don't have to do this, mom. It's *your* choice."

She knows this, but everyone around her keeps pushing for it. She feels cornered. Too much pressure. This is her life on the line, and she doesn't know what to do.

"Look, please. Do what you want, mom. This is your life. They don't know you. They are just doing what they think might work. They have no idea if it will. But this is your life. And it's about what you want, not what they want."

"I just don't know anymore."

"I'm here to support you either way. Anything you want to do. I'm here for you."

nineteen

MOM'S BIRTHDAY
April 5th, 2018

It's my mother's birthday.

I buy her favorite treat, a spinach croissant from Au Bon Pain.

"I know it's not much," I say. "When you get out of here, we're going to celebrate with a big cake."

She nods, and for the first time in forever, smiles. "Oh yeah! I can't wait."

Two hours later, they are wheeling my mom down to get a stent.

As a transport wheels her out of her room, she looks at me. She grabs my hand in her hers and clasps it tightly.

"Stef, I'm scared. I'm really, really scared."

"You're going to be okay, mom. I promise. I love you so much, more than anything in the whole world. And I'm right here."

"I love you too."

While my mother is getting her procedure, I am feeling optimistic. I want her to be happy when she gets back, so I go to the store inside the hospital, and I buy her a beautiful shawl and a Lavender eye mask. I figure when we go home, she can wear the shawl, and she can use the eye mask right now.

Hours later, she returns, but she is out of it. Something isn't right.

I try to give her her gift, but they tell me she needs to rest now.

I figure I'll give it to her tomorrow.

The hour is late, and we decide we'll give her tonight to rest. We need the rest too.

twenty

OBSERVATIONS IN THE ATRIUM

April 6, 2018…

The next morning, I'm hopeful my mother will be conscious today, and the grogginess will wear off. I'm anxious to know if the procedure worked. But when we get to the hospital, we find out she has been moved to a different room. Something happened during the procedure. Her kidneys don't look good, and she's had a reaction to the anesthesia.

"What?" My heart sinks. My body is in a permanent state of alert—my heart races, my body feels weak.

The doctor with whom I had an altercation tracks me down. She, in very little words and form, apologizes to me because of her previous behavior.

"I don't want you to think I'm not empathetic to the situation. It's just, eh, you have to understand, my job is to report things as they are."

"It's okay," I reply. "I wasn't at my best either."

At this point, I just want my mom to be okay. All I want to do is talk to my mom. I don't even care how long she has left to live. I just want to talk to her. Her words replay in mind.

"Stef, I'm scared. I'm really, really scared."

I remember her wide eyes, the look like she was pleading with me to do something to get us out of this. And all I could say was everything was going to be okay.

What if that was the last thing my mom ever says to me?

No, I shake the thought from my mind. No. No. No. No. That's absurd. She's going to be okay. I will, at the least, be able to talk to her again, even if it's one more time to say goodbye.

The doctors want to take her down for a Kidney scan. She's grumbling and not making any sense. She can't get up. She can't go to the bathroom, and her excrement is going all over a puppy training pad.

She has a catheter.

I'm worried. I start to panic.

I try to communicate with her, but she's saying strange things. She's not even looking at me. Not really. I try to give her her birthday present. She doesn't want it. She moans and pushes it away.

They take her down to get the scan, and my brother and I walk around the hospital building. Block one, block two, block three, block four. Block one, block two. It's just so cold for April; I can't stand it. Eventually, we walk back inside.

When we learn my mother isn't back yet, I sit in the atrium with my computer. I don't have anything else to do. I decide to people watch. There are doctors, nurses, employees, and family members eating. Some are laughing and talking; some are just people watching. I watch people "people" watching, and it is an unusual experience. I wonder what they're thinking, and I wonder if they know what I'm thinking. Do they know how much pain I'm in? Do they know what I'm experiencing?

A few girls who were sitting next to me keep talking about their mothers. The more they speak, the more upset I feel. Would my mother recover? Would she leave the hospital? This is the first time throughout this whole process that I doubt her going home. I had been so positive, so confident before, and now? I don't know how I feel, but I know it isn't right. Everything feels wrong. Why am I here? How did we get here? I don't even care about the cancer anymore. That she would die from that means nothing to me. I just want to speak to her again while she's still alive.

I am jealous of the girls next to me, laughing, jealous of them speaking about trivial things like weddings and bachelorette parties. Would I ever have one? Would I have my mother at my wedding to watch me marry? Would we ever go on vacation again? Would we ever go on one of our retreat trips? Would we ever go shopping again? I can't deal with the pain. It pierces through my heart on more than one occasion, but now the pain is getting deeper, so much deeper. I can only describe it as being at the center of my heart. My brain feels like it's filling with fluid. My insides are writhing with uncomfortable nausea. My heart is beating quickly, and sometimes I can't breathe. And still, I wonder if anyone in that atrium knows how I'm feeling. And I wonder if anyone else in this room feels the way I do—so worried for their loved one.

I wish I could find them and speak to them. We could discuss our feelings and support one another. But I can't recognize anyone who looks as in pain as I feel, and maybe I am taking this harder than other people. Or maybe I am actually the only one in this room experiencing it.

twenty-one

GARGOYLES AND OTHER DIMENSIONS

Between all the heart pain, fear, tears, and anguish, there are moments of clarity. Moments where my mind just stops because it simply cannot take anymore. So, it clears. And when it does, I notice the strangest things.

Gargoyles. There are so many gargoyles on this one building. I must have been in the city hundreds of times. I must have seen this building hundreds of times, yet never once had I noticed the gargoyles. *Philadelphia does have very beautiful architecture*, I think. It is one moment out of thousands of moments of anguish where I notice something beautiful.

My mom isn't back from her kidney scans, and I'm so scared. I need to walk around. I leave the building and walk around the hospital block alone about ten times. The people on the streets are a blur. They're like ants crawling across every inch of the city. I can barely see them. It's so damn cold out, it's annoying. I'm hungry.

I walk to a Mexican restaurant and sit at the bar alone. I eat a very unsatisfying meal. Then I head back to the hospital.

My mom is back, but they are still waiting for the results.

She is still incoherent.

I hate this hospital so much. I just want to grab my mom, leave, and never come back.

As we wait for the results, I sit with my mom, holding her hand.

The room is quiet, except for the beeping of hospital machines. My mother's eyes are closed, her breathing a little labored. She still has a catheter and a puppy training pad under her. I am alone in the room, and I just stare at her and pray.

I pray she comes back to me, that she speaks to me. I pray we have any conversation at all. Anything is fine. Even a hello. Anything. Anything! I'm so desperate.

I pray she heals. I pray that we still get time together to talk, to laugh, to cry. I pray for anything.

A woman who was so magnificent, always dressed to the nines, always so beautiful, and here she is, dying? She is basically unconscious but is still sitting up. She can't speak to anyone, but she nods here and there when the nurses ask her a question. The nurses leave her for a while, and it's just her and me. She's talking to someone.

"No," she murmurs, shaking her head. "Uh-uh."

She shakes her head, over and over again.

I think she's trying to talk to me, so I get excited.

"Mommy? I'm here." I say to her, but soon it's obvious she's talking to someone else. Someone somewhere else. My hope of her recovering diminishes once more, but I *am* interested in who she is speaking to.

A small voice in my head says, "She's transitioning."

"No," I adamantly say out loud to no one. "She's not."

She's still responding to questions somewhere in a different realm. I have no idea what they're asking her. I start to imagine them asking her if she wants to stay on earth. I imagine them asking her if she wants to go back.

Once in her dialogue, she replies, "Yes, he will. He will."

I wonder what the beings on the other side ask her and whom she is speaking about when she says, "He will." Are they asking her if my father will take care of me? Are they asking her if my boyfriend will take care of me? Is that permission for her to leave me?

I stop myself from getting carried away with these thoughts.

She's just out of it, I think. When she comes out of this, you can ask her what she was saying.

I get up and decide to walk around the cancer ward to pass the time. I see an old Asian man. A woman, whom I imagine is his wife, holds his hand. He is frail but alive. Another man is there, perhaps his son. He sits inside the hospital room, solemn. I can see the old man is tired. A young man, possibly his grandson, plays a game on an electronic tablet.

I see a girl my age who is enthusiastic despite her diagnosis. She continues to do CrossFit even while getting treatments. She is optimistic and enthusiastic when the nurses come in to check on her. Even the nurses are impressed. But I'm not.

Is she going to die, I wonder? Does she know she might die?

When I return to the room, the doctors are there waiting. They have even more bad news.

My mother's kidneys are shutting down.

"What?"

"She also has an infection. This is likely from the kidneys."

"She didn't have an infection or a problem with her kidneys before the procedure."

"Sometimes, this can happen from the procedure."

They are just going to monitor her overnight and see if she improves.

If I didn't hate these doctors before, I sure hate them now. It seems like they had given my mother a death-sentence a long time ago because their Book-of-the-Synthetic-Medicine did not have an answer to cancer except a non-successful poison that wouldn't have helped my mother anyway. They sold early detection for what? The whole thing was a marketing scheme. We were in a hospital wing filled with dying people that they couldn't do a damn thing to save. And they patted themselves on the back when they went home after their patients died. I am so angry, I could scream.

"Go home for the night," my brother suggests. "Dad and I will stay here."

I don't want to leave my mom. But I am so weary. My eyes are puffy, and I don't feel well. My boyfriend picks me up, and I go home. He stays by my side as I cry all night. I am on the floor, hanging on to my bed, gripping my heart as I try to catch my breath. My heart feels like it's going to drop out of my chest. I almost want it to. The pain will stop if my heart stops. I can't take it. I just can't.

twenty-two

THE PHONE TONE FROM HELL

April 9, 2018- 3:00 a.m.

Da-dit-duh, Da-dit-duh, Da-dit-duh.

A sound that would haunt me forever.

Three in the morning, that terrible, mechanical cellphone tone rings. My father is sleeping in his room; I am sleeping in mine. It is an unsettled, far-from-peaceful, restless sleep.

A dreamless, hopeless sleep.

I shoot up out of bed at the sound. Why is my father's cellphone ringing so late? I hear him answer in the other room, his voice gruff from just waking.

"Okay," he replies. "Okay."

My heart races. I feel it beating faster, faster. I hop out of bed and into my dad's room.

He turns on the light.

"Okay," he says again. "Thank you for calling."

When he hangs up the phone, I nervously spout, "What happened? What is it?"

Those hospital doctors in Philadelphia had stolen every glimmer of hope that I had of saving my mom. Their disheartening words crushed my heart over and over again. We had been trampled on, defeated, belittled, and treated like idiots. Still, I held on to hope that they would do...something. Anything.

"The night doctor said she's worsened. The procedure caused an infection, and they had to move her to a special I.C.U. Ward. Her kidneys are shutting down."

At that moment, a new fear, one that I could have never imagined in a thousand years, filled my brain. My mother may never speak to me again, never hug me again, never tell me she loved me again. My mother, whom I had just spoken to a day before, may never, ever, come home. My mother might die.

twenty-three

THE LAST TIME I WOULD EVER SEE HER

April 9, 2018

The next day, walking into the I.C.U. felt like a dream, more like a nightmare. I just kept thinking, how did it come to this? How did a healthy person who always took care of herself end up like this? Nothing made sense.

I walked over to my mother's bedside, watching her chest rise and fall. Her breathing was labored.

"She can't really hear anyone or communicate anymore," one doctor says. "She has an infection throughout her whole body. Her kidneys are shutting down." I've heard this several times at this point. "You need to think about whether you want to keep her alive or not. Her body is dying."

These hospital doctors. Still heartless, still so practical. Robotic humans with no hearts. That's all I think about them.

I sit by my mom's side, holding her hand.

And she tries to look at me. She tries with all her might. The strongest, most powerful woman I know turns her body as much as she can and forces her eyes to open to look at me.

It's okay, mommy," I say to her. "I love you so, so much."

She keeps trying to communicate with me. Even though they say she can't, even though they say she won't. I know she's trying, but the words aren't coming out. Her eyes are staring right at me, wide. Her brain is trying to communicate. I know it. Her chest is rising and falling so high, so low. She is struggling so much to breathe. It's killing me.

There is only one doctor who is kind. A male, young. I don't remember his name; I doubt I ever will. But he is the only one who offers hope and the only one I will remember fondly.

"I don't know if the dialysis will work, but listen, we have to try." I can hear the empathy in his voice. I feel his energy; he's genuinely upset.

I walk out of the I.C.U., unable to breathe. I'm sure my heart is going to give out, and maybe I would die before her. I was okay with leaving this world. Because losing her was a death I couldn't face. I fall to my knees in the hallway and cry and cry. People pass by me. I stay huddled in the corner against a wall bawling my eyes out. I lose complete awareness of where I am. I am inconsolable.

My brother takes me out to his car. I can tell he and my dad don't know what to do with me. I just keep crying. There are no moments of peace or let up from my tears. I literally can't breathe. I don't care.

"I think you need to go home," my brother replies.

"I don't want to leave her," I sob. I didn't want to leave her side. That's not what we did, my mother and I. We were there for each other always. She was there for me; I was there for her.

"Stef, you have to go home. You need rest."

My dad stays at the hospital as my brother drives me home. At home, everything feels wrong. It's an unrest I cannot describe, and I won't bother trying. If I even think of her face, how she was trying so hard to communicate with me, I break down.

I am numb, so numb.

twenty-four

MOM IS LISTENING

April 10th, 2:00 p.m.

I do not go to visit my mother today. Yesterday was too painful. I knew she would understand that it was much too painful for me. I had shut down emotionally, mentally, and physically, so everyone decided it was best I stay home.

I'll take today to balance my emotions, and then I'll be back tomorrow. *I can handle it tomorrow*, I say. Thankfully, my brother and his wife are with my mom today. My dad is going to the hospital soon, but he wants to make sure I am okay first.

At 2:00 p.m., I take a shower. I can't stop crying. I bang my hands against the shower as my head rests against the wall. I am calling out to my mom, begging her to come back to me.

"Not like this," I cry. "Please. Please."

Suddenly, I have a moment of clarity where I feel I'm being selfish. My mother would do *anything* for me. She would stay here on earth in this decaying body as long as she had to, just for me. Was it fair that I was begging her to stay in this body when it was no longer working for her?

"No, it's not fair," I say out loud to myself. Mustering all the courage that I could, and through a cascade of warm tears, in the purest of places, the shower, I say, "Mom, I don't want you to suffer anymore. If you want to leave, you can. I love you so much, and I just want you to be happy."

Even now, as I write this, I'm crying because I can remember exactly how it felt to let my mother, my best friend, go.

I step out of the shower and get dressed. My dad is standing at the bottom of the stairs crying.

"What's wrong?" I ask.

"Mommy's gone."

"Oh," I say, somewhat in shock.

"Raymond was with her when she passed."

My dad is crying, and I lose it, but not before thinking, *I let her go. I had to. And she listened.*

Imagine the sound of a biting cold wind whipping across a land amidst dull, lifeless gray skies. On a wide stretch of barren dirt, only wisps of old, yellowed grass sway in the wind. Imagine all is quiet, except for that wind. It is the end of a battle, one which you did not win, but here you are, in the aftermath of destruction, staring at the devastation before you. Still bodies are strewn across the land, and you, the sole survivor, are paralyzed by what has just occurred.

Part Two
Walking In-Between Worlds

"*I answer the heroic question, 'Death where is thy sting?' with 'it is here in my heart and mind and memories.'*"

Maya Angelou

one

THE EULOGY

Losing a mother is devastating. Losing a mother, a best friend, and a business partner all at once is beyond anything I can comprehend. As I try to come to terms with how different my life will be, I reflect on what my mother, my best friend, taught me.

I sit outside on a stone slab, overlooking our beautiful backyard. Tiny dandelions and blue wildflowers are sprouting in the winter-soaked grass. Spring is trying to burst through. I think of my mother, and I try to find the words to describe her.

A robin soars past me. One of our outside kitties jumps up on the slab, insisting on being pet. It's warm today, the only warm day. My mother loved warm weather, gardening, and nature. I start to cry. She wanted so badly to plant her garden this year.

I can't wrap my head around her death, wondering how someone so powerful and strong, someone who cared for her body so well, could have suffered as she did. I stop, reminding myself that she wouldn't want me to remember the dark days. Instead, I think of who my mother really was.

Wonder Woman.

I know. Everyone thinks their mother is Wonder Woman. But Diana, daughter of the Amazons, may as well have been Roseanne, daughter of Rose and Rocco. Born under the zodiac sign Aries, my mother's attributes paralleled those of this great super-goddess, and my mother was adamant about ingraining these qualities into me as well.

Like Wonder Woman, my mother was a warrior of life: free, rebellious, creative, compassionate, determined, ambitious, and confident. She was fiercely loyal to her children, her husband, her family, and her friends. As a best friend, her loyalty to me was unmatched.

She embodied incredible feminine strength. From her, I learned never to allow anyone to bully me or challenge my self-worth. She encouraged me to stand up for what I believe in and always to be myself. She did not believe in pleasing anyone for the sake of pleasing but instead lived her life authentically. She boldly showed and shared her personality with others and instilled in me the importance of being authentic.

She taught me always to be honest, even when people didn't want to hear the truth.

She taught me to have confidence and to always stand up for myself.

She taught me the importance of determination and ambition and to always push forward despite setbacks. I have never been afraid to follow my dreams or pursue anything I love doing because of her.

She taught me to love the arts and appreciate the beauty in everything—nature, gardens, butterflies, animals, paintings, books, the beach, and much more.

How lucky am I that I not only learned all of those qualities from her, but I can cherish and live by them?

In addition to her super-goddess qualities, my mother was (perhaps most importantly) fun and friendly. She was such, such fun and had tons of friends. I think that's why she was my very best friend. I would say, "Mom, I want to go to Charleston." She'd reply, "Okay, when are we going?" And we did go. My mother was always ready for the road trip, always ready for the adventure. And we had so many wonderful adventures. All I can say is, how lucky am I?

I have lost my best friend, and I anticipate many, many dark days ahead.

But I will carry all her exceptional qualities with me and live the most authentic, creative, ambitious, fun, and happy life. No doubt I will take a while to heal, but I will get there. My dear mother, my very best friend, and my favorite business partner, I love you. I love you. I love you.

two

DEATH, A NEW CONCLUSION

I'm trying to deal with the physical and mental effects of my mom's death. I think the fear of my own sickness and death is what plagues me most. I desperately want to release this fear and be at peace. I want to know I am safe and loved. I miss the innocence I had before this trauma—the cheerful, optimistic, happy-go-lucky view I had of the world. Now, all I see is darkness. I have to find a way to cope.

One thing that helps me tremendously is studying the afterlife—mainly, near-death-experiences. Through studying these experiences, I have come to a greater understanding of the meaning of this life. I study people like Anita Moorjani,

Eben Alexander, and Renate Dollinger, to name a few. I watch movies like *Astral City* and listen to skeptics like Raymond Moody. I listen to Neale Donald Walsch and am comforted by his experience.

I learn a lot from everyone I study. Just listening to their incredible stories gives me hope that somewhere beyond this world, my mother is existing in some form—that our death is not a final death but a transition into another, more magnificent place. It helps me realize how special our time is here. What if there is a long line of souls waiting to get back to this experience called life? Those souls know how precious this experience is. But perhaps we living folk are so immersed in our experience, we have forgotten how remarkable life is. Life is like driving, a privilege, not a right, and perhaps so many people wish to come back here and experience emotions, life through the senses, and growth of the soul.

My studies of the afterlife make me interested in mediums. Jon's sister recommends a medium named Jane that she visited in the past. The only problem is, Jane doesn't have any availability until November. Right now, it is only the end of April. *I can wait,* I think. *If she's that good, and I can connect with my mom, I can wait.* So, I make the appointment for November and decide I won't think about it until then.

I think about where my life is going from here. Could I become a positive influence on others? I think I speak well. I enjoy connecting with others, helping them, transforming them. But I'm afraid. I'm afraid to help others because I think, what if I wake up and feel hate in my heart towards myself or anyone else? What if I have a bad day? A bad week? How can I always be a beacon of light? Will I have anything good to say?

Anything that will help anyone? Plus, am I even wise enough to help anyone?

I wonder if other people feel the same. I believe we all have a story to share. We've all been in a position where we gossiped or judged someone or something. We've all been in a situation where something terrible or debilitating has knocked us off our Ferris-wheel of life—where some adversity has shaped our lives differently. We've all had to pick ourselves up after hitting rock bottom. Humans are all connected in that way, right? Some people may claim to be better than others, but all people are perfectly flawed.

There has to be a way out of the pain, I think. I have seen the other side, where overwhelming love for everyone floods me to the point that I can't contain it. *That* love transcends gender, race, sexual orientation, religion, species, time, and space. I like it there, in that space, where everyone and everything is equal, where everything is just love. But when that feeling fades, I wake up and judge my life and my experiences just like everyone else. There *has* to be a way out of judging myself and others.

Why is it that most people who preach love and equality don't do much loving or view people truly as equals? Religion pops into my mind, but there are so many other instances. Instead of *pretending* to be all-loving, there must be a way for a person to feel sincere love for all living beings.

Maybe I could wake up every morning and say, "Today, I love myself, and today, I will find something beautiful about everyone I see." And at night, I will go to bed and ask myself, how much did I love myself today? How much did I love everyone else?

Maybe it isn't a cure-all. I know it's not, at least not right now, but it's a step in the right direction.

When I look at people now, I'll try to find something beautiful about them. One quality that makes them unique.

Don't we all want to be in love with ourselves, our lives, and the people in our lives? Isn't that the point of this whole experience here? Maybe that's what death teaches us—that our experience here is the ultimate privilege, and we should do everything we can to love and enjoy it to the max. We should love everyone around us and be *in love* with our lives. We should have gratitude for just being able to have this experience. Because maybe there *is* a long waiting list to get back here. What if we—all of us on the planet right now—are the privileged ones experiencing this part of human existence that will never again repeat in this way? Perhaps we ought to spend our time seeing the inner beauty of the people with which we surround ourselves. Because maybe those people can offer us a small glimmer of ourselves. Perhaps life is about connection—real, genuine relationships with other human beings, animals, and plants. And the more connected we are, the more in love with life we are.

three

THE IN-BETWEEN WORLD

End of April 2018....

Why is it that loss leaves us feeling so alone?

Inside the abyss, I feel like I'm walking in two worlds: one, my old, familiar world, the other, a strange, dark, sad place in which I do not want to be. My whole world has changed. From April of 2017 through April of 2018, I've lost my cat, dog, and mother.

This life cannot be mine, can it? It feels as though I've time-traveled to another dimension where I don't know anything, not even myself.

But I do recognize some of the figures in this new world. My dad, my brother, my grandparents, my aunts, my uncles, my cousins, my boyfriend, my friends, my three other cats, my rescued cats outside—they are all the same. But they are different too. Do I even know them? Are they even real?

I do not know this world, yet I walk through it as if it is my own.

This vessel, is it mine?

How did I get here?

The familiar-unfamiliar, a term I first hear from my therapist, Anna Marie, makes the most sense to me. It's as though I'm caught between two worlds, in a purgatory of sorts. I walked into the death realms with my mother. Am I still there? This world is a dark, fearful place. It feels like I'm walking in the underworld, watching the living world through a glass globe. *Look at all the people living*, I think. I used to be in that world, but I am not in it any longer. I can barely breathe where I am. I just want to get out of this place. How do I get out?

There is no way out of it. It just is.

"It's not real. This can't be real," I scream. Tears choke my words. "It can't be. This isn't my life. It's not my life."

Who am I crying to? There is no one to answer.

four

DARK THOUGHTS OF MY INNER WORLD

April is a blur. I am in a complete state of confusion. People are at my house almost every day. They bring us food, tons of food. I try to be as pleasant as possible, but I am dying inside. I just want to be alone. I want them to go away. I don't want anyone near me in this unfamiliar world.

Every night, my three cats sleep on me. They have never done this, but it is apparent they feel my emotions. My one cat, a long-haired Maine Coon tabby, sleeps right on my chest. He gently takes his paw and touches my face when I cry. Then he snuggles deeper into my chest. He will not leave my side. My other cat, a buff color, snuggles on my left shoulder, and my Siamese mix sleeps on my feet. They do not move. Night after night, they assume their positions, like guardians, protecting me.

At night, I cry myself to sleep. When I wake, something strange happens. For just a couple of seconds in the morning, I am at complete peace, but then I remember everything. The memories come flooding back into my brain like a rush of water. It's as if they burst out of a tightly bound box. For that one second, though, before remembering, I am no one. I am nothing. And I feel at complete peace.

During the day, I walk around like a zombie. It's an effort just to get up in the morning. I cannot eat. Nothing means anything to me—not my house, not my animals, not my relationship. I have no desire for any pleasures, not even sex. I have a sweatshirt, one I call my "I don't give a fu*k sweatshirt," and I wear it most nights. I cannot watch anything on television that is violent or sad. The only show that gets me through my days is *Fuller House*.

Mostly, I am in a constant state of fear of my death.

I refuse to go anywhere. Going to stores is the hardest. My mom and I always used to shop together. Even walking into a store can set me into a deep state of sadness, so I avoid it at all costs.

Meanwhile, I keep working to keep myself busy. I work in the music industry and am about to leave for Nashville for an event we put together every year. Throwing myself into this work is all I can do to forget what's happening, even if it's only for a little while. My dad is also going to Nashville for his company, so we will both be there. And the event falls on Mother's Day, so I won't have to worry about feeling so sad because the week will be busy.

In Nashville, I try to be pleasant—it's my job to be. It's a necessary escape from the darkness. But I am in a daze. Some people in the industry who know both my dad and me tell me how sorry they are for my loss. I appreciate their kind words, but I also feel numb as if this life is not *real* life. I feel like I'm acting, pretending to be living in this world when really, I am from another one. I am from another time, and this time is just a movie I am starring in for a short while.

I am present to do my work, but that is it. Otherwise, I am completely lost. I hardly remember the days. There are moments in Nashville that I laugh and smile. I allow myself that. I try to be my cheerful, optimistic self. But that charade ends when the nighttime comes, and I am alone in my hotel room. I am far from home, and when I return, it will not be to the comforting place I always knew. It will be to the unfamiliar world that I detest. *This cannot be my life. This life must be a dream,* I think, as I stare at Nashville's twinkling Batman Building. (It's AT&T.) *This cannot be my life.* That is the thought that repeats in my head over and over again. But if this is a dream, how come I am not waking up?

five

CELEBRATION OF LIFE

May 18ᵗʰ, 2018

In May, we have a celebration of life for my mother. It's what she wanted. Even though I am still in a state of shock and numbness, I help plan the celebration at our house. I walk around like a zombie, cleaning and getting the house in order. My dad and I clean out the weeds from our gardens. I order butterflies for release (it's a wish my mom had) and spend a ton of money on things my mom would have wanted.

On the day of the celebration, I am in a strange place emotionally. At least 100 people gather in my backyard on a cloudy, warm day. We pitch large white tents on the lawn with a host of tables and chairs. My brother and I plan to sing Leonard Cohen's "Hallelujah" because my mom loved it when we sang it. As people arrive—my friends, neighbors, family, mom's friends, dad's friends, and co-workers—I feel detached from the whole experience, like this event isn't for *my* mother. It's for someone else's mother. I am just that good friend who helped plan the celebration, so my friend would feel comforted during such a tragic time in her life.

People are smiling, happy that such a celebration is taking place. They're asking me if I'm okay. Meanwhile, I'm just worried about whether there's going to be enough food. I am busy making sure people have full plates and that the desserts haven't melted. I am going around asking anyone if they need anything.

"You don't have to do that. You don't have to make sure everyone's okay," someone says. I don't remember who. I am in an emotionally detached state and spend the celebration running around like a wedding coordinator.

At one point, we release the butterflies into the air. They all fly out, landing all over the lawn. My mom would have loved it, I know this, but I still feel numb, lonely, and sad. Children who have come to celebrate my mother marvel over the butterflies. The butterflies enjoy the butterfly bushes, while some leave the property altogether.

When the celebration is over, I am affected the most. It feels like time suddenly slows down—that I've been sucked into a black hole. There, every emotion is in full force: the anger, the sadness, the longing.

The pain is overwhelming, so I decide to try drinking my blues away. I drink an entire bottle of Riesling. I rarely drink, so I'm drunk quite quickly and am very sick a short time later. I cry my eyes out as the wine exits me via a vicious, involuntary exorcism over our pearly pink toilet.

I wake up the next morning with a colossal hangover and decide I'm never drinking like that again!

"No," I say to Jon, shooing my hand at the bottle of empty Riesling on the countertop. He jokingly asks me if I want more wine. "I think I've learned one thing. Numbing the pain is not for me. I'd rather feel the pain than escape from it this way."

six

A GLASS OF ICE WATER

I am having lunch at Turning Point in Moorestown with a good friend of mine, Al. Al is a film-director, a musician, and a comic book writer, and I've worked with him for many years. Every once in a while, we meet for lunch to discuss our creative endeavors. Trying to get back into the swing of things, I meet with him on a warm day at the end of May, a month after my mother's death.

I am still floating through life. I'm only half-invested in this new world. I am still in shock, but I'm trying to keep my mind and body moving. I'm too afraid to slow down because I am paralyzed by emotional pain and traumatic memories when I do.

I explain this to Al as we eat. We talk about my mother (he knew her quite well), and we discuss our creative projects.

But halfway through my meal, I suddenly feel hot. So hot, I feel like I'm going to pass out. Now the room is spinning. Al is still talking, but I am no longer listening.

This incident isn't the first time I've had a panic attack, but it is the first time my mother isn't there to calm me down. She had a remedy for this feeling. Once, when I was at the grocery store, and this happened to me, she gave me a pack of frozen peas and said, *"Put this on your wrist. You'll feel better."*

This was back when my mom had the "You'll always be all right, just do this" mentality. She always felt like nothing was that bad. And why shouldn't she have had that mentality? Both of her parents were in their nineties with no real health issues. She didn't have a reason to run to the doctor for every little thing because she had longevity and good health in her genes. She always had the natural remedy—a long line of natural remedies from my grandparents and their parents (who also lived until their nineties).

So, her answer was always, "You'll be fine."

And that's how I grew up. But now, now that my mother was dead, things had changed for me. I used to be the "Everything is fine, person." But now that I no longer felt confident in my longevity and wellness, I was afraid of everything.

"I feel like I'm going to pass out," I blurt out to Al. "I think I'm...having a panic attack. I don't know."

"It's okay," he says. "Just relax."

I'm confused, scared; my heart is racing. I can't breathe, and the room is still spinning.

I take my glass of ice water and put it on my wrist. Perhaps my mom got it all wrong. Maybe everything wasn't always okay, but she didn't get this wrong. At least not for me.

She knew how to calm me down. As soon as the ice water is on my wrist, my body returns to normal.

seven

WONDERFUL THINGS ARE HAPPENING
June 2018

Wonderful things happen even when a tragedy occurs. A lot of incredible things are happening in my family. My cousin, one of my closest friends, is pregnant with a precious baby boy. My sister-in-law, my brother's wife, is pregnant also.

In June, my brother and his wife decide to have a gender reveal party. I should be happy, but instead, anger and sorrow consume me. It's not that I'm unhappy for them. But I am so angry that they are moving on to a happy event when I'm still neck-deep in sorrow that I cannot yet process. It's too soon for this big of an event. It's too soon to be happy!

I show up to the gender reveal, the house full of my sister-in-law's family and mine. My brother is happy. My grandmother is happy. My aunt is happy. My cousins are happy. Everyone is smiling. *Why are they smiling*? I'm dying inside because I want them to be sad. I want them to remember they lost their mother, daughter, sister, and aunt. But they're *smiling*. I don't want to be selfish. I want to be happy too. But I'm not ready to forget my mom. For God's sake, it's been two months. Why is everyone moving on? Have they no feelings? Aren't they sad?

My mind is raging, and I start to cry in front of everyone. I hide my face into my brother's wall so no one sees. As usual, Jon is right by my side.

"Are you okay?"

"No," I shake my head. Now I am full out crying.

My brother sees me.

"Come on," he consoles. "Why don't you go upstairs?"

"Want me to go with you?" Jon asks.

"No," I shake my head.

I hurry through the crowd of guests, make my way up the stairs, and sit alone in my brother's office. It's filled with his guitars and his recording equipment.

I break down. Alone.

I don't want to be selfish, I think. *I just don't want to just forget my mom is gone and be happy. It's not right. It's not fair. They are selfish for forgetting her. Did they not love her? Are they glad she's gone?* My heart is overwhelmed with emotion again, and I sit in that room and cry until my eyes are puffy.

Then I collect myself. It's time to go back downstairs, where everyone is still happy, smiling, giggling. I don't look at anyone. I breeze right by everyone and find my cousins and my boyfriend.

It's time to do the reveal. I look around me. An outsider, that's what I feel like. These people are my family, but I don't feel connected to them. There's a buzz of happiness around me. Everyone is talking. The voices mesh together, making it seem like white noise. I feel alone, not in a "woe is me" way but more of an "alone on a sailboat at sea, trying to reach the shore, but never coming close" kind of way. There's plenty of life going around me, but I am alone. It's a strange feeling, hard to describe.

The pinata breaks and pink candies fall out.

It's a girl. My brother is having a girl.

My mother isn't here to see this. My heart aches. But Lauren's mother, Annie, isn't here either. She died a few years ago, also of cancer. *This isn't fair*, I think, the tears threatening to start up again. This little girl will grow up with no grandmothers to teach her wisdom. I didn't know Annie well, but I knew she had powerful energy and a ton of wisdom like my mom. I never met my dad's father, and I know how that felt not to have my grandfather. There was always a hole where that relationship could have been. I couldn't imagine if I never had my grandmothers. It feels wrong.

It takes everything I have to keep my shit together at this moment and paint on a smile for my brother and his wife. But I do it.

eight

THE BLUE DAWN: A POEM

One morning at 5 a.m. I am sitting downstairs in my favorite room, staring out the window. I planned on meditating, but instead, I am captivated by the world outside my window. The dawn makes the morning world a cool shade of blue. I hear songbirds and see a deer ambling across the lawn. It is so peaceful here in the blue dawn. I have not felt a peace like this in a long time, perhaps even before my mother's illness and death. *When was the last time I felt this peace*, I wonder? I realize it has not been for years.

I have my journal nearby—I planned to write about my meditation experience in it. But instead, something else comes to mind. I open my notebook and write,

The Blue Dawn

The Blue Dawn is quiet
except for the songbirds
whose morning songs
call our souls to remember.

The Blue Dawn is quiet
except for the deer
who gracefully amble
along dew-touched grass,
careful not to stir a sleeping world.

The Blue Dawn is quiet.
It is here truth exists,
in the quiet, majestic dawn.

The Blue Dawn is quiet
but soon, the world will wake
and the quiet will be gone.

When machines wake their masters
truth disappears.
Sounds drown out the songbirds
and the only sounds left are the lies of man.
While our minds fill with noises of a broken world,
our souls long for the quiet of the Blue Dawn.

nine

KALEIDOSCOPE DREAM

June 2018

I am emotionally, physically, and mentally exhausted by two in the afternoon, so much so that I can barely keep my eyes open. I figure a nap may help, and I fall asleep within minutes of my head hitting the pillow.

THE DREAM

I remember the exact moment I become lucid in the dream. It is as though my spirit intercepts my subconscious mind.

"Ah, here I am, in the place where I am both asleep and awake," my spirit silently notes.

My spirit watches the subconscious movie running in my mind, ready with some purpose to intercept further.

Meanwhile, in my subconscious movie, my dreaming self carries on a conversation with a thin twenty-something blonde-haired male. I am sitting at a desk, working at our annual music conference. I am saying to the man, "Wouldn't it be so funny if people were coming up to get their credentials, and I kept telling them to take this mug and that sticker, but nothing was actually there? Like, make people think they're crazy that they can't see what I'm talking about? I have to tell Evelyn [my co-worker] this."

For some reason, my dreaming self finds this statement hilarious and laughs.

The blonde-haired guy politely smiles but does not respond.

My spirit does not find the statement as funny as my dreaming self. She does not judge either way but simply waits for my dreaming self to finish laughing so she can merge with her. And when she does, I become lucid in the dream. Now, my lucid-dreaming self stands up and turns to see a tall staircase behind me.

"This means I can visit my mom!" I say out loud to the blonde-haired guy. He smiles again.

In the dream, I am aware that I am half-child, half-spirit. I understand the human being is always a child, governed by an incredible range of emotions. Sometimes, those emotions are out of control. That is my human existence, an emotional child here to learn and grow. I also understand that the spirit in me is old, wise, and forever-poised. When my soul and human existence merge, the child always has more control.

I run up the stairs to see the most incredible sight.

At the top of the stairs is a long stretch of iridescent mirrors. The best way I can describe it is a kaleidoscope fun-house laboratory.

Sure enough, my mom is there—miles away—walking with a very tall, about 6'5ish, light-skinned, bald male. I am not certain who this man is, but he looks very much like the famous author and spiritual teacher, Wayne Dyer, who passed away just a couple of years before my mom.

Dressed in all black, with a crisp black long-sleeved shirt tucked into black pants and a belt, the man gracefully walks alongside my mom. I sense whatever the man is telling her is significant because she is intensely focused on his words.

"Okay," she nods. I hear her loud and clear, but the man's voice is softer, serene, calm. "Okay," she replies again. I sense she is making sure she understands what he is telling her to do.

"Mom!" I scream, tears streaming down my face. Suddenly, I am weightless, like a ghost, able to float freely. I start floating toward her, fast. "Mom!!"

I am faceless, body-less, but she recognizes me anyway. As she turns to see me, a smile spreads widely across her face.

The man does not stop my mother as she rushes toward me, and despite my lack of form, when I finally reach her, we hug close.

"Mom, where are you?" I ask angrily. "Don't you know I need you? I need you, and you're off doing what?"

"I'm sorry," she says. "I'm just really busy right now. I have a ton of work to do."

"Too busy for me? I need you. I need you!" I scream. I am sobbing.

"Just let me finish this, and then I promise I'll be there for you."

My eyes dart open.

I am sobbing when I wake also.

Even though I am awake and the dream is over, I know I have connected with my mother. Out loud, I scream, "What could be so important there that you wouldn't be here with me?"

I sob, and sob, and sob.

"How dare you!" I yell. I punch my pillow.

I'll never forget the kaleidoscope laboratory, upstairs in the convention center of some unknown place, in an unknown time. And I'll ways remember a blonde-haired man who smiled and nodded, a bald man in black, and undoubtedly my mother, who had never been too busy for me on earth, but on the next plane, in the next realm, was on a mission.

One day, I hope she tells me what she was doing that was so important.

ten

CAROL AND STEVE

In late June, I eat lunch with my good friend and fellow author, Carol. Carol calls me her guardian angel because I helped her publish her book, but she is, in fact, mine. She is always imparting wisdom unto me—one of those things she writes about in her memoir about her mother, *Rosie (and me).*

Carol's wisdom is steeped in her Jewish upbringing— every time we speak, I leave with some life advice to consider. And she's always right.

"Remember what I wrote in my book, when my nephew died," Carol says one day when I visit her and her husband, Steve. "The Rabbi said, 'Death is like a ship, sailing past the horizon. You can't see the ship, but you know it's still there.'"

Carol and I talk about my mother still being here, but maybe just in a different dimension or realm. I think about the fact that none of us truly know what's beyond this life. Perhaps there is something more magnificent than we could ever imagine. Maybe this life is covered by a veil. We cannot see the truth of what is. And perhaps what *is*, is better than anything we could ever envision.

I cannot help but think about the synchronicities between Carol and me. Her mother's name was Rosie. My mother's name was Roseanne. Both of our mother's birthdays were April 5th. Carol and I are cosmically connected, meant to find one another and be friends.

But Carol is more than my friend. She and Steve feel like my family. I call Carol one of my "seven mothers" because I have seven powerful women that profoundly influence my life, especially now that my mother is gone.

I am going through some sort of post-trauma from my experience with my mother. The trauma grips me at any moment in time, and I am all consumed by it. When it happens, I am immediately crippled—caught in an intense fear or crouched on the floor, balling my eyes out. I also have developed a type of eating issue where I am afraid of eating anything. I keep thinking food will kill me, even if it's broccoli. And lastly, I am desperately trying to figure out why my mom died. I still have no answer as to what could have happened.

I talk about all of this with Carol's husband, Steve.

"The only thing my mom did do was drink bottled water," I say. "My mom rarely ate meat, never ate a hotdog or sausage, and disliked ground meat so much that when she was little, and they got hamburgers, she would take the patty off."

That's why, while everyone is selling vegan as the healthiest way to live because red meat causes cancer, I am over here wondering where my mom fits into this. She ate red meat on a rare occasion. I could probably count how many times on my fingers. Maybe red meat *is* a carcinogen, but it doesn't have to do with my mother's cancer or death. That's for sure.

Carol's husband, Steve, reminds me not to fall into the abyss.

"Remember that quote by Nietzsche," he says, "And if you gaze for long into an abyss, the abyss gazes also into you."

I understand what he means. I'm not ready to climb out of the darkness, even though I desperately want to.

eleven

A Song to My Mom

I have always been a very creative person with love for many arts. I remember as a child, the first creative art I enjoyed was painting. On one particular day when I was eight, I was off from school for an in-service holiday, and when my mom asked me what I wanted to do, I told her, "I want to sit on the back deck and just paint in the warm sun."

Of course, my mom, an artist herself, set this up for me. I remember the day so vividly. It was a warm, Spring day in March, and I sat on our back deck with a tall easel and some watercolor paints, staring at the beautiful greenery of the backyard. I don't remember what I painted that day, but I do remember how I felt. Peaceful.

But painting was just one way I found peace. Even as a child, I wrote imaginative stories and poetry. Growing up in the music industry, I loved all kinds of music. As a child, I played the flute, and I sang in the choir from elementary school through college. I taught myself how to play the piano, and I wrote my first song at twelve. Throughout my teens and twenties, I continued to paint and write songs, stories, and poetry.

Creativity has always been a source of happiness for me, a way to throw myself into the present moment and escape, in a healthy way, whatever unpleasant things are going on in my life.

Even when my mom was sick, I wrote in my journal, worked on a novel, and wrote some songs. I started one song in the hospital in the last days before my mom's death. Now, I try to channel my creativity into finishing it. It's difficult for me to play the piano without crying, but I do it anyway. As I sing the words I wrote during that time, I once more remember her last days and all the emotional pain I felt. But I need to connect in this way and put my feelings onto paper, no matter how it turns out.

I finally finish the song. It's haunting and full of the rawest truth I know.

10th Street

I lost my faith on 10th street.
I lost my mind there too.
I lost my faith on 10th street
I lost my best friend too.

I tried to keep calm,
I tried to be strong
and keep it together.

I tried not to break.
I took all I could take.
I thought it would get better.

Then I fell to my knees,
begging God, please, please, hear my prayer.
And I fell to my knees,
begging, don't leave me here. Don't leave me here.

I lost my faith on 10th Street
I lost my heart there too.
I lost my faith on 10th Street
I lost my life there too.

I tried to keep calm,
I tried to be strong
and keep it together.

I tried not to break.
I took all I could take.
I thought it would get better.

Then I fell to my knees,
begging God, please, hear my prayer.
And I fell to my knees
begging, don't leave me here. Don't leave me here.

twelve

ONE MORNING WHEN I WAKE

August 2018

An August morning, I'm awake at five. My room is dark. Only a slight ray of light shines through my white blinds. I hear the hum of my fan. Curled next to my legs are two of my cats, fast asleep. I stare up at my candle-light yellow ceiling, processing my dream from the night before.

I am still in a nightmare; only it is when I am awake, not asleep. My life feels like the aftermath of the battle, a feeling of peace, sorrow and loss, and great uncertainty. But in my dreams, all is well; all is perfect. Last night, I dreamed my mother was still alive.

THE DREAM

The doctors send my mother home, saying there is nothing they can do, as they usually do, as they did to us, but she simply smiles. We take her home, and she decides she will cut all the stress from her life. Six months later, she is well. In my dream, I am going to buy her a plaque that says, "Congratulations on being well- six months cancer-free. I'm so proud of you, Mom."

I am so genuinely happy for her. I am pleased that she is playing computer games and running her successful business.

And then I wake up.

As I have done many, many mornings, I have to remind myself that my mother, my best friend, is dead, and once more, all the horrific memories of trauma from the last six months flood my mind.

I decide meditation may help, and it does in its own way. Not in any way I could describe, except to say my mind settles a bit, and I am able to clearly and consciously remind myself that my mother is in another realm somewhere and likely is happy, so to dwell on the traumas of her passing will not change anything. The trauma is simply a memory.

I push myself to get out of bed, make my way downstairs, and share some quiet moments with my good old friend, coffee. Then I meditate for a short time. After I finish, I listen to my most recent audiobook.

I try to read a book a day or a book a week. I've just finished *As a Man Thinketh*, by James Allen, and now I am listening to Julia Seton's *The Ultimate Guide to Success*.

Reading keeps me sane, as do yoga, the gym, and meditation. But reading keeps me focused, determined, and striving to be a better person.

Adversity is a funny thing. I'm sure I am not the first to say this. But it *is* funny because it hurts more than anything. Hurts like absolute hell. There are days when I don't think I can go on, days when I have to use every bit of strength I have just to get up in the morning. But there is also this strange, deep knowing that I am meant for greatness, and the adversity I experienced plays a role in me achieving that greatness.

Greatness in what? Book writing? Songwriting? Baton-swirling? Cat-Ladying? I have no idea yet. All I know for sure is that the "knowing" is there. And even in my darkest moments, I feel a pull toward a life that is beyond anything I could have ever imagined.

So, I keep going. I keep pushing. I keep reading. I keep learning. I keep writing. I keep striving.

Maybe one day, I'll look back at this post and say, "Ah, yes, that was what it was all for." And I'll thank my mom for all the wonderful gifts she gave me. I'll take the worst tragedy of my life, and I will thank it for being my motivation to become the best version of me.

thirteen

Jumping in the River

It's August. I am trying to meditate, but it's difficult to sit still for any length of time. I'm still a hot mess mentally, but the thick mists of the death realms are beginning to clear. It's strange to think I am coming out of them. But I am not returning to my old world. I am most definitely in a new one. I'm reminded of a South Carolina sunrise on the beach on a beautiful, warm, clear day. At first, the world is dark, but one can see the slightest hints of light. Then that light grows brighter and brighter.

As I write, I think about the many trips my mom and I made to South Carolina. We would drive, just the two of us, down to Myrtle Beach and Charleston. We would spend the week trying to find ourselves, reading inspirational books, taking long beach walks, visiting the magic art and nature at Brookgreen Gardens, going shopping, and lying on the beach. Those were some of the best trips of my life. It's hard for me to process that those trips will never happen again, not in the same way, at least. My biggest fear is losing the memory of how incredible those trips were—the thought tears at my gut.

I feel like a defeated warrior, looking to pick up the pieces of my life. But I do not want to be this way. I do not want to be a victim. Instead, I want to pick myself up, rise from the ashes of my old life, and embrace this new world.

One night, Jon and I go to a ping-pong bar in Philly with some of his friends. I'm sitting on a couch next to one of Jon's friend's girlfriends as the guys play ping pong.

"How are you so wise and calm?" She asks me. "If it were me, I wouldn't be able to be out having fun just a couple of months after losing my mom."

"I don't actually know," I shrug. "I guess it's because humans are more resilient than they realize. You would be surprised just how resilient we can be. But to be honest, if I hadn't had ten years of studying higher awareness and enlightenment, I'm pretty sure I'd be at home right now under the covers. And there are days I want to do just that. There are days that I do. I put on my 'I don't give a fu*k' sweatshirt, and I sit, cry, sleep, or watch movies all day. But eventually, I push myself to rise."

"It's been three years for my mom. She still can't get over my grandfather's death. I have to drag her out of bed some days. It's so sad. It's like she's paralyzed in time."

I nod.

"I can understand her. Even though I push myself, I can understand why people don't. People say that grief heals in time, but I don't believe it does. I think the people who say that haven't really had anything bad happen to them. They're the hopeful ones—the ones who give in to the internet memes that somehow, one day, you wake up and poof; the pain is gone.

To me, life is like a river. Imagine the river just flowing, and imagine we are all just flowing with it. And then a tragedy happens, and it's as if we're catapulted out of the river and thrown onto a rock in the middle of it. But the problem is that the river is still flowing. Even if it isn't for us, at that moment. Even if our life feels like it's ended, it's going on and on for everyone else. And it's at that point that we're faced with a decision to stay on that rock forever or jump in the river and keep flowing with life, knowing that by the time we jump back in, life looks nothing like the one we had before.

I find it hard to process that while my old life has ended, it is continuing for everyone else around me. People have to choose to embrace a new life. And if people have awareness, they can use their adversity and trauma to rise to greatness or become a better version of themselves and fulfill an extraordinary destiny. Rising above our hardships is a choice. It is not guaranteed and does not come naturally. We choose to keep going or not. And sometimes we have to do it every single morning."

"Again. I do not know how you are so wise."

"I'm not sure that I am. I think I just know this from the raw experience and the willingness to learn from what happened to me."

fourteen

MUSIC FOR MY WEARY SOUL

I continue to write music to keep myself sane. I don't know if I'll do anything with these songs—hopefully someday, but just writing them keeps me from flying off the deep end. I am sitting at the piano on a relatively warm summer day—the piano is a keyboard that my brother's friend gave me. I am in the basement, my three cats sitting patiently by the piano as they always do, waiting for me to play them something. Luckily, they don't care what noises come out of the piano. It's as if they enjoy the concert regardless.

I write a line:

My mind streams thoughts onto pages.

I think about all the wisdom I've learned in ten years since I began my journey toward spiritual awakening at twenty-four.

My heart keeps the wisdom of 1000 sages.
I missed my mark a couple of times.
I got back up, now I feel fine.
I didn't bend; I didn't break.
But I sure had as much as my heart could take.

The words pour out of me easily and effortlessly like water filling a glass.

And now there's nothing in the world that I won't do.
I'll live my life in color—
vibrant shades of every hue.

I remember my mother's words as I write—begging me to live, to *truly* live. Would I fulfill her request? I hope so.

I'll climb a mountain, feel the breeze.
Swim the oceans, and sail the seas.
Fly with eagles above the trees.
I will do it all.

I'll watch the sunset; watch it rise.
Run with wolves a couple of times.
Moonlit dances, Paris nights.
I'll ask myself, have I lived life?

Have I lived? Oh-oh
Have I, Have I, Oh-Oh

Have I (lived), Have I?

fifteen

ANOTHER DREAM: BE READY

I never really know when I'm going to have a powerful dream. I do ask the Great Spirit to connect with my mom through my dreams, and while it does not happen every night, I find that when it does, especially now, the dreams are more powerful.

THE DREAM

In this dream, I arrive outside of a house. My mom's cousin and her husband help me figure out the prettiest bushes to plant in front of the house. It is their house (not in real life), and they have a daughter who is about eleven.

The house is slightly bigger than a single standing row home.

I watch as their daughter hurries out of the front door.

That's when I see a boy.

The boy is thirteen, extremely skinny, brown-haired with many freckles. He is malnourished; his eyes are narrowed as he circles the house like a shark.

Meanwhile, my mom's cousins have disappeared into the house. Now, I am outside with the girl and the boy.

I warn the girl to stay away from the boy because I sense he is bad. Very bad. In his company, I feel intense fear.

I yell for him to go away.

The girl is smiling at first, and then she's angry. Angry with me. She hides in the back seat of a neighbor's car. The girl wants me to go away so she can speak to the boy alone. But I won't move. Not until he's gone.

Eventually, he leaves. Suddenly, the house fills with people, tons, and tons of people. It's Christmas.

I hurry inside. I don't recognize anyone except my sister-in-law. She is standing by a pile of wrapped gifts with an *A* on them. Handing me one, she smiles.

I take the gift, turn around, and that's when I see my mom. Dressed in a beautiful electric-blue and black sweater with shoulder pads and wearing matching blue eye makeup, my mom is young, mid-30s, and looks gorgeous and healthy.

We both sit on the floor, and she starts speaking to me.

"Here, put these on," she says, handing me a box. Inside is a pair of beautiful, long electric-blue and black earrings. I immediately put them on.

"Thank you!" I exclaim. The earrings morph, first into pearls and then into diamonds.

Someone hands me another gift—a little girl's dress. It is white and lime green.

"Does this mean I'm having a baby?" I cry.

"Well, no. It means something else," my mom replies. "But it's good."

As always, I become lucid in the dream.

"Mom!" I cry, suddenly realizing my mom will not be there when I wake up. I rush in and give her a long, tight hug.

She hugs me but then pushes away and pretends like a hug is a foreign thing.

"I'm sorry. I don't know how."

"Why?" I ask.

"I don't know. Stef, you have to be..."

My mom tells me something so wonderful, something so profound that my life is changed instantly at that moment. The problem is, being so lucid, my brain begins to think in the dream.

Instead of paying attention to what my mom is saying, my mind screams, "Wake up and write everything down. Right now. Wake up. Write this down. Your mother is speaking to you, and it's really her."

My mother still speaks, but my mind is too anxious. Because of my waking mind, I miss her profound message.

She finishes her message. "...ready."

My spirit has heard what she said and tries to repeat it to me. My mind tries to process the words, but they become fainter and fainter.

I've missed everything she said between BE and READY.

Lastly, my mother says, "You've been jumping in your sleep lately."

And although I want to stay and hear more, my brain has won, and I wake up.

Now awake, I write every detail I can remember down. After I do, I sit in bed, trying hard to remember what the message was between *be* and *ready*. I know it's magnificent. I know it is meaningful and wise, and a message that will help me in the waking dream we call reality. But I cannot remember. I'm angry with myself for doing what we humans always do, rushing the moment. If I had been more patient and recognized the marvel occurring at that moment, maybe I would have heard the words more clearly.

Please, I whisper. *I need to remember.*

But I can't.

I research key points of the dream: the earrings, the boy, the girl, the dress, the house, etc.

But I am still interested in what I cannot remember.

I plead with the guardians of the spirit world and to my mother to resend the message.

Later, I consider that maybe her message simply is, "Be ready." *But for what,* I wonder? *Be ready for what?*

sixteen

FEAR OF THE FAMILIAR

Jon and I go out one night to a country club to see one of his co-workers sing. The country club isn't far, only ten minutes away. Once we get there, we eat. I order a salad, and Jon orders a pulled pork sandwich. His coworker's voice is pleasant, perfect for the scene around us. As we wait for our food, I am lost in thought as I watch other females around me laughing.

"I used to be carefree and happy once," I tell Jon. "I feel like that person is dead."

"Why?"

I want to tell him that I need to figure out who I am. Because I no longer know myself. Who is this new woman? I am wearing her skin, but I do not know her. Is she fun? Sexy? Lovely? Bitter? Cold? Unfriendly? Joyful? Sad? Right now, all I know is that she's lost in thought and unable to figure herself out.

"I have so much anxiety about going back to work," I suddenly blurt out. "I'm afraid. And I feel so insecure lately. It's like I've lost my confidence completely."

"Maybe you could just be in the now, in this moment."

"Yeah," I agree. After all, I've read the *Power of Now* about fifteen times cover to cover. I knew about the present moment. I'm the one who repeatedly talked about living in the present to Jon when we first met when he wasn't into anything higher-awareness. Now here he was, wiser than ever, and throwing my words right back at me.

"I want to write. I want to help people, but I'm in the middle of the storm still. This is the storm. This is the unfamiliar life I don't know. How am I supposed to...I don't know how to navigate through this? It feels like I'm living someone else's life. Like I just popped into this body one day and had to assess my surroundings and deal with it."

He doesn't reply now. He just stares at me.

"Do you think..." He treads carefully a few minutes later. "Maybe you feel like you need to be somewhere other than where you are emotionally? You're putting too much pressure on yourself to be in a better place?"

"Yes," I reply. And then, with more intensity, "Yes."

"Why?"

"Because that's what...that's what I've done my whole life. I've been an actress my whole life. And in show business, the show must go on. It's like, I've trained myself to not be vulnerable. Pretend like everything's okay, even if the whole world is crashing down. And I'm someone who feels my emotions deeply, deeper than most. I'm just really good at not showing those feelings to people when I choose not to. I get

THIS SIDE OF THE DREAM

that no one expects you to just get over a death, I get that, but people do, actually. In a way, they do. They don't say it to you. They would never say it to you. But it's almost like they're thinking, 'Okay, are you done? We all have lives to get back to.' Meanwhile, I don't even know what life I'm returning to. It's like this feeling makes you feel damaged or something because it's a current that courses through you every day, and you're not your normal self, and I feel like you're still forced to be in normal situations, working, going out with friends, and it makes you feel like you *have* to put on a show. Because you were never the sad person. No one knows you as a sad girl. You were always the one bringing joy to others. And now you're in this place—this dark, inescapable place. And no one wants to be the downer or the sad person, especially if you're happy by nature and usually so bubbly and friendly."

"Maybe just think about tomorrow…tomorrow. And try to be in this moment. Maybe it will allow you to just feel like your normal self. But you don't have to be better, Stef. You can be however you want to be."

We pay our check and start to walk out to the car. I am driving home, and then we are taking an Uber to Philly.

"I just have all these fears all of a sudden."

"About getting sick?"

"No. Actually. More about relationships. It's hard to explain. And I really want my mom. I don't want to talk about this stuff with you. I need my mom."

Tears well in my eyes, and I start to feel that emotional build-up that I've felt so many times before. It's a longing for what can never be, mixed with nerves and anxiety.

"You can talk to me, Stef," Jon assures me.

He knows how to disarm me.

"It's just I never wanted to become too familiar with a man, you know? It feels so much better to keep just a bit of distance from him."

"What do you mean?"

"Like couples who become too familiar, I mean some say it makes you more in love, but doesn't it just...doesn't it make you look at them differently? Like instead of looking at them as this hot, sexy lover, now they're this *familiar* person? And being too familiar, can't that ruin a relationship because you don't see them the same way anymore? You don't lust over them, or you just take them for granted. For instance, I had this thing happen, and now instead of going out with your happy, bubbly, sexy girlfriend, I'm just whining all the time. And sad. It's so annoying to me, and yet, I can't be anything else."

"You're not whining all the time, Stef. You're dealing with losing your mom. And I think I sometimes help. I try to make you laugh, and it works, so..."

I smile. Jon is right. He always makes me laugh.

"Plus, if by familiar you mean like ripping a fart or something, I'm okay with that," he says. "I mean, I do it."

I laugh again and say, "Now you've just gone too far. Girls definitely don't fart."

seventeen

WAKING UP IN SEPTEMBER

I'm awake. The time is 4:38 a.m. I am nodding my head as I come out of a dream. Nodding because I just received a message. Who is the message from? An unnamed man.

I have a holistic viewpoint of the spiritual world—that we're all in this together, and no religion outshines another.

If one were to call this unnamed man that visited me God, I would be okay with that. Perhaps she would call it an angel or spirit guide, and I would also be okay with it. Maybe she would say it was Jesus, a loving ancestor, a scientist outside of a simulated earth reality, or a benevolent being from beyond. The possibilities are endless. And I've studied and embraced all of them.

The point is, **He**, whoever he is, had a message for me. One that I've had to sit with for a few weeks.

THE DREAM

In my dream, I return home to see my mother is still alive. She has come back to life. What I'm most worried about in my dream is telling everyone the funeral didn't mean anything because my mom is alive after all. But I am thrilled she is alive and well.

We are all so happy. But suddenly, my mom gets sick again.

Our two-story home morphs into two unfamiliar homes. I am standing outside in the night. To my left is a small cottage where my mom is growing weaker. To my right is a white farmhouse, where my dad resides. A mighty oak tree is by the white farmhouse; one of its branches scrapes its white siding. A dimly lit dirt path leads from the dark farmhouse to the cottage.

My mother emerges from the cottage, failing fast. She falls, and I run to her, but I know I can't help her, just as I couldn't help her before. I scream for my dad, and he runs out of the farmhouse.

"I can't go through this again. I can't!" I scream as I fall to my knees, sobbing. "Please, help," I beg to whoever will listen. "Save my mom."

My arms are wrapped around her, holding her tight.

I can see and feel her fading from me, dying right in my arms.

But right before she dies, a man's voice interrupts. He is a man I do not know. Suddenly, I am lucid, very lucid. Time stops in my dream. Everything is frozen, including my parents and the large oak tree. Everything stops as though someone pushed pause on the remote control in the middle of a movie. Only the man (who is faceless and nameless) and I can move.

"Stefani," he says, his voice calm, serene. "This is what I wanted you to see. I wanted you to see why people don't come back after they die."

"Why?" I ask.

"Because, the pain of losing them again, after they have resurrected, would be unbearable to every human."

I nod.

And then I wake up. Nodding.

I think this is the first time anyone ever spoke to me directly in a dream. Was this a literal inception? And if that's possible, well, only one person could be responsible, and his name is Leonardo DiCaprio. All jokes aside, the man's voice was calm, yes, but I don't feel comforted by him, as in, this dream hasn't made me feel much better about my mother's passing. What I know for sure is that the man isn't wrong. Having our loved ones return to us seems ideal. Come back to me, we pray, scream, and beg.

But if our loved ones did return in human form and had to leave us in some other terrible way, it would be too much for us to bear.

And, as much as I love my mom, I won't be Doctor Frankenstein-ing anyone.

I've always believed dreams are powerful, but now I'm beginning to wonder if they serve a much higher purpose than most of us are willing to accept.

Maybe the person in that dream was my higher self. Perhaps it was a spirit guide, guardian angel, or God. What matters is, I will stop begging for my mom to be back here. Because while the grief is still here, the tragedy is over, and I would never want to go through that again.

eighteen

FOLLOWED BY FEAR

I break out in full-body hives on Monday, September 24, 2018. To say that stress could be a cause is an understatement, but I still try to eliminate things from my diet and everyday use that are new. I remove Omega 3 pills from my diet first, then B-Vitamins. I stop using my organic deodorant. Still, the hives do not disappear. I am using a new face wash cleansing cloths. I decide I'll try to stop those as well, but my face is perfectly clear. In fact, it's the only part of me that is.

In addition, pancreatic cancer seems to be following me. I don't know if it's just showing up more on television and in life, or I'm just more aware of it now. But for some reason,

I keep seeing it everywhere. I guess that's the Law of Attraction at work.

"You have to block it out," Jon says when I tell him I'm afraid.

My cousin's friend has just died of pancreatic cancer at thirty-five, and it has brought a host of pain and trauma back to me—not to mention a load of fear.

I listen to Jon. He is right. I do need to block it out.

"Trust me," he continues. "I know it's easier said than done, but…or never mind, don't listen to me. I don't know what I'm talking about."

"No, I get what you're saying," I nod. "And I don't want to focus my attention on that. I do have to block it out."

"It's like people will constantly repeat to you, "Oh, that's in our family, or that happened to so and so, so it could happen to you or me, but honestly does it have to? What about one person who smokes for thirty years and gets lung cancer and another person who does the same thing and lives a long, happy life with no illnesses? If one person can be fine and another not, what does that say?"

"You're right. I mean, sometimes people with the same genes in the same family will express them differently."

Jon is reminding me of what I already know. I've studied epigenetics for some time. I understand how an environment can influence gene expression. I know that you can down-regulate not-so-pleasant genes and up-regulate good ones. I spend a lot of my free time studying the research done by Bruce Lipton and Joe Dispenza. But maybe I just don't fully practice what I know. I'm still letting fear drive my life.

"I know these hives are from stress. What I need to do is find ways to de-stress myself. And I know that I need to practice what I preach. I know this stuff, but it's like the fear still wants to take over for some reason. I guess it really is all about what you think and believe," I reply, "what your brain is willing to accept or how you think about disease."

"Exactly." Jon nods. "I mean, none of us know for sure, but how do you want to live? Believing the bad is possible or just living your life happy?"

nineteen

REACHING A MILESTONE

In late September, we have my sister-in-law's baby shower. The event is a milestone for me. From the gender reveal where I could not stand to look at any smiling faces to her baby shower, I have made huge mental and emotional improvements.

I walk into the baby shower feeling happy, something that has eluded me for a long time. I sit with my aunts, cousins, and grandmother, and I am cracking jokes and being silly. I haven't felt that way in so long.

For the first time, I am excited to meet my niece.

I try to stay positive and happy the whole night. I also try not to think. If I think too hard, I dip back into the shadows of my soul, where I think about how my mother should be here for this event. I think about how I won't have her for my wedding or my children, and I feel the sadness well inside me again. I know one day I'll shift my perception, but it still tugs at me for now.

It's okay, I tell myself. It's okay to be upset.

When I get home that night, Jon and I discuss our plans for a trip we want to take. Well, I want to take the trip, and he is willing to accompany me. My mom and I talked about going to Sedona, Arizona, together for years. We were going to plan the trip for this year, but clearly, that was never going to happen. So, I told Jon I wanted to go, even if I had to go alone.

"There are energy vortexes there. My mom always used to tell me there's an energy in Sedona that is unlike anywhere else."

My mom had been to Sedona, and she always raved about it. Because she was a crystal expert, she couldn't wait to go again and visit.

"Also, there are a ton of crystal shops."

Jon tells me he's interested in going with me.

"I really think I can find a piece of myself there," I say. "I need a retreat trip to connect with my mom, and I believe this trip will be a source of healing for me."

Jon and I plan the trip for early October. We find a nice hotel just outside of Sedona and book our flights. We don't have a ton of money, but this trip is an exception for both of us because he knows how much I need this and also wants to get away.

"I can't believe we're going," I say when it's all booked. "I hope you know what you're in for. I don't even know what I'm in for. But I know it's going to be great."

twenty

THE DAY BEFORE SEDONA

October 2018

The day before Sedona, I research the Sedona vortexes, all the crystal shops, the different scenic places, museums, restaurants, and more. Going through my mom's photographs, I realize how important it is to keep these memories. So, I create a binder to bring with me. I figure any literature I collect on Sedona I can include in the binder and create a cool scrapbook or photo album when I get home.

My hives are still in full force.

I think about my intentions for this trip.

I intend for my body to heal physically.

I intend to receive insight and wisdom.

I intend to release trauma and pain.
I intend to clear my karma.
I intend to be open to new possibilities.
I intend to cleanse and clear my energy.
I intend to balance all my chakras.

I can't help but feel a stir of excitement, an anticipation of what I'm going to experience. Of course, I'm frightened too. I always feel anxious right before a trip. I hate leaving my puppy and my cats. I have so many reasons to be frightened, especially because I'm still recovering from trauma. But I'm still going. I have to go. It's non-negotiable.

I'm up most of that night with hives. They itch so badly. Here I thought I would get a peaceful, restful sleep before my trip, but instead, I am up crying most of the early morning. I begrudgingly climb out of bed, go downstairs, and take an allergy pill. Then I go back to bed and stare at the ceiling. The itching is unbearable. I try to read a book to distract me. It doesn't help. I repeat a mantra over and over again in my mind that my body is healed. Eventually, I fall asleep.

twenty-one

SEDONA: DAY ONE

On the plane, I read *One Spirit Medicine* by Alberto Villodo. I am really into the book, but my mind begins to wander. I close the book and my eyes. Maybe I can meditate. Instead, my mind is searching for meaning in life.

I think about how I am still walking between two worlds, but my studies lead me to a realization. The two worlds I am walking in, the ones I am so focused on, are on the physical plane. But what about the invisible plane, I wonder? I am aware of the invisible plane, but I am too immersed in my physical existence and spend most of my time comparing my new, unfamiliar world to my old, seemingly better one. I seem to have forgotten there is another existence beyond this physical one. It is the place from which I am observing this existence. Sometimes I am so aware of the wiser, non-judgmental observer me—a me that came from a distant place to subtly guide the wild and unruly, immature physical me in the right direction. That "me" is all-loving, all-accepting, and immensely patient. She never criticizes me but simply lets me be. She is my inner voice, my inner tour guide of the earth. She is my all-powerful self, my true-life Wonder Woman. And she reminds me, especially when I am at my worst, to just breathe.

When we reach Phoenix, we pick up our rental car and head on our way. I am nervous when I arrive in new cities. I'm afraid of the drivers, so I make Jon drive. The skies are dark gray and spit rain as we drive along.

"It looks like California," I say. "With the palm trees and the mountains."

"It reminds me of Florida, too, kind of."

"It definitely doesn't look like the desert," I say.

"Nope."

"The skies are like Jersey thick gray."

Jon and I laugh as the rain pummels down a bit harder. As we continue along the highway, I silently pray to my mom.

Please, mom, please keep us safe.

Jon turns on the radio, and we look at each other with wide eyes. Toto's "Rosanna" is playing. My mother's name was Roseanne.

"It's my mom," I smile between tears. "She's here with us, to keep us safe."

"Yep," Jon nods. "You need to write this down. There's no way you would get in the car, and when I turn on the radio, the first song is Rosanna."

We both are in shock as we head onto North 17 towards Flagstaff. Now I see magnificent cacti.

"I just realized I've never actually seen a cactus before except in that one room at Longwood Gardens, but never just doing its thing on the side of the road."

"Me either," Jon replies.

I snap photos of the mountainous countryside, marveling at the sight before me. I've never seen so many mountains. They look like they're touching the thick billowy dark clouds.

Halfway through our drive, I realize how exhausted I am. Between not sleeping well the night before and the plane ride, I can barely keep my eyes open.

The cacti become sparse as we travel north, deeper into the mountains. As we reach Sedona, we see the famous red-rocked mountains of breathtaking, almost indescribable beauty. The landscape looks fake, like someone set up a green screen or a tapestry backdrop. The rain has dwindled up here, and while it is still cloudy, one can still see the mountains.

The view of the landscape at our hotel is unlike any I have ever seen.

We overlook beautiful canyons in the distance. I am immediately snapping photos.

When we check into the hotel, I am surprised at how beautiful it is. For some reason, I think it's going to be less attractive inside, but it is so much more than I could have asked for. It's perfect. The concierge explains a host of activities we can do on our trip. She tries to get us to book a tour with her friend.

His name is White Wolf.

Wolf energy, I think.

I think of Anna Marie telling me just a few days before that I will meet wolf energy in Sedona. Is this the man with that wolf energy? He sounded perfect for what I needed, but a part of me hesitated. Did I want a tour guide and healer through these mountains? Or was this journey mine (and Jon's) alone?

I had come to Sedona to heal. That is what I want. This man could help me heal. I do not doubt that. And yet, my inner-self wants the journey to be my own. My inner voice speaks to me.

All healing comes from within. You can use people, situations, and things as a crutch to get you there, but the healing comes from you, not them. You must trust yourself.

"I don't think I will see White Wolf," I tell Jon after he and I discuss it. We are getting ready for dinner. "I think if I come back, I will. But this trip is about me. There are things I need to discover on my own. I think. At least, that's what I'm going with for now."

"Okay," Jon supports me.

Suddenly, a wave of anxiety washes over me, and I start to cry. I miss my mom so desperately. I can never control when these feelings are going to grip me. I'm back in that space again, with all those horrible memories. They cripple me. I crouch to the floor, trying to shift myself to the now.

That night my hives are so bad again I can't sleep. Luckily, I buy an anti-itch cream and slather it on my legs. I need sleep and am willing to get it however I can, no matter how many products I need to put on or in my body.

I keep thinking maybe I should see White Wolf. Perhaps I did need a healer after all.

twenty-two

SEDONA: DAY TWO

My hives are even worse when I wake up. My legs have welts everywhere, and now, I have cuts and bruises because of all the scratching. It's pouring when I look out the window.

"Welcome to the desert!" I say. "What should we do today?"

Jon shrugs.

"As long as breakfast is involved, I don't care."

I start to panic.

"What if it rains for the whole week? I knew the rain would ruin our time."

"Stef, stop being so negative. No matter what, we're going to have a good time," Jon says. "We just have to make the best of it."

"You're right," I reply. "I think I'm still going to wear hiking gear. What if we decide to go in the rain?"

Jon nods and gets dressed.

As we are about to leave, my inner self says,

Try to think of a centering thought to keep with you for today.

"Today, I'm going to practice patience," I blurt out to Jon, who is trying to get reception on his cellphone. "I also want to be open to possibilities and messages."

Jon agrees, and we go to breakfast.

As we wait for the hostess to seat us, we see a family with a small child also waiting.

"I want to be seated now!" The curly-haired blonde boy yells. He reminds me of Verruca Salt in *Willy Wonka and the Chocolate Factory*.

"William," the mother scolds, "You must have patience. You need to wait your turn."

I smile. The Universe is reminding me of my centering idea of the day.

Patience. I needed it just as much as William.

After breakfast, Jon and I decide to shop. The clouds are so thick they cover most of the mountains. Some of the mountains aren't even visible anymore.

"I feel like we're in *King Kong* with these mountains."

"Me too!" Jon agrees.

"Or some crazy island...if I hear a T-Rex roar, I'm out."

Jon laughs. We snap a dozen photos of the mysterious looking cloud-covered mountains and then head through an archway toward the shops.

Sedona has a generous amount of crystal shops. They're everywhere, and I can't help but think of my mom.

"Gosh, my mom would have loved these shops," I say, tears coming to my eyes. "Please don't think I don't love being here with you. I'm so grateful. But I really wish I could have made this trip with her."

"I know," Jon says, hugging me close in the rain.

In one of the stores, we meet Lydia, an employee. I see a bunch of healing lotions on the sidewall.

"These lotions are on sale," Lydia says. She has a calm, soft, soothing voice. "And they're all made by a local woman. She uses only organic products."

"That's great," I reply. "I have an issue right now, so I'm afraid to use any lotions." I found myself telling Lydia my whole story. Lately, I was willing to tell everyone everything. I explained about my hives. "I think they're stress-related because, honestly, I've eliminated things in my diet and life that could have been a cause."

Lydia, a beautiful middle-aged woman with blonde hair and aquamarine-blue eyes, just nods as I speak. When I finish, she responds.

"The liver," she responds. "It is overloaded with anger. I would try a primal scream. You have to release your anger somehow. Otherwise, it will stay inside you and wreak havoc."

"It's funny you mention that," I reply. "I feel like ever since my mom died, I've been expressing sadness. But I'm angry. I have a lot of anger toward the doctors who traumatized me and gave us no hope. I'm angry with my mom for pulling away from me in her last month. I have anger that my life changed in this way, while other people in my family just kept living their lives as though nothing happened. It sucks. I'm angry, but I don't know how to express it because most of the time, I'm just sad."

"You *have* to release your anger," Lydia says. "Too much anger expressed as sadness can turn into depression. You have to find a way to release it."

Lydia is right. I know this.

She gives me a few gemstones to hold. I explain to her that my mother and I worked with stones all the time.

"I'm sure you know a lot of these."

"Honestly, there are some I haven't worked with." I point out a couple of them. I hold onto a piece of Morganite. Its energy is so powerful, I know I need the stone. Lydia and I chat for several more minutes.

"In addition to working here, I am a healer," Lydia says. "If you're interested in a healing, I'll give you my card."

"Thanks. That's great," I reply. "I've been looking for some kind of healing. My therapist says I will meet a wolf-energy out here."

"Very odd," Lydia replies. "My dog, who was part wolf, just passed away, and I ask him for guidance in my work every day."

"That is strange."

I can tell Lydia is genuine, and I am open to possibilities. I am aware of the synchronicity here and make a mental note to write it down later.

"You both have earthy energy," Lydia notes.

"Yes, we're both earth signs. Taurus's actually, although my moon sign is Pisces, my rising sign is Pisces, I have a trinity of Scorpios in my chart, and my Chiron is in Gemini, so I'm all kinds of things. Besides my sun sign, I can especially feel the influence of Pisces, Aries, and Scorpio."

"So, you *do* need to release that anger," she laughs. "And you," she turns to Jon. "You have this very angelic quality about you. You hold a space for her to let her be who she needs to be."

"Oh," Jon replies. "Okay. I don't know about this stuff."

I end up purchasing a Ruby in Fuchsite heart necklace that is beautiful. Then Jon and I say goodbye to Lydia and head on to the next shop.

"I like her," I reply.

"Yeah, she was nice. Do you want to book a healing with her?"

"I don't know yet. I mean, ideally, yes. But my inner-voice is still saying I need to do this on my own. I don't know why."

"Well, whatever you decide."

"She is right, you know."

"About what?"

"About you. You do have this amazing quality. You let me be who I need to be without ever getting flustered, and I am crazy, impulsive, and erratic sometimes."

Jon laughs.

"You're fine."

"No, I mean it. Thank you for letting me be myself. Or, not really myself, but whoever this person is right now. I think you do that with a lot of people. You let them be who they are without judgment. That's an amazing quality, Jon."

The rain is coming down harder as we make our way into the next shop. I change the subject.

"I need to find gifts for people."

"Let's go across the street," Jon suggests.

In one of the shops across the street, there is a sign. In big letters, it has PATIENCE and then a quote underneath.

"Jon, do you see this right now? It's like the Universe or my mom, or something is driving this message of patience."

"That's pretty cool."

We find a discounted Native American Jewelry store across the way.

"I want to get Anna Marie a gift."

I find the perfect gift for her, a Turquoise dragonfly pin. As I purchase it, Jon and I start a conversation with the woman working behind the counter.

"This rain isn't typical, you know," the woman says. Her long gray hair is in a ponytail, and her reading glasses rest on the tip of her nose. "I mean, we have Monsoon season, but that usually begins in July and ends in September. But this? Well, I'm thankful for it because my water bill is so darn high sometimes."

"I just look at it as if my mom is cleansing Sedona for me."

"Well, thank her for me, would you?"

We all share a laugh.

"Wasn't this leftover from a hurricane?" Jon offers.

"That's what they say," the woman replies. "Anyway, it'll move out, and then it will be beautiful. Speaking of water, make sure you drink plenty of it. I found out the hard way that at a higher altitude, you are breathing less air in, but you're pushing more air out. So, the air is thinner. You need more water. Much more. In fact," she gets out a calculator, "this doctor told me you have to take your weight, divide it in half, and then divide that by thirty-two, and that will give you the minimum water required."

"Interesting," Jon says.

I take out my phone.

"So, if I weigh, let's say 133…" I calculate my minimum water intake and find it is two quarts. "I need two quarts minimum of water. And I've had about a quarter of that today."

"Yes, you must," the woman replies. "You can tell if you're dehydrated. First, you'll get a headache, and then you can get nauseous, dizzy…"

"Yikes."

"So why did you come to Sedona?" The woman asks.

I explain to her about my mother's death, how I was honoring her by coming to Sedona.

"It's a hard thing to lose your mom," she says. "To lose anyone. If I can give you one bit of advice, it would be to trust in yourself. Believe in yourself."

Once I pay for the gift, we leave. Outside the store, I say to Jon.

"So, I saw the little boy and the sign about patience, and then that lady tells us about the water. And then she tells me to trust in myself, which is exactly what I was talking about yesterday. That all healing comes from within."

Jon doesn't reply this time, at least not about my revelations. Instead, he is preoccupied.

"I have to pee," he says. "Like, really bad."

I laugh.

"Okay, let's find you a bathroom, and then we need more water."

twenty-three

THE FIRST VORTEX

It's still pouring after we finish shopping.

"What do you want to do now?" Jon asks.

"I don't know. Should we try to hike?"

"I think so. Look, we can't stop our whole trip because of a little rain. What was the first vortex you wanted to visit?"

"The airport one."

"So, let's go."

"All right," I shrug.

We drive South on 89A around two roundabouts and make a left onto Airport Road. We pass a few houses, and soon the road narrows. The rain has eased up a bit, but the skies are still cloud covered. We are driving through a mist around winding curves.

"Right here," I say, following the directions; the airport vortex is a half-mile down the road. I had printed out a paper map of the vortexes as they didn't exactly show up on a GPS.

Locals had told us that if we were to continue all the way up Airport Road, we would come to a scenic overlook that had the best view of a Sedona sunset. With all the rain, we know there will be no good sunset in Sedona on this day.

Jon pulls into the parking lot, and we gather our backpacks and raincoats. When we step out of the car, we realize we aren't the only people braving the rain to see this impressive overlook. We step out of the car, our hiking boots hitting the wet pavement. As we make our way up the short trail, I note the red clay crunching under our feet.

"Woah, do you feel that?" Jon asks.

"Yes," I nod.

We both feel an incredible surge of energy and see the twisted junipers that are said to represent the presence of a vortex.

The airport vortex overlooks much of Sedona. It's a beautiful view, even in the rain. We stay still for a few minutes, watching the misty rain and the thick clouds reaching down onto the mountains. We notice some people have hiked up a mountainside to the top of a tall red rock. I wonder if the rocks will be slick and wet, but we decide to climb the mountain anyway. It only takes us a couple of minutes. My hiking shoes have a good grip, and despite being wet, the red rocks aren't too slippery.

From the top of the mountain is a beautiful view of all of downtown Sedona. It is lovely even through the rain.

"It must be so amazing on a sunny day," I tell Jon.

"Yeah," he replies.

Only one other person is up there with us now. The rain has picked up again, and everyone has left. The man up there with us is about our age, snapping photos of the landscape. Jon and I take photos of each other in the rain. We smile and laugh as the rain pelts our faces. Soon the man comes over to us.

"Excuse me," he says.

"Yes?"

"I'm taking photos for the Sedona newspaper. People enjoying Sedona in the rain is the top story. You guys are going to be in it."

"Really?" Jon and I smile.

We hope to get a copy of the paper, but it publishes Friday, and we would be long gone by then.

The photographer says he will try to get us a copy of the newspaper and then leaves.

Now Jon and I are alone at the top of the mountain. We decide to sit on the edge and look down at the thousands of feet below.

"Let's meditate," I say.

Jon agrees, and we just sit there with our eyes closed. I smell the fresh, clean air. It's cool and crisp. The wind picks up, and so does the rain. I hold my mother's gold necklace that says Roseanne in my left hand and an Apophyllite crystal in my right hand.

Mom, connect with me, please.

I draw in deep breaths, hold for a few seconds, and release the breath out through my mouth.

My energy is cleansed and balanced.

I repeat the mantra silently over and over.

There is something oddly peaceful about this experience. Almost lovely, even. Here I am at the top of the mountain, wet drops of desert rain whipping against my face, meditating. It feels like when I walk outside on a snowy day. All is quiet, except for the wind and the wet snow hitting my face. It feels as peaceful as that, only less cold.

We sit in this peaceful meditation for several minutes. Then the rain picks up to a point past comfort for me, and I am ready to go. Oddly enough, Jon wants to stay.

"I'm really enjoying this," he says.

Meanwhile, I'm shivering now.

"Can we come back when it's nicer?" I ask.

Eventually, he agrees, and we head back down the mountainside, careful not to slip as it is now very wet. Thankfully, they have a metal railing at this mountain, and I hold onto it to climb down.

Once we are back in the car, I realize I do feel calmer. Maybe it is the vortex energy, the meditation, or taking time to breathe in the fresh air on the top of a mountain in the rain. Perhaps it is allowing the rain to cleanse me. Maybe it's a combination of everything. Either way, I feel at peace, a peace I haven't felt for a very long time. With my anxiety gone, I am ready to be open to new experiences.

Jon and I end up at Whole Foods and stay there for a few hours. When we finally get back to the hotel, we are so exhausted, we shower and go right to bed. I am looking forward to the next day.

twenty-four

THE SECOND VORTEX

Let Mother Earth heal you.

This is the thought I wake up with on the third day of the trip. Jon and I are going to Cathedral Rock today. Yesterday was the masculine vortex, and today is the feminine. There are still a ton of clouds, but we can see a bit of blue peeking through them. Jon and I make a sandwich for breakfast and are ready to go hiking shortly after. We pack a couple of protein bars and lots of water and then climb into the rental car.

Cathedral Rock isn't too far from our hotel. We make a left onto Red Rock Loop Road. The road is long, winding, and has some of the most spectacular views of Sedona I have ever seen.

"Slow down," I say to Jon. "You're making me miss a breathtaking view."

To Jon, he's just trying to get to the park. To me, he could be going ten miles an hour so we can take amazing photos.

"Do you want me to pull over?" He asks.

We see how muddy the pull-offs are.

"I guess I wouldn't. The car will get really dirty."

We follow the directions to Crescent Moon Park by making a left onto Chavez Ranch Road, then a right onto Red Rock Crossing Road. A short way down, we see the entrance of the park on the left.

"Oh, no," I say. There is a red stop sign on the front of a gate. The park is closed due to flash flooding.

"Now what do we do?"

"I don't know," I shrug. "I really wanted to go here today. What if the other places are closed?"

"I don't think so," Jon says.

"Okay, should we go to the vortex at Boynton Canyon?"

"Okay," Jon nods. "We need to get more water first, though."

We stop at Walgreens and then head toward Boynton Canyon.

Boynton Canyon is on the other side of 89A. We make a left onto Dry Creek Road and follow that down to Boynton Pass Road. The scenery is breathtaking. The sun is out now, shining onto the mountains and making them look more beautiful than anything I have ever seen. The light highlights parts of the mountains casting shadows on other parts of the land. We turn into the little parking lot at Boynton Canyon, gather our camera, backpacks, and waters, and exit the car. There is a bathroom at Boynton Canyon, and the foot of it is close to a resort.

Outside it is sunny and hot, but I wouldn't describe it as dry. Yesterday's rain had undoubtedly left the air a bit humid. As Jon and I begin on the canyon trail, we see a deer, or at least what we think is a deer.

"Look at him," I say, watching the deer graze. He has large antlers, and he is grayish-white.

"Is he a deer?"

"I don't know. I think so? Maybe he is an antelope."

Jon shrugs. I'm sure neither Jon nor I know what an antelope looks like or if they even exist in Sedona. We decide he is a deer and keep moving.

The hike up Boynton Canyon is pleasant. I'm grateful for the warm air and sunshine. The air is clean, and every once in a while, I get a faint smell of pine from the trees. I love the sound of the twigs and rocks crunching under my boots. I feel myself breathing a little heavier as I climb and stop to take some water.

Halfway up the canyon trail, I feel a surge of energy, but I can't tell if I'm just feeling light-headed from the altitude change or it's the vortex. I see the twisted Juniper trees.

"Is this a knoll?" I ask Jon.

"I have no idea," he laughs.

From what I've read about the Boynton Canyon Vortex, it is on top of a knoll.

"What is a knoll?"

"I don't know."

"We can't even look it up because we don't have any wi-fi."

"Nope," Jon says.

We stop to take a few photos of one another when we see a man walking toward us with a quick pep in his step.

"Here's a red rock for you, and for you," the man says as he approaches us. "It's a red rock from the hills of Sedona, and it's filled with love, light, and blessings."

"Thank you, I say. This is beautiful."

"If you ever feel unhappy, angry, or sad, just hold this stone close to your heart and remember all the love stored in this rock is washing through you and removing the negative energy."

"Thank you," I say again. "Do you mind telling me your name?"

"It's Robert," he says. "Have you two been up this canyon before?"

"No. actually, we came to see the vortexes and feel the energy."

"Well, you've come to a beautiful spot. There are actually two vortexes. That one right there," he points to the taller one, "is the feminine vortex. She's known as Kachina woman. There's a story behind her that she's the divine protector of us, a symbol of peace and love. And then there's Warrior Man, symbolic of divine Masculine energy. It's really a wonderful place to be."

"I'm really excited!" I explain the story of my mother's death and why I am in Sedona.

"Now, you see," Robert says, "like all of us, your mother had human consciousness. Human consciousness is what causes us to hurt each other. It's the reason we have wars and don't treat each other with love and kindness. Everyone has human consciousness, but we can evolve past it. All we have to do is fill our hearts with genuine love and kindness and spread that out to the world, and as we continue to do this, others will spread more love, and so on and so on, and slowly we will change the planet. There are beings all over the universe, and sometimes when we are pulsing out negative energy, that energy reaches them, and they just shake their heads and say, 'Oh, it's those humans again.' But we'll get it eventually. That is our purpose as beings on the planet. Love is the purpose. If we invite positive energy into us and spread it to everyone, we can make the world a better place."

"I agree," I smile.

"And I want to tell you this," he continues. "If you get an idea from the Creator, I want you to go with it. Even if it doesn't make sense, even if it doesn't work out the first time, go with it. Try again. That idea is meant for you."

When Robert is gone, I look at Jon.

"What do you think about Robert?"

"I think he had some good stuff to say."

"Honestly, someone else might think he's crazy, but you know I'm all about it. From a practical perspective, though, when you look at what he's talking about compared to reading people's negative rants and angry hate spreading on Facebook, even if I didn't know anything about what he was talking about, I'd rather listen to what he's saying any day."

"Agreed."

"What Robert said, the idea from the universe, that's how I feel about the book I'm writing. I have this feeling about it that I'm supposed to write it, even though it's different from anything else I've ever done."

"That's good then," Jon says.

"Yeah."

By now, we've reached the top of the hill. To our left is Warrior Man, to our right is Kachina Woman.

"I can see why people love this. The balance of feminine and masculine energies."

"It looks incredible."

We snap photos of ourselves, marveling at the beautiful landscape before us.

"Can I just say you are so beautiful?"

I turn to see a pretty, middle-aged brunette standing with a gray-haired man.

"Thanks so much," I reply.

"Just a beautiful girl. I just had to tell you."

"Thank you so much," I repeat.

"Is it your first time up here?" she asks.

"Yes," I nod. Then I launch into the abridged version of what we planned to see today, about my mom, and about the heart rock I just received.

"Oh, you met Robert," she replies.

She says it as though she knows him well.

"He's a nice guy," she continues.

"Yeah, I was thankful to meet him."

"You guys have to go to Antelope Canyon."

I write it down in my journal.

"It's so beautiful there," the man she's with interjects.

"You guys will love it."

"We'll definitely put it on our lists of places to go. What are your names?"

"I'm Lisa."

"Alan."

The woman and I chat about my books. She wants to buy my fiction novels. Then she steers the conversation back to my mom.

"Did you bring your mom with you?"

"Yes," I nod. "I brought her gold name necklace. She wore it every day. I needed her to come with me."

"That's very good," Lisa says. "Also, don't discount any sign your mom sends you, no matter how crazy it seems. She's sending you messages all the time. Just be open to it."

I tell her about my mom playing "Rosanna" on the radio.

"Exactly," she says. "Just like that. But there will be tons more."

After Lisa and Alan leave, Jon and I decide to climb higher on Kachina Woman. A couple is meditating by the foot of the rock. Jon and I sit with them and meditate too. After several minutes we decide to hike up the rock on the other side a little more. By now, most of the people who have been up there with us have left. It's quiet, with only one other couple around, and they are at the Warrior Man vortex. We take some photos of the breathtaking landscape. Below us is a vast, green valley. Sedona is incredibly colorful. In this one scene, I can see bright orange-reds, browns, and greens against a clean, bright blue sky and puffy white clouds.

Jon grabs my hand.

"You know I love you, right?" He says.

"Yes," I nod.

"And I want to be with you forever?"

"Yes," I reply. I can tell he's nervous, and it makes me nervous. "Are you proposing?" I laugh.

It was something we joked about before, but this time Jon pulls out a ring, gets down on one knee, and at a 10,000-foot altitude asks,

"Will you marry me?"

twenty-five

Keeping Meaning in the Journey

"Of course," I reply, hugging Jon close. Now, my heart is racing.

"Whew," Jon says, "Thank God that's over. Now I can just relax."

"Thank goodness I said yes. I mean, we are at the top of a cliff. If I said no, you could have just pushed me off."

"True," Jon nods.

"I like how I ruined your moment. I felt you get all nervous, and I was like, he's either going to tell me something horrible, or he's going to propose."

"Yeah, you're like, 'Are you going to propose?'"

We share a laugh. My body is still shaking from being nervous.

The one couple that is up there with us, previously by the Warrior Man, is making their way toward Kachina Woman.

"Let's ask these people if they'll take our photos."

"Yeah."

"Excuse me," I say to a beautiful blonde woman about my age. "We just got engaged. Would you mind taking our picture?"

"Not at all," she says brightly. "Congratulations! Tom!" She calls to the man she is with, "They just got engaged!"

"Oh, wow," Tom replies. "Congratulations!"

I never learn the blonde woman's name, but she snaps a ton of photos for Jon and me.

"Why don't we move over here, and you stand there," she moves Jon into position by a tree. "And you come here."

I walk over and stand next to Jon by the tree.

"Did she tell you we're professional wedding photographers?" Tom asks.

"Really?" I say, exchanging raised eyebrows with Jon.

"Yep, we do this for a living all day."

"Where are you located?"

"Canada."

"Wow, that is so awesome," I say.

After a ton of photos, we say goodbye to our photographer friends and make our way down the canyon.

"What are the chances of meeting Canadian wedding photographers, the only other couple up here, immediately after our proposal?"

"I would say as slim as could be."

"I think that's the Universe at work, a sign from your mom."

"I agree. I don't believe in coincidences. Not like this."

Jon and I reach the bottom of the canyon about five minutes later. By this time, my mood changes from happy to morose. I'm keenly aware that I'm wearing Jersey resting bitch face. Jon doesn't seem to notice, or if he does, he doesn't say anything.

"Can I say something?" I say after we climb back into the car. "Most girls dream of getting engaged and having this incredible wedding, and they're so focused on it, the venue, the dress, the proposal, all of it, but when you have a tragedy, it's all just bittersweet. You want to be happy, you do, but there's a part of you that is so deeply unhappy, it...you just can't be that naive, carefree, happy girl that other people are."

"I know," Jon says.

"It's like the one person," tears stream down my face now, "that I want to call and tell this to, I can't even talk to. Not really. All I get are energetic signs, but I want to talk to my mom."

"I know, I know."

Jon hugs me close.

"And, I love you," I continue, "I love you so much, and honestly, there is no better proposal than this one. This is unmatchable. But this trip is about finding myself. It's about going on a journey to heal, and even though we got engaged, and I am really happy, I don't want the whole trip to be about that because I am still searching for something."

"I understand."

"But I don't want you to think you didn't do the very best because this was the very best. I don't think there is any place better you could have proposed, in any way better, than on the top of a mountain in Sedona at a vortex, and on the feminine side."

Jon laughs.

"Well, maybe if I had millions of dollars and flew you around the world or something, that would have been better."

"Maybe," I smile as I wipe tears away.

"What should we do now?"

"I guess we should go back to the hotel, take a bit of a rest, call my dad, your mom, and then we can go to Bell Rock?"

"Sounds like a plan," Jon says.

Back at the hotel, we are getting texts and posts on social media about our engagement. I don't want to post anything about it, especially the ring; I don't want any bad mojo from people who might be jealous for some reason, but Jon insists, and I give in.

I talk to my friends and my dad, and Jon calls his parents and sister.

Then we are back on the road again toward Bell Rock.

We drive down 89A and then make a right at the roundabout onto 179A. I see a slew of shops I hadn't seen before.

"I want to go into these shops at some point," I say.

"We can do that," Jon replies.

We head down 179A further, passing another two roundabouts. A little way further down the road, we see a parking lot.

"This is it, I think," I say, and Jon turns left into the lot. There are bunches of people there. I'm feeling exhausted from our Boynton Canyon hike, but I don't say anything to Jon.

We get out of the car and make our way on to the trail. Jon hears a rattling noise.

"Is that a rattlesnake?" He asks, stopping in front of a bush.

"Don't know, don't want to know," I said. "I'm pretty sure we should keep moving."

I read a sign that says the earth is a living bacteria.

Jon, not reading the sign, picks up a handful of dirt.

"Oh, my God! Put that down!" I yell. "It's bacteria, a living organism. And who knows if it's good or bad."

"Sorry. I didn't know."

I laugh. "Well, it said so on that sign."

"Oh no," Jon replies. He drops the dirt.

We continue up the pathway to Bell Rock. The closer we get, the steeper it gets. Now we are climbing up the rock. We aren't even a quarter of the way up the rock mountain, and we come to the point that is too high for me.

"I don't know if I want to go up there," I say.

"Come on," Jon says. "You can make it."

"It's too high," I reply. "How would I even get down?"

With Jon's encouragement, I reluctantly follow him up the mountain. I step on one part of the rock, wedge my right foot on the other part, and he lifts me the rest of the way. We keep climbing until we reach a flatter spot that is great for picture taking. I try to meditate there, but I see a fire ant, and I can't keep my eyes closed for long without peeking to make sure the ant isn't coming near me. When I see him getting close, I open my eyes.

"Let's keep moving," I say. "I can't concentrate with this ant following me around."

We climb a bit further, about a quarter of the way up the rock. Looking upward, we see people at the very top. We want to go up there, but now we are just sitting looking out at more scenery.

"You know what?"

"What?"

"I can't climb anymore," I say.

"Why?"

"Because I'm so beat. And now it's 5:30, and I'm going to be sleeping on this rock if I keep going. Maybe if Cathedral Rock isn't too crazy tomorrow, we can come back here after and hike up the whole way."

"I'm actually really tired too."

Jon and I agree to climb down and start on our way.

That night we eat dinner at an Italian restaurant to celebrate. I have shrimp scampi, and Jon gets lasagna. We get gelato afterward. I don't want to tell Jon, but that meal is making me feel a little sick.

When I finally tell Jon, he says, "Really? Me too. It started before the gelato."

We are both in bed by 9:30 p.m. It isn't food poisoning, just an uncomfortable feeling we both have. My legs start to itch so badly; I cannot sleep. I can't stop thinking about Lydia's words about how I may be holding anger in my liver. How, maybe because of this pent-up anger, I need to detox or release it somehow. I look over at Jon, who is already fast asleep. I can't believe I'm engaged. I have such mixed feelings. On the one hand, I am so excited; and on the other, I am so sad. My eyes eventually close, and I fall asleep with a million thoughts racing through my mind.

twenty-six

THE BUTT-CRACK OF CATHEDRAL ROCK

In the morning, I am tired, having gotten such terrible sleep. Still, I am showered and ready to hike well before Jon is. We are going to Cathedral Rock today. I am bringing the heart rock Robert gave us with me.

"Should I wear my ring? I don't want to ruin it hiking."

"You have to. You're engaged now."

"But, wearing it to hike up a tall mountain? Is that a good idea?"

"Yes."

I shrug and put it on.

We do the same drive as before to Crescent Moon Park. This time it is open. We pay a small fee to park and drive into the large parking lot. A decent amount of people are already in the park. We continue on a short trail, and suddenly we are in a forest.

"This looks like…New Jersey," I say, laughing.

"Yeah, what the F," Jon replies. "I didn't realize there was a forest in the desert."

"We clearly don't know anything about this place. I just know I've seen this river in New Jersey."

"Yeah, it's like Palmyra Park here."

"Or Pennsylvania."

"Yes." We are walking through small winding trails through woods when we see a clearing. Before us stands the mighty Cathedral Rock, but we can't climb it. The water is too high, and we can't get over the rocks.

"How do we get over there?" I ask.

Jon and I decide to follow the woods parallel to the river, thinking we could find someplace narrow enough to cross.

We head several hundred feet down the path through tall green plants that graze our arms and legs. Then Jon stops.

"There's no way over," he says finally. "The river is too wide."

Jon and I agree to look on the other side to see if there's a way back. That's when we see two women coming from a different trail.

"Do you guys know how to get over the river?" One of the women asks.

"That's exactly what we're trying to do. We've walked up and down the river, but it's too wide to cross."

"The lady at the front said usually the river is so low you can walk over the rocks, but because of the rain, it's too high."

"Maybe we can walk to the other side and see if there are any rocks to climb over."

"Sounds good. We'll go with you."

"I'm Stefani, by the way," I say. "And this is Jon."

"I'm Sue."

"I'm Dee. Nice to meet you."

As we walk back through the trail toward the opening near Cathedral Rock, I explain why Jon and I came to Sedona and about our engagement.

"Wow! Congratulations," Sue says.

"Have you guys been here before?" Jon asks.

"Well, yes and no. Actually, we were in Utah, but this is our third stop on our journey."

"We're here because Sue is going to a conference."

"Nice. Which one?"

"A Deepak Chopra conference."

"Deepak Chopra? I love him. I've read all his books."

Sue and I are instant friends. It's obvious we know about and study a lot of the same authors. We chat about 'higher consciousness' books, Deepak Chopra, and a book by David Hawkins called *Power Vs. Force*. We have so much in common.

"Stef writes books," Jon says.

"So do I," Sue smiles. "Do you have a publishing company or..."

"I self-published, actually."

"So did I!" Sue laughs.

"I think it's clear we were meant to meet. The Universe conspires in mysterious ways."

"Absolutely. Anyone who has read *Power Vs. Force*. That's a sign."

"I've read so many books. So, so many. Gregg Braden, Louise Hay, Joe Dispenza, Bruce Lipton, Don Miguel Ruiz, Sandra Anne Taylor; I don't think I have enough time to say how many authors I've read on the quest to find whoever it is I'm searching for."

Sue laughs. We reach the clearing where the river is high.

"There really doesn't seem to be a way over this rock," she says.

"Maybe that rock out that way?" I say, pointing to a large rock in the middle of the river. "If we can find a rock closer to the bank to hop on, then get on that one, maybe we can get over."

"Might as well try," Dee says.

We climb through the trees on a trail that is visibly not widely traveled. The bushes brush our legs and arms, and I am thankful I'm wearing jeans.

When we reach the rock in the middle of the river, we see the water is running pretty quickly downstream, and there is no way to reach the rock unless we step on one that is slightly submerged underwater.

"I don't think we can get over this," Sue says.

"Yeah, it's too dangerous," Dee replies.

"What can we do then? To get to the other side?"

"Hey, there's a guy over there," Dee says. "Sir?"

She calls over the rushing water to an older, gray-haired gentleman.

"How did you get over there?" she yells.

It's hard to hear him over the water, but he uses his hands as he speaks.

"I came down from this way," he says, pointing his hand to the top of the mountain.

"How do we get there?" Dee asks.

"You have to drive around," he yells. "Leave that park and follow the road like you're going to Bell Rock."

"Thank you!" Dee yells back.

"I can't believe the water is so high from the rain we can't get over these rocks."

"It's just crazy. Well, I guess we're going to leave now and head over to the other side. We are climbing a mountain today. How about you guys?"

"I think we'll stay around here for a while," Sue says.

"There's a nice little meditation spot up this way," I say. "It overlooks the river."

We walk back the way we came and come upon a bunch of red rocks overlooking a river. We sit on the rocks.

"I think we should take a photo before we go. To remember this moment."

I get out my camera and snap a photo of Jon, Sue, and Dee. Then I switch spots with Jon.

Sue and I exchange information, and then Jon and I leave the park.

On our way to Cathedral Rock, the other side, Jon and I get lost. We end up at another park, and the ranger tells us how to get to the mountain.

"You have to go up this road, get back on 89A, then get on to 179A. Go down until you see the roundabout, and take Back O Beyond Road. That will take you to Cathedral Rock."

We thank him, do a u-turn, and then are on our way to Cathedral Rock.

We follow Back O Beyond Road. The road narrows, and we drive slowly to a parking lot filled with cars. A couple across from us is putting on sunscreen.

"I should have thought about sunscreen," Jon says.

"Ask them for some."

"No, I can't," he says.

"Just do it. Give them five bucks or something. Who isn't going to take money for a squirt of sunscreen?" Really, I am thinking, who *is* going to take money for a squirt of sunscreen, but you never know people.

Jon takes the money, climbs out of the car, and asks the couple if he can use some sunscreen.

"Of course," the woman says, shrugging away Jon's money. "I forgot last time, and that was a huge mistake. I don't want your money, though."

Jon sprays himself down as I adjust my boots and make sure my water bottle is secure on my backpack. I step out of the car, and Jon and I follow the trail up to a bathroom.

"I have to go before we climb," I say.

"Me too."

In the bathroom, which smells incredibly bad as it is a glorified port-o-potty with a bottomless hole, I make the mistake of looking at the ceiling. There, in the left-hand corner, over the door, is a spider half the size of my palm.

Don't panic, I tell myself. *Just breathe. Don't look at it. Don't look at it.*

I finish up and run out the door. There's nothing to wash my hands anyway, but I brought flushable wipes with me.

"There's a huge spider in there. Like huge."

"How big?"

I show Jon.

"F-that. I'm not going in."

"I went in."

"Yeah, so?"

"So, hold your pee, or don't look at the spider when you go."

"Whatever," Jon says and hurries into the bathroom. He returns quickly.

"It must have moved a little because it's scrunched up now."

That it moved gives me the heebie-jeebies. I shudder.

"Glad that's over with."

As Jon and I make our way up the trail, I smell the air. Sometimes it feels hot, sometimes cool. That faint scent of sweet pine fills our noses, not always, but when the wind is just right—the red rocks and clay crunch under our feet as they have so many times on our journey.

Jon and I playfully climb the mountain with ease. Then the rocks become steeper. Soon we reach a part of the rocky mountain that is about three stories high and extremely narrow.

"There is no way to get up here," I tell Jon.

"Maybe if we wedge our foot in the rock and place our hands on either side to balance ourselves."

"Are you kidding me? I'm not doing that. If we fall off here, we are really high up already. It'll hurt. Really bad."

"I think we should do it."

A father and his daughter were coming back down. They shimmied down on their butts.

"How bad is it to climb?" We ask them when they reach the small edge of the rock where we are standing.

"It's not too bad. Just brace yourself on either side to go up, and sit on your butt to get down."

"Let me go in front of you," I tell Jon. "That way, I can't look down."

"Okay," Jon says.

He hoists me up to the first rock, which is about four feet tall. Once I'm on it, there's no going back. I wedge my foot into what I name "The Butt-crack" of the mountain. Keeping my hands braced on either side, I continually push myself upward. I'm moving quickly, so I don't think about looking down. Soon the narrow path widens a bit, and there are small grooves to place my feet. Now I am crawling up the mountain with ease. I stop when I come to a fork in the climb.

"Which way?" I ask Jon, who is right behind me.

"Uh, I don't know, left?"

The air is tighter; it's harder to breathe at the top, and I draw in deep breaths.

I take the left path and hoist myself onto one of the rocks to reach the top. The top of this mountain is a round flat circle. I breathe heavily, take out my water bottle, and drink a bunch of water.

"Well, we did that," I say breathlessly.

"Yes, we did. Now what?"

I look at the time. "We should probably go soon. But...look."

Behind us is the rest of Cathedral Rock. We've only climbed up halfway.

"Now that we're here," I say, "We should probably climb up more."

"Are you sure? I thought you wanted to get back by a certain time."

"I think we should just climb for five more minutes. Then we can head back down."

Jon agrees, and we keep climbing. We are moving steadily upward, but it is pleasant. Nothing is as difficult as that tall narrow pathway.

Five minutes pass, and Jon and I are still climbing.

"We're not just climbing a mountain," I say, breathing heavily. "We're on a sort of pilgrimage to honor my mom. Well, I am anyway."

We reach a point where we stop to drink some water. A couple is walking down from the top of the mountain. As they pass us, they say, "We know you're tired, but if you keep going to the top, we promise you, it's worth it."

"Thanks," I smile. "Looks like we're going to keep going to the top, Jon."

We climb and climb, and soon we reach the top.

It's quiet at the top of the mountain and more beautiful than mere words can describe. There is a peaceful breeze, and as we look down, we can see a valley of green. Birds fly over the trees. I feel like I am in the middle of a jungle. Jon and I sit on one of the rocks and just breathe in the fresh air.

We climb up onto another rock and sit in quiet meditation. The sun is shining over us, and there are still taller, unclimbable (at least to our knowledge) mountain tops on either side of us.

After a while, I pull out my journal.

What is today's mantra? I think.

If you don't push yourself, if you don't take a chance, you can never reach the top.

Yes, that is the perfect mantra.
And the thought of the day?

Believe in synchronicity.

I look down. There, below my left foot, is a large Lemurian crystal. Someone had wedged it in between a crevice in the rock. I grab at it.

Synchronicity.

My mother and I worked with Lemurian crystals for many years. I still work with them. We even became Lemurian Seed Facilitators, which helped us connect with incredible energy during Reiki and mediations.

Is this a gift from my mother? Had someone left this crystal to charge in the feminine Cathedral Rock vortex? I feel bad taking it, but I know the crystal is meant for me.

"Look, Jon. Look at this."

"Wow," he says.

"I can't take it unless I replace it," I say. "There's an old saying with crystals. That if you lose one, never be upset. That just means it is meant for someone else. If you find one, well, it's likely meant for you. I'm going to take this, but I have a cleansed Lemurian also, and I'm going to replace this one with that one, so maybe the next person who comes looking will find this, and it'll bring them charged Cathedral Rock energy."

"That's a good idea."

I replace the empty crevice with one of my Lemurians, which is slightly smaller in size but is still extremely beautiful and memorable to me.

Jon and I sit at the top of the mountain for about fifteen minutes, then decide to make our way down the mountain.

As we do, people are struggling to reach the top.

"Your shirt is the only thing keeping me going," one man says as he breathes heavily. My shirt, which says, 'Don't Ever, Ever Quit,' gains even more popularity as I descend.

"Thank you. That's just what I needed to read," another person says as she passes.

Jon and I continue downward, reaching the "Butt-crack" about ten minutes later.

"So, how do we get down?" I ask.

"On the butt," Jon says without skipping a beat. "And then when it gets super narrow, use your arm strength to move you. I'll go first."

By night, my hives have subsided. This moment is the first on this trip that I am not scratching like crazy. Maybe a mountain climb is what I needed. Maybe connecting to the earth is what I needed.

As I'm journaling, I am halfway on Jon's pillow.

The anxiety of returning to New Jersey in the morning fills me.

I'm not healed. I need more time. But would I ever be healed? What was I looking for anyway? There is no miraculous pill for grief any more than there's a magic pill for disease. Even the best modern medications fail time and time again. Maybe the problem is we are so disconnected from the body, so disconnected from our emotions, from our true nature, and each other. We are always looking for a quick fix, but the real healing comes from within.

"Um," Jon says, looking at me. "I have a serious question."

"What?"

"Did anyone say you can journal on my pillow?"

I start laughing hysterically.

twenty-seven

THE UNFINISHED ROOM

October 2018

I felt magical in Sedona, but now I am back to my everyday routine. In this routine, my mind starts to wander into unhealthy thoughts and emotions. I no longer feel connected to the earth (understandable, considering where I live is mostly industry), and I no longer feel connected to my mom. I don't feel or sense her. Toto's "Rosanna" is not randomly playing on the radio. I am not meeting people who may bring me a higher message. I'm not receiving that guidance from my higher-self or a higher power, either. Or at least, I'm not perceiving these things are happening, even though they may be.

On a semi-warm day in October, I am driving to work. Sometimes I can't write in my journal, so I speak into my voice memos on my phone and record my thoughts. I push record before I leave, throw my phone on the passenger's seat, and as I drive, I just talk. I hit stop when I reach work. I probably look crazy to anyone who would see me, but I could care less.

One of the things I talk about is how I realize that I am measuring the progress of my transformation by our laundry room, which we started renovating months ago. We painted a lot of it a robin's egg blue, but it's still not complete. I just want it done, but Jon and my Dad are both working all day, as am I. None of us can finish it. So, every day, I return home to this unfinished room, which feels a lot like myself—messy, half-painted, incomplete.

On my drive to work, I think about the unfinished room and imagine what it will look like when it is complete. Then I start thinking about my mom and how I feel. I conclude that death feels like I'm moving forward, but I'm doing so with anticipation that one day everything will go back to normal—that my life is going to be the life I had before.

I'm not in denial. I know my mother will never return. I understand what death is, but that's not what I mean when I say return to normal. It's the zest I had for life, the wholeness I felt, the safety and security of life, the joy, the peace, the innocence. That is what I think is going to return. That this situation is all a bad dream, and someday the cloud will lift. Even though right now I'm navigating this unfamiliar new world that I don't want to be in, I still think one day I'll return to that old life. And I feel this longing and this intense need for it.

My mind knows that that life is over, but my body doesn't. A part of me died with my mom, and I need to accept that this is the new world now. There is no returning to the old. Like a hero crossing the threshold in Joseph Campbell's *The Hero with A Thousand Faces*, I had entered a new world and would never return to the old. The only option now is to keep going forward.

There is no putting life back to the way that it was. It is what it is now. And it's never going back. Every hero goes through trials and tribulations. He or she must survive and change, never to return to the old self again. But when we look at heroes, we don't see them as broken because of it. We see them as stronger, better, wiser. We want to be them *because* of what they went through. We want to emulate their strength and power. But they've only gained it because of their mastery of pain and struggle. So, maybe this new self, this person I did not yet know, doesn't have to be a worse version of me. Perhaps humans evolve the same way as superheroes. Maybe they become stronger, more powerful, and wiser with every struggle they master. Maybe, if I allow it, I can become that version of myself. And if I do, will I even want to return to the old me?

twenty-eight

A New Baby Arrives

My niece is born on October 29. It's the first time I have to visit a hospital since my mother passed away. I am having tremendous difficulty, but I know I have to do this. As soon as I walk into the hospital, a flood of memories fills me. It doesn't matter that we are in a different hospital, town, and hospital wing. It's the dimly-lit halls, the smell of antiseptic, the nurses, the doctors. It all triggers those terrible memories for me. I stop and lean against the wall as a flash of the cancer ward fills my mind. I'm taking deep breaths. My dad is well ahead of me. He doesn't notice I've stopped.

"You're not there," I say to myself, reminding my brain that I am not in that terrible moment anymore. I am in a different moment, a much more pleasant one. I draw in another deep breath and keep moving.

When I finally meet my niece, she is beautiful—the most beautiful baby I have ever seen, with large beautiful hazel eyes and a full head of black hair. She looks exactly like my mother. As I stare into her large eyes, I am so sad neither of her grandmothers will meet her. What upsets me is how much wisdom and guidance this poor child will never receive from her grandmothers. To me, the tribe of women that guide other women through life is so important. Grandmothers hold the keys of immense wisdom for their granddaughters. And once again, I reflect on how my poor niece has neither grandmother to guide her.

Now, my mind remembers when my mother found out my sister-in-law was pregnant. I am thrown into the memory, crippled by the intense pain she felt at knowing she'd never meet her granddaughter. She cried and cried and cried. I let the pain wash over me and then collect myself again. I cannot let these memories paralyze me today. I don't want to be a Debbie-downer. I want to be happy for my brother and sister-in-law. I want to be happy for this baby. So, I do my best to be happy.

twenty-nine

THE FIRST MEDIUM

November 2018

On a chilly day in early November, I sit in my car on a side-street in Collingswood, waiting to meet with the medium, Jane. I'm nervous—I've never been to a medium, and I am so desperate to connect with my mother. I pray out loud.

"Mom, please, if you can hear me. Please be here today. Please talk to me. Tell me the things only I would know. I need to feel my connection to you."

Still sitting in my car, I start to wonder about what to expect. I promised myself I would be open to whatever I experience, but I can't help thinking about what I need from my mom. I think I expect my mother to come through and tell me she's okay, that she's sorry for leaving me, and she knows I'm going to be okay because she's watching me every step of the way. I also think she's going to tell me the cause of her illness because she knows I need to put my mind at ease.

I stop myself. If I keep doing this, I know I'm going to be disappointed. I can't control what's going to happen. And I don't want to get my hopes up.

I watch as two older ladies walk out of Jane's office. Their hair is unmistakably teased and full of hairspray. I feel like they just stepped out of an episode of *The Sopranos*. One has blond hair; one has black. They are gibbering away about their experience and using hand gestures to do so. Now, it's my turn to go inside.

When I walk in, Jane meets me in a waiting room. Jane is a professional in her approach. Once I am in her office, she starts talking. Her energy is high, almost too high for me to deal with in the depressed state of mind I'm in, but she's very nice. She explains how she's going to do the reading, says a prayer to connect to the angelic realm, and then begins.

Jane starts drawing an image. Mountains. She's talking under her breath as she does.

"I have two people here that want to say hi to you," she says after she finishes the image. "Sometimes, spirits will fight to come through, and whoever wins gets the floor."

"Okay," I reply, praying it's my mom who comes through.

"I have a male here who is stepping forward. He's making this gesture."

She's rubbing her chin. "And he's on the father's side. He has a pointed nose, and you know what's interesting is the way he's coming through to me is that..." She snaps her fingers continuously. Her sentences are incomplete as she processes what she sees. "He is a male on your father's side, like a father figure to you?"

"My grandfather," I reply. I'm not sure if by saying this, I'm leading her on. I realize at this moment how skeptical I am of mediums.

"Your grandfather, okay." She nods. "Now, he crossed younger than one might think, right?"

"Yes."

"He crossed at fifty-eightish?"

My heart jumps. My grandfather died at exactly fifty-eight.

"Yes."

"He comes forward right away, and he's saying hi. Was his crossing quick? Because he's saying unexpected. Because he's like, 'I was here, and then…shit, I'm *here.*'"

I start to laugh. Although I've never met my grandfather, from how my father describes him, that is precisely the sort of thing he would say.

"Now, who lives in Arizona?" She asks.

"No one that I know of, but…"

"Hold tight. Because there's a female here that wants to talk about that, but he had to come forward first. He's telling me cute stories about you. Was there something about where you were born that's unusual? Or the date of your birthday?"

I scan my mind for possible connections. The only thing I can think of is that my birthday is April 26th, he died on April 15th, and my mom died on April 10th.

"Date is special," she nods. "'The date is special to me,' he's saying. He's trying to signify that the date is special. You need to celebrate both dates. Birthdays, yes. But also, death days. They're important too."

She says that my grandfather is so proud of my dad, establishes that his name is Salvatore, and talks about how he visits my dad's cousin's pizza shop.

"Is his wife still here?"

"Yes."

"Because he keeps saying, 'My bride. My bride.' And he is thanking your dad for looking after her. 'Thank you for looking after my bride.'" She pauses for a moment. "July. July, he's talking about something there. He says two dozen long stem roses. That's my symbol for Happy Anniversary."

She draws a tent.

"I'm getting married in July."

"He's going to be there. Now there's a female with him. He's saying, 'I've got her. I've got her.' So, Salvatore helped your mom cross over, okay?"

She describes my mom, saying she resembles Theresa Caputo because of her really blonde, full hair.

"Your mom went with you to Sedona," she says. "In fact, there was a plane change, so I'm telling you this to let you know she was with you. Mom had an illness, yes? It's interesting. She keeps talking about spreading. She keeps talking about her skin, like blackened. She's trying to communicate something about her skin. And she keeps talking about her head. What happened to the back of her head or her hair? Did you cut it or do her hair?"

"I used to do her hair."

"She's showing it to me. She's saying how pretty she looks. How you always made her feel so pretty. 'I love you. I love you. I love you, and I'm always with you,'" she says.

I can't help but feel emotional when she says this. I dab my eyes with a tissue as she speaks.

"Listen, every soul before it's born is given these two golden books," she says. "And we have to sign them with dates. The first golden book we sign is our birthdate. And the second golden book we have to sign contains our death date.

We get the breath of life to get here, and then we get a life plan and life lessons. Some of us get to stay a little longer. Your mom is saying she's so sorry that her crossing over date was so close…was so close to her anniversary and birthday. But this is really, really important because this date that she crossed over is a big date of celebration. The worst thing you can do is close the drapes and forget about life. Angels want you to *live* life. You have to celebrate her angel date. It is so important."

I try to keep up, but my mind is whirling with thoughts.

"Mom's like throwing you all kinds of signs, and I don't usually talk about signs because they're so personal but, you know, she's saying 'it's me and the butterflies.'" Jane is drawing a butterfly as she says this. "I'm like, are those dragonflies? No butterflies. You'll be at the weirdest place, and a butterfly shows up. Like you'll be in the city, and a butterfly will fly past you."

I explain how we did a butterfly ceremony for my mother and how she loved butterflies.

"Mom is talking about your ear. Do you hear her?"

"Yes. Sometimes I can hear stuff. It's faint, but…"

Jane is nodding.

"She's saying 'I'm always with you. You'll be all right. I'm okay. I am so happy to be out of that body. I did *not* like this body.'"

"My mom always used to say that when she was alive," I laugh. My mother did. For years she would say that her vessel was not working properly with her spirit.

"'I'm so glad to be out of this body. I get to just fly like a butterfly.' There's another woman with your mother. I feel like she crossed younger. Did she have a sister cross, younger or a sister-in-law?"

"No," I shake my head, "But *my* sister-in-law's mother died."

"Okay, that makes sense. She's pushing me to this side, which is the female side. Is she a new crossing?"

"No," I shake my head.

"She's showing me younger. She's showing me Florida and Disneyworld. 'I have to tell you; I'm dressed in blue.' Is someone pregnant?"

"My sister-in-law just had a baby."

"Is she a girl?"

"Yes."

"And I'm getting the letter 'A.' She's showing me two girls, this woman. 'Please know I have two girls I love,' she says. This baby's pretty. She's real pretty. So please know when the baby doesn't sleep, it's my fault because Grand-mom is playing with the baby. Also, you should know, any soul before it's given the breath of life, the grandparents get to hold the baby until it's ready to be born. And she's not with the letter A?"

"She *is*. Her name is Ariabella."

"'My two girls,' she keeps saying. 'She's such a good mom. Such a good mom.' She's talking about her daughter."

"*Your* mom thinks Ariabella looks like you. She keeps saying, 'mini-me; it's a mini-me.' She's beautiful. She doesn't stand a chance with the two grandmoms watching over her."

I'm happy Annie is there and that they're talking about Ariabella. I know my sister-in-law will want to know that her mom is with her and my niece. But I'm waiting for her to leave so my mother will speak to me again. I don't feel like she's told me what I needed to hear. But then Jane tells me she feels the energy pulling, and the spirits are ready to leave.

I can't help but feel a huge disappointment. It's not that I didn't want to connect with these other spirits, but I thought, with how deeply connected my mom and I were in this life, that she would be eager to connect with me too. Instead, I feel like she was willing to give the spotlight to anyone who came through.

And now it's over, and I don't have the answers I came for. I feel let down, not by Jane, but by my mom and the whole experience. My mother and I were so close, we were inseparable best friends, and now I feel so disconnected from her. I honestly thought that if she were to come through, it would be with such a force, and she would tell me everything I needed to hear. I walk out of Jane's office, feeling mixed emotions.

On the one hand, I feel like Jane knew incredibly detailed things. I don't doubt Jane's abilities at all. On the other hand, I question the process of connecting to the other side. How come the connection is so distant and impersonal? Why didn't my mom tell me what I prayed for her to? Did she not hear me? If she's always with me, why doesn't she just communicate with me and give me the answers I need to be okay?

I feel more confused and more disappointed with the idea of death than I did before my reading. Maybe I'm looking at it all wrong, but I desperately want to connect with my mother on a personal level. Perhaps I'm too much of a skeptic. Or maybe I'm too gullible. I have no idea. All I know is, I'm hungry, and I need to decompress from this experience and reflect on it at another time.

thirty

THE SECOND MEDIUM

It's a few weeks after my first visit to Jane, and I'm deeply unhappy. When anyone asks me how I liked Jane, I tell them how I feel. I wonder if my expectations were too high. One day, I'm talking about it with my dad.

"You know how close mom and I were," I tell him. I'm sitting on a stool around the island in our kitchen; my dad is putting dishes in the dishwasher. "It doesn't make sense that she wouldn't clearly communicate to me more. I mean, we talked about this all the time when she was alive. We would have conversations about this. About all the ways, God forbid one of us should go, that we would be in contact with one another."

"Did you ever think that maybe the rules are different on the other side? Maybe she's trying so hard to communicate with you, but it's hard to bridge the two worlds. I know your

191

mother. She would do anything to try to bridge the worlds and communicate with you."

"I know. You're right. It's possible. I wish I could understand more, though. I feel like I just really need to communicate with her."

When my friend Theresa texts me that a medium named Jonas is coming to her house, and there is an open spot left for a reading, I take it. *Maybe this one will be different*, I think. *And it's good to try out other mediums.* If mediums interpret visuals, symbols, sounds, and feelings, then every one of them must interpret them slightly differently. Perhaps this medium can connect better with my mom.

The night of the reading, I am sitting with Theresa around her kitchen island. There are three other people with us, and Jonas is doing one reading at a time in Theresa's library. We decide to let those people go first.

When it's my turn to be alone with Jonas, I'm nervous. I'm wondering if I should be doing this so close to the last reading. The one positive is, this time, I am not expecting much. He lets us record the session. I decide that in this session, I am going to be more reserved. I won't say anything to lead him on.

As soon as I sit down, he says, "You have a lot of people who have passed. Are you from Philly?"

"No," I reply.

"Do you have a connection to Philly? I'm seeing relatives from the 30s and 40s—during that time period."

"Probably," I say, thinking about the research I did on my ancestry. There were absolutely roots from Philadelphia, but mostly from Camden, NJ.

"Your great-grandmother is here," he says. "Do you have a confirmation name?"

"Yes. It's Catherine. I think with a C."

"Yes, it's with a C," he confirms, "Your great-grandmother is here."

My great-grandmother's name is Catherine. Now, I'm starting to believe something is happening.

"My grandmom is still alive," I reply. "Believe it or not, she's 92."

"Is her birthday coming up?"

"Yes. In February."

"It's not the 17th, right?"

"I actually don't know. I know it's close to that." I pause. "It's the 19th."

But seriously, close enough.

"My sister Joanna just showed me that date. Joanna passed. She's in Heaven. But she showed me that date. Your grandmom knows my sister. Isn't that weird?"

Jonas's energy is high too, but it's different than Jane's. I feel so calm with Jonas. I make a note in my mind to ask if my grandmom knows Joanna.

"Is that on your dad's side?"

"No. My mom's."

"Did your dad pass?"

"No. He's still alive."

"I keep hearing Dad. Just over and over again. Dad. Is there someone close to your Dad, who is a male figure who passed?"

"My grandfather."

"That's it. Because they're pulling me to your dad's side, and there's a male there. He wants you to know he's here as well. And he's saying the same name. So, what's his name?"

"His name was Salvatore."

"Is there another Salvatore?"

"Well, when my father was born, he was named Salvatore, but my grandfather didn't like his name, so he changed my dad's name to Ray."

"Ray," Jonas says at the same time as me. "Yeah. Gotcha. Because he's talking about the same name as your dad, so that makes sense. Uh, he loves you. He loves you. He keeps talking about how beautiful you are. How smart you are, like, he's talking about all this stuff." He pauses for a minute. "Did you spend a lot of time with him? I'm getting that sense from how he's talking."

"No, I didn't. I never met him."

"Do you feel a connection with him?"

"Yes."

"Was he artistic? He's showing me that he is artistic like you and that you both have very similar qualities. He's showing me a comparison of how much you two are alike, which is why you have a deep connection. Did he die right before you were born?"

"No, he died in 1982. April 15th, 1982."

"Okay," he nods. "He says there's something significant with his date too."

"Yeah, mm-hmm."

"Other than it being tax day."

I laugh.

"Yeah, umm," I try to gather my thoughts. "April is a huge month for me."

"You're not married yet, right?"

"No, I'm going to be, though."

"I know. I was going to tell you that. Because he's bringing up the wedding, and you don't have any children yet or anything yet, right?"

"No, I don't."

"Do you want children?"

"Yes."

"Good, because I'm getting children around you too. So, now your great grandmom, she's your grandmom's mother. There's a grandfather on that side as well. So, your grandmom's father is here too. And then I'm getting a J name like John or Joe. And he's coming through with your Grandmother's father. And I'm getting an Ed."

"I don't know an Ed. I mean, there could be, but…"

"Ask your mom about this Ed."

"My mother is deceased."

"Oh, okay," he says. He's quiet for a minute. "Oh. She's here. But she isn't talking yet. I didn't know she was here because she was so quiet, just hiding in the background."

"Why is she doing that? I don't understand."

I say this, knowing Jonas doesn't have the answer.

"She just wanted to let your family members say hello. But okay, now she's stepping forward. Did she die of cancer?"

"Yes."

"And she looks exactly like you. Same face. It's giving me chills."

"Yes," I say. "We looked a lot alike."

"Okay, now she's talking. She says she's always around you all the time. Um, she's very funny too, your mom. And she's young. She's young. Did she pass young as well?"

"Sixties."

"That's young. No, well, everyone is young in Heaven. But she's actually coming through younger to me. She's not coming through even in her sixties. She's coming through like as if she's in her early thirties. What's your mom's name?"

"Her name is Roseanne."

"Did anyone call her Rosie?"

"My dad."

"Cause she's saying, 'He called me Rosie,' but I didn't know who she was pointing to. She says you're taking good care of your dad."

"Yeah."

"Are you one of two children?"

"Yes."

"Okay, because I'm seeing two children."

"Did your mom miscarry, do you know?"

"I don't think so," I reply. "I actually don't know."

"Okay, because I'm seeing a baby that passed with her as well. She has the baby with her. She says you get dreams from her. She says you saw her in your house. Like you saw her standing there."

"I see shadows, and I know it's her."

"She loves that you know it's her. And she sends you songs too. She sends you songs to let you know she's with you."

I think about the song "Rosanna," and I start to cry.

"She loves your dad." He pauses. "He loves her, right? Because she's also showing me how much he loves her."

"Yes," I nod.

"They had to still be married when your mom passed because she's showing me this."

I nod again.

"Your mom says you hear her, you feel her. She gives you all the messages. She loves you, and I can't tell you how much she loves you. Your mom is talking about how you were by her side the whole time. This went fast, though, her cancer? Like less than a year. She's showing me five to six months."

I nod through tears. Jonas goes on to talk about my brother. We talk about how he has a baby and how my mother is concerned about how he's handling everything. Jonas tells me he sees my brother had a baby girl.

"Your mom says she knew she was going to pass that day too. Was she unconscious?"

"Yes."

"She said she heard you, and she knew that you were there. She said you knew when she left. You're very in tune with the other side. You have a lot of psychic abilities yourself. Do you know that about yourself?"

I nod, but I can't speak.

"Yeah, you're very in tune, and you knew when she left her body. That's a thing. Some people are sensitive to that. And you said goodbye to her at that time."

"I did," I say between tears. "And I wasn't even there."

"I know," Jonas says. "That's what I'm saying. So, you knew that she had already left before you found out. So, she wants you to know that." He pauses. "And she says you're doing a beautiful job with the gems. Now, do you have your own business?"

"Yes, it was her business, but I took it over."

"Does she have a shop, like a place?"

"Uh, not a physical store, but online."

"Very cool."

"Your mom is saying you were there for her every step of the way. And this was hard. This was really, really hard. Like, cancer is always hard. Some people pass really quickly from it, but your mom isn't showing me that. This was tough for everyone. And your mom hears your prayers too. And what I mean by that is she also hears your thoughts. And, um, did you used to take your mom places?"

"All the time."

"Okay, because she's always sitting in the car with you. And she said you girls had fun. So much fun. Like the best times that a mother and daughter could have."

"We did."

"And what do you do for a living again?"

"I write books, and I make the gemstones."

"The books. That's what I'm seeing. That's going to do really well. What kind of books have you written?"

"I've written adult mysteries, children's books."

"Have you published any of them?"

"Yes, seven. I self-published them, though. But I haven't written anything since my mom died."

"Okay, well, she's saying you have to. You have to keep writing. I'm seeing three books. That's what she's bringing up. Your books are going to do well. There's another book coming, Stef. There is definitely another one. But I think it's more about your life. So, that's what I think. And I think you're going to help out a lot of people with that book. And, I also see you sort of opening a place. But in the future. Not tomorrow. Opening a place where it's more of a spiritual thing or that kind of thing. That's what I think you're going to do. You just have a whole lot of psychic ability, so when you get a vibe, stick with that. I know you already know that, but really, you know people, about who's good and who isn't and that sort of thing. Okay? But your mom, she wants you to know that she's grateful that you were there with her and grateful that you helped her with her getting to the next spot that she had to go in her life. Please tell your brother and your father how much she loves them too."

"Okay."

"You really did. You really did help her with everything. She said that there was never a time that she wasn't happy with you. You guys were just best friends. You know how girls and their moms fight, like when they're teenagers? I'm talking to her, and I'm asking her, and she's like, you never did that. She is showing me that you guys were *always* best friends. So, that's what she's saying, and that's really nice. And she's saying, 'you always have me.' You always have her as your best friend. And you do throughout your whole life. She says she'll be there at your wedding; she'll be there at all your life events. And she says she already knows who you're going to have for children. She knows them already."

"Are they girls?" I ask.

"I think one is," he chuckles.

"And you know, you're going to be around for a long time. You have a lot to do here, so I think that's cool. Pay attention to your dreams, okay? You remember being with your mom when you dream, don't you?"

"Yes."

"I mean, these are vivid, vivid dreams that you get."

"Yes."

"And she says you get a lot of them. That's cool that you get them. And see, you remember every little detail of your dreams, don't you?"

"I do. Every detail."

"Isn't that cool?"

"Yes. Every color, every smell."

"Yeah, and when you have them, you remember them forever. I can remember dreams I had when my father passed. Those dreams stick with you. It's amazing. Because your soul is with them. Your soul flies, do you know that? You have out-of-body experiences, is what I'm getting at."

"Yes," I nod, remembering the few occasions that I remember astral traveling.

"And that's what vivid dreams are. When your soul leaves your body. Your father gets them too."

"Yes, he does," I reply, remembering the stories my dad told me about how when he was six, he left his body, and God told him he had to go back down to his body and live out his life. And then there was the time he woke up and turned around and saw his body was still lying in bed.

"And she takes him in her dreams too. She says not as often as yours, though. Your mom is really open. And that's the reason you're so in tune with her. You're very in tune with her, like, you know that she's around just because she's that open. For instance, you have psychic ability, she does as well, so you have that connection whether she's on earth and you're on earth, or she's in Heaven, and you're on earth. You still have that connection because it's beyond this world. It really is. It's a soul thing. A telepathic thing. That's why you feel so connected to her. And you always will. It's just like when people are on earth together, it really is, and when people have psychic ability, they get different kinds of messages than other people do, with people that they love. It's clearer. That's why you get them as much as you do. And um, but that's her. She was like that on earth too. She'll always be with you. Always."

Jonas and I finish up our conversation, and when it's time for me to leave, I stand up feeling very different from my last meeting. I feel my mom came through stronger to Jonas than Jane, and my mom understood that I needed to hear from her. While I still don't have the answers I initially sought out to find, I do feel comforted. I still feel connected to my mom in some way. I think about how Jonas talked about my mother in the present tense. At this moment, I feel that death really *isn't* the end, but it is merely a transition to another dimension, another realm. And while we can get glimpses of how it may be, through mediums and dreams, none of us really know what it's like on the other side. That's what plagues us. The "not knowing." Because if we knew how great it was, we absolutely wouldn't be sad. We would be happy for our loved ones, knowing that they are truly in a much better place. But then, life here is special and meaningful too. So maybe our loved ones aren't in a *better* place; perhaps they're in an equally great place. And what if that place is just a stepping stone to another place that's slightly different but is just as great as Earth and Heaven? Maybe part of the magic of life, whether it's three-dimensional or some other plane, is not knowing what happens when we die. And maybe the connection between souls transcends space and time. As I ponder this, I feel the dense pain inside me transforming into wonder and possibility. And that's something I'd like to hold on to.

Part Three

Braving this New World

"The wound is the place where the light enters you."

Rumi

one

CARRYING ON TRADITION
Thanksgiving 2018

When I visit with Anna Marie one day, I tell her that I don't know if I can carry out the traditions that my mom did, specifically Thanksgiving. Anna Marie tells me I am at a significant crossroads where I will have to choose to continue my mother's tradition for Thanksgiving or to change it.

I decide carrying on this tradition is extremely important to me. It is the one day that always made us feel happy, our "early" Christmas celebration. I spend weeks decorating the house. It is a lot of work, but I enjoy it. I try to keep it as my mom did, but I change some things and add my own flair. A week before Thanksgiving, the house decorations are complete.

THIS SIDE OF THE DREAM

On the day of Thanksgiving, I wake early. Instead of awakening to the smell of the turkey, I am the one who wakes early to get it in the oven. My dad and I stare at the raw turkey.

"Do you know what to do with it?" I ask.

He shakes his head.

"Not a clue."

"How do I get out all the giblets? Do I get it from this side or this side or both? Do I have to stick my hand down there?"

"We better call my sister," my dad says.

We call my aunt, and she walks us through the process of getting the turkey in the oven. Once that's done, I begin on the potatoes. My fiancé and dad help me with as much as they can. I decorate the tables just as my mom did with gold-vined table cloths, fine china, and gold silverware. I shower and put on the Sounds of Seasons music. I'm too busy to be sad today.

When the guests arrive, I work hard to serve everyone in the same way my mom did. We eat and enjoy all the delicious food.

I think I am going to feel sad, but I don't. I don't because I feel my mom is there with me that day, as though she is helping somehow. She makes the day completely flawless, from every bite of food to the little gifts for everyone.

It is a beautiful day, and by the end, all of my family exclaims how perfect it was.

"It is exactly how your mother did it," my cousin says. "I don't know how you did it, but you did."

I know how I did it. I had a lot of help from my dad, my fiancé, and my mom.

two

THE ANNUAL COOKIE EXCHANGE
December 2018

Every year, my mother would sell her gemstone jewelry at a cookie exchange Anna Marie held at her house around Christmastime. Everyone loved my mother's gemstones and couldn't wait for this cookie exchange to buy their friends and families gifts. My mother would go all out, creating the prettiest angel charms, exquisite bracelets, and purse clips. She would design her tables around each theme.

There was an angel table, a Rhinestone "Bling" Bracelet Table, and various tables for each Chakra. My mom had a magical way of talking about gemstones and how they could influence one's life—her passion for gemstones and her deep desire to help others always translated through her artistic creations.

After her death, I decided to keep her work going, although it was very difficult for me. Every gemstone was a reminder that she was gone.

This year, Anna Marie asks me if I would be willing to continue my mom's work and sell all my gemstone jewelry at the exchange. I decide to do it, although I know it can never be the same. Somehow, I feel it's important, as though my being there, carrying out her work allows all her friends to feel closer to her, if even just for a night.

I spend weeks preparing jewelry. I decide to use the chakra system as my blueprint. I begin at the root chakra and make a host of bracelets and charms. I use red coral and black obsidian. Then I move into the second chakra, known as the sacral chakra, and create pieces with orange gems—orange calcite and orange fire crackle agate. I continue to the third energy center, known as the solar plexus chakra, and make citrine bracelets and earrings.

The night of the cookie exchange, I am nervous. I am going to see all my mom's friends for the first time. What will that be like? Will they cry? Will they be upset? Jon helps me set up the tables. I try to envision how my mom would set them up. Even though my mother is gone, I want to make her proud. I want people to feel like her essence is still there, working through me.

We are just finishing setting up the last couple of tables when guests begin to arrive. Some of them I don't know, but soon I see people I do know. My heart is racing. A few people come up to me and say how sorry they are about my mom. I do everything I can to hold back tears.

As the night continues, I feel more at ease. In a way, I feel comforted being at the cookie exchange. I feel safe here with these people. I feel like they know me because they know how close I was to my mom.

At the end of the night, both Jon and I are exhausted. But I am happy. I feel I have honored my mom, and I feel closer to her.

three

Rosanna On the Radio

Today I'm having one of those no good, terrible Sundays where I am longing for my mom to be here. I almost can't stand this skin or this new life without her. I am in deep need of feminine connection. Losing my mother was like losing a direct line to the purest feminine energy, wisdom, and creativity. I think about how any female who has a close connection to that feminine wisdom, whether it's a mother, grandmother, aunt, or friend, might feel the same. The loss is suffocating—I literally can't breathe sometimes. Jon and my dad cannot understand this loss of connection. I've been crying all day, but I need to go to the store to pick up a few toiletries. It's snowing, and I don't want to drive myself.

"Will you take me to the store?" I ask Jon, who is watching an Eagles game on television.

"Can we go at halftime?" He asks.

"Yeah," I reply. My eyes are puffy and sore from crying. I remember how my Sundays revolved around reading books on enlightenment, taking walks in the park, meditation music, and making Sunday dinner. Now, all I hear is a football game. Not that football wasn't on the television on Sunday before the tragedy. It was. It was just that there was a balance between feminine energy and masculine. Now, the house is a bachelor pad. The kitchen is a mess; the lights are dark and cold. The warmth is gone.

I try to clean up a little. Half-time comes and goes, but we don't go to the store. I'm feeling worse and worse. The feeling of longing is so intense now; I feel the rage build inside me for this alien life. The rage passes, and now I'm in a state of anxiety. The tears flow once more.

We end up going to the store during the second half of the game.

"Do you want me to go in with you?" Jon asks.

I shake my head. I'm not even able to speak without the tears flowing.

As soon as I step into the store, I head straight to the body wash. Suddenly, I hear the music in the store. The song "Rosanna" is playing. I stop crying, knowing that this is not a coincidence. I realize that this isn't the second time I've heard this song. I remember now that back a month or two before Sedona, I was grocery shopping with my grandmother at Whole Foods, talking about my mom, and I mentioned that this song was playing, and wasn't that a coincidence? How would Rosanna come on exactly when we turned the radio on in Phoenix? How would it come on exactly when I step into a convenience store on a day I am feeling particularly sad?

I know it's my mom, telling me it's okay and that she's here with me.

four

DROWN OR SWIM

At the end of January, I learn I am $16,000 in debt and climbing. I am in such a state of constant anxiety that I can barely get out of bed most days. I am working at a job that I don't mind, but I don't feel fulfilled because I have stopped pursuing my dreams. I have given up on all my creative pursuits. I have zero ability to write, except in my journal. I do not even try to sell the seven books that I've already published anymore. I am severely depressed, mostly because of my mother's death and my financial debt.

I have a tough time planning my wedding because I cannot deal with the fact that my mother will not be there. People are so excited to help me plan this wedding that I care nothing about. Although I am no longer in the death realms or living in survival mode, I am still walking in a daze. When we look at a venue, I am in a fog. Dress shopping? In a daze. So many nights I spend crying, wishing, begging my mother was there. I am envious of everyone whose mother is there to help pick out the venue, dress, have the bridal shower. I feel isolated and alone. My aunt helps me tremendously. She's pushing me along to make decisions, but I'm still so apathetic about it. What was the point of some big wedding when the person you needed most wouldn't be there to enjoy it? Yet, somehow, I manage to pick out a stunning dress and book a venue.

Every time someone learns I'm engaged, they say, "Aren't you so excited?"

"No," I say. "I'm not. I'm sad."

I have lost my ability to care what anyone thinks.

I long for my old life. I feel an intense pull each time I think about all the things that would never be again: no more shopping lunch dates, no more wisdom and advice, no more trips, no more homemade dinners, no more holiday celebrations, no more calling my mom when I feel alone and need the one person who would always love me unconditionally. I am living in a world I don't know, and I don't like it.

I have hit some kind of rock bottom. Rock bottom is a strange place to be, but when you're there, you know it. It's the place just beyond our most incredible suffering where we can step outside of our pain to see we face a choice—to surrender or endure.

I contemplate the place I am in as I sip coffee out of a white "Bride to Be" mug on a cold, January morning. One of my cats, Mr. Bugatti, is snuggled on my lap.

Time and time again, we hear adversity is a calling for greatness. Recalling my journal entry about the hero's journey, I remember suffering comes first. Always. The choice is what comes second. Once we know real suffering, it is as if the universe presents us with two boxes. Our "choice" is to open one box or to open the other.

In the first box is the act of giving up. In the second box is the chance to endure, which leads to transformation. The second box allows us to become the best version of ourselves.

The question is, which one do we choose? Do we give up, or do we keep going? It's not an easy answer. There are days I want to give up. This life is so foreign to me. I don't know if I can pick up the pieces. And sometimes, I don't feel supported in the way I need to be by the people I thought would be helping me. There are other times when I know I can transform my adversity into greatness when I receive clarity and wisdom. And those moments keep me going.

It takes strength not to surrender. It takes incredible courage to pick the second box.

I can say, "I simply can't go on." I can wave my white flag and surrender. Or I can tap into my inner power and *refuse* to surrender.

I finally understand how *not* alone I am in this situation. I know so many people are going through this same experience or a similar one and face this same choice. At some point or another, the choice comes for everyone.

Giving up sounds like the easy way out, but I know it's not. I can empathize with people who feel so hopeless. When all hope is gone, and the fear of never finding happiness is in full force, life is empty. You do all these things to make yourself happy and feel joy, and nothing works. If depression takes hold, you feel apathetic and uninterested in life. Your pain leaves you feeling anxious hopelessness that permeates into everything you do. The feelings are so intermingled; they are indescribable. And you wonder, what's the point of all of this? What is the point of living?

I do all the things people say. I join a gym, working out about four days a week with Jon. I read books on enlightenment, do yoga when I can, meditate as much as possible, eat well, take supplements, write stories and song lyrics, paint, play with my puppy, and spend time with loved ones and friends. I watch comedies and laugh as much as I can. I genuinely believe these things will bring me back to happiness. But they don't. Not really.

There is still an unfillable void within me. So, I am faced with the choice to drown or swim, to pick one box or the other, just like so many other people before me. And this choice isn't just one day; it's every moment of every day.

Every day, when I wake up, I choose to open the gift of transformation and strength. I choose to swim. And I realize this gift is available to all those who suffer. Suffering ignites a primal warrior in us if we allow it. A warrior who would not put down his sword and surrender when almost all is lost but instead would rise from his suffering and say, "I will not be defeated!"

I understand now that choice is the most important part of suffering. Suppose there is any reason for our suffering, any positive at all. In that case, it is this: Trauma and tragedy have the capability of transforming us into the best versions of ourselves—more compassionate, grateful, loving, and sometimes even more successful people. The keyword, though, is capability. It is not a guaranteed transformation, but one we must be willing to undergo; one we must choose every minute of every day. In quiet contemplation on this morning, I think, *what a gift that in our darkest moments, in our most profound suffering, we are given the tools to become the most powerful version of ourselves.* Our pain invites us to be the most powerful, the strongest, and the most successful beings we can be.

In our culture, we spend a lot of time praising superheroes. They're great, but what I know now is that the most extraordinary version of us does not come from some outside power but from the inner power unleashed when we embrace strength through suffering. And those super strengths, which include more love, compassion, gratefulness, and wisdom, are available to each and every one of us.

five

WELCOME TO EARTH SCHOOL

Often, when I dream of my mother, at some point, I stand in her old office by her computer. When she was alive, she spent so much time in there, creating her beautiful gemstone bracelets and earrings, designing beautiful boxes, chatting with friends, or playing computer games.

THE DREAM

In this dream, I am in her office, standing there looking around at an empty room. That's when I hear it. Her voice, coming from downstairs in the kitchen.

I cannot run down the stairs fast enough. But when I get to the bottom of the stairs, I slow my pace. I act as though nothing is different as I stroll into the kitchen. My hair is freshly wet from a shower, and it forms into tight brunette curls. I see my beautiful mother, young, dressed in all black. With her hair teased up, she is looking as flashy as ever.

She is on the phone with her sister. My aunt must ask her if she's doing okay because my mom replies, "Everything's fine. I'm fine. The only thing that sucks is, they make you clean out your locker when you're done, and they send everything back. But I don't really care about that..."

I think nothing of the response; I'm too preoccupied with my own desires.

"Mom, do we have any chocolate?" I ask innocently.

"Yes," she replies, still holding the extend-a-phone to her left ear. "Right behind you."

I turn behind me to see two things: a red rectangle (which I believe to be dehydrated beef in a red package) and an orange pumpkin bowl. Inside the bowl are a bunch of Cadbury Eggs. They fill the bowl to the top.

I take one, noting its vibrant blue, red, green, and yellow wrapping. I unwrap it and eat it. Then I eat another.

As I eat the second one, my stomach feels sick. Without a word to my mom, who is still talking to my aunt (although now I cannot hear what they're saying), I exit the kitchen and head back up the stairs.

I enter her office once again, and then I wake up.

As usual, I need to remind myself that my mother is dead.

As peaceful and lovely as the dream is, I awake to a different life. An unfillable void. The nightmare.

"The only thing that sucks is, they make you clean out your locker when you're done, and they send everything back."

My mother's peculiar statement makes me question so many things.

I wonder about the locker and people sending stuff back.

Have we just come here to learn lessons and master them? Once our life ends, do we graduate (if we've passed), and they clean out our lockers, and off we go?

Is Earth just spirit high-school?

Perhaps the spirit world is much more complicated than we think. Maybe we do come upon the pearly gates of Heaven at death, or maybe we wake up in a laboratory and realize the whole time we were actually in a simulated reality.

Perhaps the afterlife is a mixture of both ideas—a little science and a little spirituality—and our young human minds cannot possibly comprehend how vast and wondrous it is.

Knowing crushes Fear into dust and watches as Fear's infinitesimal particles drift away in the wind. Fear, adamant and persistent, still tries to destroy the man, but Fear never fully regains its power over him because of Knowing.

I've mostly been living in fear since my mom's passing, but this dream is the first that makes me feel safe.

Whether my mother is now walking in an eternal peaceful garden with our ancestors and God, or her consciousness has disconnected from *this* reality, and she has finally restored to her original form, at least I *know* she's happy and safe. I hope she is celebrating her many accomplished earth lessons with afterlife cake. I know wherever she is, she has successfully "graduated" earth-school. And this "knowing" helps to eliminate all questions, speculations, and inferences. Whenever a fear of death grips me, I remind myself of what I know for sure.

six

A NEW VIEW ON DOCTORS
February 2019

Sometimes trying to find the why of someone's death is as productive as filling a water bottle with a large hole at the bottom of it. With some deaths, the pursuit of "why" is completely useless, at least in the traditional sense of why.

I know this, but I still go down the rabbit hole anyway, trying to figure out *why* my mom died. Yes, I know *how* my mom died. The *why* still plagues me after many months. It weighs on my mind every damn day.

I define my life by that now—trying to figure out what happened to my mom. It permeates everything I do. I'm also fearful of my death again. The feelings subsided when I studied the afterlife, but now I feel like I've taken ten steps backward in my healing. The worst feeling a person can have is the paranoia that everything, especially food, will kill him. And I have that phobia.

I'm still as afraid of broccoli as I am of bacon. Everything on the internet conflicts with everything else. At this point, I thoroughly believe the internet is a bunch of lies.

220

None of my family understands this phobia of food that I have. They just kind of cock their head to the side when I say I'm afraid to eat carrots, chicken, fish, or oatmeal. Yep. Even Brussel Sprouts. "Et Tu, Brussel Sprouts? Et Tu," I say, shaking my fists to the sky.

No, I'm not starving myself. *Please*, I'm a *Taurus*. We will eat no matter what. (If you're a Taurus, you know what I'm talking about.) I just happen to question every single thing I put in my mouth and worry it's going to kill me. I chew on the food, in a state of stress and fear that this piece of broccoli will do something terrible to my body, and I shouldn't be eating it. I eat it anyway.

This issue is very upsetting and a huge source of anxiety. Some days I'll find myself breaking down because I don't know what's safe to eat. Sometimes I won't eat anything for a little while. I don't trust the carnivores or the vegans. The sad part is, I don't think my mom's illness had anything to do with the food she ate.

Getting back to the "why" of my mother's death, one theory I haven't quite looked into yet is how emotions play a role in our bodies. I've flirted with this notion, studying authors who talk about this, but I haven't done the work. I haven't immersed myself entirely into it yet. For some reason, it sticks in the back of my mind as something I should investigate, if not jump wholeheartedly into studying.

In February, I go to an event with Evelyn about how food is our medicine. The people running it are doctors from the hospitals my mother went to, so naturally, I am nervous when I go. I don't know if I can be around them. What if one of the doctors that treated my mom is there, I wonder? This event is different from anything I have ever seen; if one of those doctors is there, they are there for a good reason.

When we arrive, a host of speakers talk about how chronic diseases are mostly coming from our diet and lifestyles and how we can prevent or even reverse some of these diseases by changing our diets. For the first time in a long time, I feel uplifted. And I'm seeing a different side of hospital doctors that I didn't know existed. These doctors are very different from the ones I met in February of the prior year. It's as though I'm in a completely different reality. I feel validated when one of the doctors points out that most medical schools do not require students to take nutrition courses, which even he feels is scary. Many of the doctors standing before me are against, "take the pill to stay ill" philosophy. They want to change the system. They see the connection between disease and nutrition. They want people to heal, and their prevention and treatment plans involve changing their patients' eating habits. They even express contempt for the insurance companies who are blatantly open with those doctors about how using nutrition to prevent and treat disease will never happen because "good health loses them money."

I feel further validated when these doctors point out that only 50% of doctors genuinely care about their patient's health. The others are like robots going from patient to patient. There is no real concern if one will die because he or she is just a number in their book.

Hearing these doctors speak is exactly what I need to forgive the hospital doctors who treated my mother. So, I decide right then and there to forgive them. Why? *Because,* I think, *first, there are many good doctors out there dedicated to wellness instead of illness. Not all doctors are the same. Secondly, those doctors I encountered are part of the 50% that focus on disease instead of wellness.*

Perhaps those doctors are merely following a "system" that has taught them to manage symptoms instead of making people well, or they're not strong enough to stand up to the system even when they feel it's wrong. Thirdly, they may be in medicine for the wrong reasons (although I believe this percentage of doctors is probably the smallest).

All I know is that those respected doctors who work hard to promote wellness instead of manage disease show the apparent flaws in our current medical system. And this system, like so many others under scrutiny in our country now, needs a cleanout and a cleanup. Thankfully, intelligent, compassionate doctors out there are taking the initiative to change the system.

When my dog died, the animal hospital called us to say how wonderful Bella was and how they would miss her. I think about all the cats I cared for and how the hospital called every time to give their condolences when one passed, even if it was feral. I think about how I wished and wished just one person from the hospital would call to say, "We are so sorry you lost your mom, but we are so glad her final moments were at our hospital, where we were doing everything we could to save her." But no one called, no one sent a letter of condolence. My mother was indeed a number to them, and I think that fueled some of my anger.

But what do I gain by being angry with them? And how do I know what those doctors were actually feeling? Suddenly, I realize I can't be responsible for how much empathy and compassion *they* show, but I can be responsible for how much *I* show. Is it possible that I need to talk less about what they need to show and be more empathetic myself? Perhaps I need to see the situation through their eyes. Could I do that? Yes, I could. I had the ability too.

At least 50% of doctors are trying to do their best, I reason. And it's difficult to change what you can't see or you don't *want* to see, especially when your school and system trained you a certain way. Perhaps seeing what they see every day is hard for these doctors—maybe they're worn down and sick of not being able to save people. Maybe some of them feel hopeless about certain diseases.

Maybe some doctors aren't brave enough to speak out, and because they can't say what they really want to, they can't help in the ways they really want to. I know some doctors have breakdowns when they lose a patient. I know I would too.

When I think about the hospital doctors that treated my mom, rather than hold an ounce of anger, I decide right then and there to send them as much love as I can. Because love is so, so much more powerful than anything else, and I know that is true.

Seeing these doctors standing here at this event, many of whom may have previously been like those doctors I encountered in the hospital, gives me hope that the system is already changing. After the event, I begin to study other doctors dedicated to this reform. I realize there are doctors dedicated to the cause of disease and to wellness. I feel uplifted and a surge of excitement. Then, I realize something else.

I have always had the gift of reading people's energy. When those hospital doctors walked into the room, before they even uttered a word, I felt the insecurity and hopelessness they felt about this disease. I telepathically picked up their helplessness. I read their body language and perceived their lack of knowledge and ways to help. And while I may have sensed their true feelings with my extrasensory ability, that didn't mean anyone else did. Then again, my ability to perceive energy continues to increase. If it is for me, perhaps it is happening for many other people as well.

My intuition tugs at me, saying, this is the beginning of the reform. Things are beginning to change, and like all change, it starts with denial. Anger follows, then a little bit of resistance. But eventually, the change happens. People everywhere, in every profession and walk of life, are waking up and becoming more aware. They are tapping into their intuition and ability to feel energies. I believe that we will all be so authentic and communicate with one another on such an energetic level one day in the future, we'll know how to help those around us and ourselves.

Even doctors. As the field begins to change, and more doctors "wake up," they will continue to learn and perfect the many-pathed route to wellness. It is quite apparent, when it comes to diseases like pancreatic cancer, the current way of doing things is outmoded, highly ineffective, and in need of deep reform. But I also believe the tides are turning. And in the years to come, doctors will sell wellness, not illness. They'll authentically deliver a path to excellent health instead of pills and poisons. I now know that so many doctors are rekindling their desire to help people—first, to prevent disease in the first place, and second, to shift the masses from illness to health. It's already happening, and I can't help but feel excited and hopeful for the future of wellness.

seven

SHIFTING TIDES IN MARCH

I finally clean out my mom's clothes. For some reason, both my dad and Jon are too busy to help me. I don't know if they are subconsciously putting off helping me because it makes them feel sad or uncomfortable, but I am a little resentful at their unwillingness to just get it done.

So, I do what many women do when men don't help. I do it my damn self. I take out every piece of clothing and all her shoes from her closets and drawers. I get big large trash bags, and I pack everything up in them. It takes me days to get everything into bags. I am crying as I do it.

Everyone has a smell, or so I thought. But as I smell my mom's shirt, just to breathe in the essence of her one last time, I am *severely* disappointed. There is *no* smell. My mother's perfectly preserved clothing has no scent. Her clothes don't smell clean either, like laundry soap or some fabric softener. It just smells like nothing. I don't know why this disturbs me so much, but it does.

When I finish, nine sizeable black trash bags are sitting in our upstairs hallway. They sit there for weeks. I walk past them every time I use the bathroom or go into my room. Jon and my dad just let them sit there.

It isn't entirely their fault. I haven't asked them to move the bags. Then again, I don't feel I should have to. One thing is for sure. I'm proud of myself for doing that all myself without having too much of a breakdown. And now, I can look at the one positive that comes from all of this. When my dad finally takes the bags to the clothing drop-off, I realize someone out there who doesn't have many clothes will get to wear my mother's well-preserved, designer ones. That is something to feel good about.

eight

THE BEST DREAM I HAVE EVER HAD

It's February 18th, 2019. One night, I have this dream. It's the best dream I have ever had. In my dream, it's nighttime.

THE DREAM

I'm walking down a dirt path. There are lanterns and torches lit around me as I come to a clearing filled with picnic benches and classmates from high school. I am at some sort of camp. I understand that I'm supposed to find my group, and I'm searching for them. I see them up ahead, led by my beloved teacher. [He looks similar to Mark Wahlberg. It's not him, but I wouldn't have been upset if it was.] I haven't seen my teacher in so long, in so many years [this is a dream—I have never seen this teacher in my waking life], but when I reach him, I am ecstatic to see him. He looks the same as he always did in my dreaming life—ear length, brown curly hair peeking out of a white cap. His hazel-brown eyes burn into mine, and I listen as he communicates telepathically to my group. All he does is look at us, and we know what we have to do. We have to go

228

through an obstacle course and reach the top of this building. My team and I head off. We are against another team.

The way this game works is this: one must tag someone on the other team. If they tag them first, they're out of the game. So, immediately three people from my team are eliminated. But we eliminate a few from the other team as well.

The other team loses another player, so now we are down to four, they are down to two. Because we are winning, the people in charge of the game give us guns. [I know, this seems violent, but it turns out they are just water guns.] It is a huge advantage. Now, instead of tagging someone out, all we have to do is spray them with the water from the gun, and they will be out. I hit someone on the other team and watch as he falls dramatically.

Josh, my very animated teammate, and I are still climbing to the top. We are running up a steep ramp actually, helping one another climb. We're almost there. We're going to win. We reach the top and yell.

"We've won!"

We hug out of happiness. Now we have to find our other teammates. The rest of our team is celebrating at one of the picnic tables by the obstacle course's starting point. They cheer for Josh and me as we make our way to the table. I sit down, and I look across the table. There is my teacher again, his eyes burning into mine. Suddenly, an all-pervasive love consumes me. It fills me so completely. I feel so safe, so secure, so loved. The feeling is expansive. It's unconditional love, and I know it. My teacher doesn't say a word to me, but he communicates to me telepathically while simultaneously passing me a note that says,

You know how much I love you, right?

"Yes," I nod. The feeling is incredible. I never, ever want it to end.

When I open my eyes, I just lay there. The feeling of unconditional love is still with me. It tingles my heart and sends a cooling sensation throughout my whole body. I never want it to end. I would do anything to go back into that dream and be with my teacher. I think about who he could be. Perhaps he is a guardian angel, another being, my mother in a different form, my higher self, Jesus, or God. I don't think who he is matters. What matters is the feeling. I think about my studies of near-death experiences, where people have talked about this all-pervasive love, something that is entirely unexplainable to another human. I cannot explain it either. I just know what I felt in the dream. I am holding on to the remnant of it now, trying to remember every detail of the feeling. Every pain is gone; every doubt, every negative emotion completely is gone. I feel complete wholeness and security. I don't need anything at all, and I could stay in this space forever. Now, the feeling is almost gone. I pray that it comes back again.

nine

ONE-YEAR ANNIVERSARY

April 10, 2019, is the one-year anniversary of my mom's death. Five days before is her birthday. I already warn everyone that I do not want to be bothered for that entire week. I am incredibly sad and depressed. I can't even think about what life was like the year before because I don't want to spiral downward again. I need to order invites for the wedding, get to the venue to deliver a payment, go for a dress fitting, and order my centerpieces, but I'm not interested in any of those things. Sometimes I think Jon and I should have waited for an entire another year before jumping into planning this wedding.* If we had, then maybe I would be in a better frame of mind by the time we are planning it. But it's too late for that now.

---

*Thank God we didn't wait, as we wouldn't have been having a wedding due to the COVID19 pandemic.

Right now, I feel like the pressure is all on me to make this event happen. Weddings are stressful enough without trying to deal with grief. I thought it would be a pleasant distraction, but instead, I am miserable.

Jon doesn't seem to understand. He thinks that I want to be in charge of all this and plan it. But I don't care about it. As horrible as it sounds.

On top of that, it's my busy season at work, so I'm struggling in more ways than one. Of course, no one sees this. I always hide my feelings.

On the day of my mom's birthday, I take the day off. I go for a walk and try to be nice to myself. It's hard to imagine never buying someone a present again, never celebrating their life again. It's so hard to stomach. But I try to relax.

On April 10th, I am trying hard to stay present. If only I can stay present, I will not think about the year before and how horrible it was for me. I decide to write and begin to compile all my journal entries, songs, and dreams into a book.

I walk through the next couple of weeks of April, feeling anxious. Wedding planning, working, and dealing with my mom's death are causing me a lot of pain.

I don't even celebrate my birthday because it means nothing to me anymore.

By the end of April, I am at my wit's end. Jon and I still haven't planned a honeymoon, so we take one night to iron out all the details. We are sitting on the couch for hours discussing where we should go and when. Initially, we choose to go to Sardinia. It's considered a "blue zone," a place where people tend to live to a ripe, old age. I love Dan Buettner's book "The Blue Zones Solution," and I plan on visiting Sardinia. The problem is, I am not familiar with where the best place in Sardinia is to go.

"There are so many places to choose from," I tell Jon, a twinge of impatience in my voice. For some reason, I want *him* to choose. He wants *me* to choose. We are both sitting on the decision, throwing the decision ball back into each other's court, waiting for someone to throw it in the damn hoop already.*

"We could go to Italy, Greece, Spain, or France."

"Or London or Scotland," I say.

"I'm fine with whatever," he says.

"Oh…kay," I roll my eyes. By this point, I'm boiling at the fact that he threw the ball back in my court once more. "I'm making a decision. We're going to Italy."

"Okay, fine. Sardinia?"

"No. Mainland. My favorite place is Florence, so I definitely want to go there."

For an entire week, Jon and I try to figure out where else we're going in Italy. We still don't know 100% by the time I leave for my annual work trip to Nashville. We need to send out invitations for the wedding, I have a dress fitting, and I'm extremely busy at work. I'm exhausted, stressed, and emotionally distraught by the time I leave for Nashville. But I collect myself, as I always do, take some deep breaths, and decide that everything will work out fine.

---

*This is how we are when we order dinner also—it's about a two hour, "what do you want?" discussion that usually leads to a mediocre eating experience.

ten

MAY IN MUSIC CITY

For the past four years, I have been going to Nashville for work. The week is long and busy. From the moment we step off the plane and into the Southern heat, we are working. At nighttime, when we are officially off the clock, I sit in quiet contemplation in my hotel room, staring at the twinkling Nashville city lights. The city is unusually noisy these days. I think about the first time I visited Nashville. The only knowledge I had of it was Miley Cyrus's line in her song "Party in the U.S.A.," where she says L.A. is not a Nashville party. When I stepped off the plane the first time I visited, I expected real cowgirls and cowboys, southern hospitality, country-music-everything, and lots of wholesome folks. Back then, I could pick out some parts of Nashville's country life, but Broadway blew my mind. It was like Las Vegas met Wildwood, NJ.

Over the next few years, the cranes kept coming in, demolishing buildings, and new buildings went up.

Now, four years later, the city is so different, and so are the people. Everyone is a transfer—finding a native from

Nashville is rare. The city is part New-York, part L.A., and a dash of Vegas. If you aren't having your bachelorette party in Nashville, are you even getting married? Actually, now, a Nashville party probably isn't all that different from an L.A. one. The noise of the city at nighttime is almost unbearable. There are sirens all through the night that keep me awake. Nashville is having a massive identity crisis, and yet, so am I. *Nothing is the same for me either, Nashville*, I think. *Maybe we're working this out together. Who am I? Who do I want to be? What do I want in life?*

I ask myself these questions as I stare out into the twinkling Nashville lights. Suddenly, I feel cold and alone. I am missing my best friend tonight. I need so badly to talk to her. With a familiar pang in my gut and tears in my eyes, I hug my pillow close and cry into it. And then I fall asleep.

My co-workers and I do share a lot of laughs this week. Nashville helps me realize something important about myself. I like to make people laugh, and for some reason, the Universal Creator has given me the ability to respond at the right time. I know how to lighten a mood—brighten a day—say the most inappropriate thing at the right time to make people laugh. I've been this way since I was a child. My mom used to laugh and say, "You're so silly." But she never judged me, no matter how weird or goofy I was.

The funny thing about suffering—losing the person I loved most makes me no longer care what people think. I have become comfortable telling people "no" and being unapologetically myself. I care nothing about people's opinions of what I should or should not do. It isn't their life. What they think of me, what they want me to do, how they want me to live my life means nothing to me anymore. My life is my own, as are my decisions. Pleasing other people means not pleasing me. And my happiness comes first. That's non-negotiable in my sudden "no fu*ks given" attitude.

So, I start cracking jokes. Betty White is my idol anyway. I always say—even in my twenties, I said this—that it would be in all of our best interests to stop emulating these younger celebrities and start emulating Betty White. She's outlived everyone, and that is a campaign I can get behind.

I feel in alignment when I'm in a place of humor—I feel free. I don't go around offending people, and I try to keep it as natural as possible. I'm just trying to keep things light for my sanity. It works.

The conference is the largest I have ever seen. By the end of the week, I am so exhausted; I don't think I can take another day. I am ready to go home. My co-workers feel the same.

People are talking about Mother's Day and their plans. I don't even want to think about the day, even though I know it's coming.

I return home from Nashville on a Thursday, my mind preoccupied with some minor work-related issues. On Friday, I can't get out of bed. Saturday, I am bed-ridden also, so tired from the week.

Jon and my dad have finally taken all my mother's clothing and shoes and given them to charity. Finally, the hallway is free. The worst is over, I think.

When Mother's Day finally arrives, I am depressed again.

Jon's mom lives far away, so we are on our own today. He is trying to keep me smiling. We decide to make homemade Gnocchi's. I don't know why we do this, but it seems to occupy our time and keep us busy. As long as I don't think about it, it can't hurt me. I don't know if this is healthy or this will backfire on me someday.

THIS SIDE OF THE DREAM

eleven

THOUGHTS IN A DRESSING ROOM

Mothers and daughters are everywhere. I am out this week trying to find a dress for my bridal shower. Shopping for the dress on my own is hard enough. When my mom was alive, we would go shopping once or twice a week. We would get a light lunch somewhere, and even if we didn't end up buying anything, we would try on clothes. I remember the countless times in the dressing room wishing we were more fit, getting excited about buying an outfit that really looked good on us, and finding the perfect dress for an event we were going to. Now, here I was in the dressing room with a host of mothers and daughters on either side of me. I counted at least six. I can't help feel jealous, angry. I desperately want to go back in time—to be at the store with my mom, just talking about nothing important and trying on outfits together. I long for the days when my only "problem" was the extra ten pounds of weight I wanted to lose. I'm in the dressing room, half squeezed into a little white number that definitely wasn't going to zip, and I start crying.

The intense longing for my mom that I feel cripples me. I realize it's something I know can never be—an unfillable void. I have felt this feeling many times since my mother's death, but never before that. The feeling is quite unique, like "if I could just get this back," but much more intense. There are no words in the English language to describe this feeling accurately. Intense longing is the only thing that comes to mind, and that description truly pales in comparison to the feeling.

Perhaps the answer is to accept and embrace this new world I am in. The old world is gone, and it will never return, but this doesn't mean I can't live in this new world. I just can't see it through the lenses of the old world. If I do, I'll always be sad and longing for something that can never be. Maybe I have to look at this new world as though I've been plucked out of my old one and placed in a new reality. The idea reminds me of those movies where some person from the past travels to the future and has to make sense of the new world around him.

Still, even though my mind is sharing this wise way of looking at my situation, I am crying alone in the dressing room, depressed at all the mothers and daughters around me. I guess that's what I get for shopping for my bridal shower dress at prom time.

twelve

THE THORNY PATH

Jon and I finally book the honeymoon. We are going to Florence and then to the Amalfi Coast. We're going to Dublin for a day also. I don't believe in bucket lists. They sound morbid. But I do believe in "living" lists, you know, doing things that make you feel alive? Well, on my living list is a trip to Dublin. I have a very strict un-negotiable plan for Dublin. I want to go to a local Irish bar and have a Guinness. I don't even drink beer, but when in Dublin…

Italy excites me. I haven't been there since high school. I think about how my mom pushed me to go on that trip, even though I was so scared. I remember her words exactly.

"I'm making you do this because you'll always travel then. If you don't do it now, you'll be too afraid to do it when you're older. You'll find some reason not to. But if you go now, you'll go anywhere."

She wasn't wrong, and I'm thankful she pushed me to go.

I often ponder (mostly in the shower for some reason) about everything that has happened over the last year.

Sometimes I think about why I was the fledgling who never left the nest. I used to feel weird about it—like how come I didn't leave New Jersey and move to California and live some extraordinary life? Why didn't I live in some cool apartment and pursue my acting career and become this huge somebody? Now, I understand.

I do not regret one day of my life, staying with my parents. To me, I was living with my best friend. My mom and I were roommates. We were like sisters. I do not regret one day being a caregiver to my mother and for being by her side during the scariest and worst time of her life. I often wonder what life would have been like if I had moved far away—if my mother and I hadn't been best friends—and if I hadn't been her caretaker. I would have missed out on the most precious of moments with my mother and best friend. I would not have visited the death realms and perhaps would not see the world how I view it now.

I also think about this pain I've gone through—how my childhood was so innocent and carefree. So beautiful. Did I have that childhood because I was going to go through this terrible time? Maybe the Universal Creator wanted me to experience the very best, so I knew what was possible in life when the worst came. I think about other people too—how some people have adversity in their childhood that shapes their lives.

I realize that choosing to persevere instead of surrendering unites us, for suffering presents us with the opportunity to view the world differently. Suppose we accept the gifts our tragedies and tribulations have to offer, like the ability to feel extreme empathy. The ability to see other people from that level of compassion and understanding and to live our lives in complete gratitude for just existing is an incredible gift. Only our adversities can bring about this gentle awareness and understanding. Suddenly, the things that truly matter become the only things we care about, and all the false-mind junk that has infected our social media timelines, our emails, and our brains dissipates. No, I don't care about trivial politics or if you vaccinated your child or not. I care about how you treat people, if you're grateful, and how much you love and connect with others.

Don't get me wrong. I wouldn't say I'm doing a great job. One day I'm doing well; the next, I'm on the floor crying. But still, every day, I choose to stand up and keep going. Maybe this willingness to prevail when it's so easy to surrender is a calling to do something great. It's a re-direction from the heavens. Or an intervention. Was the trajectory I was on before not serving me? Am I being called to do something different in this new world I live in? If so, what is this world calling me to do? And why?

I reflect again on this "choice," and I think a lot about Ralph Waldo Emerson's poem, "The Road Not Taken." I believe when something terrible happens, we do go through a significant amount of rightful victimhood. Then we are faced with those two choices; to fall or to rise, swim or drown, choose to be a victim forever, or transform.

But I realize why it's so tricky to make the right choice. It's because the victim's path is the clear one, while the path to greatness is like an untamed, unworn path with thorny thickets blocking the entrance. We can take the path of surrender and victimhood, defining ourselves negatively by what's happened to us. Suddenly, a mile down the road, that clear path becomes a dangerous cliff, with nowhere to go. To take the less-traveled road or the path to greatness, we have to cut down a ton of branches and thorns and carve our own path. It's harder, no doubt. Much harder than I previously thought. But I'm betting that our efforts will lead to a clearer path, and the more we choose to break through the thorns, the clearer the path becomes until we're strolling down a clear dirt path in a meadow of wildflowers.

Even though I know this, reflecting on this concept yet again, I'm still cutting through those thorny branches. But I *can* say, with unwavering knowing, that one day, this path will be clear.

thirteen

ON THE LAST DAY OF MAY 2019

My mom is a trendsetter, even in her death. Here I am at the third funeral within a year and six weeks of my mother's death. This time, it's for my grandmother's sister-in-law. My mom's cousins decide to do the same trendy service that my mother had—no viewing and a celebration of life at some later point in time. I am thinking, "Wow, my mom knows how to set a real trend even from beyond the grave," when suddenly my dad says it.

His exact words are: "Your mom sure knows how to set a trend, doesn't she?"

While I'm at the cemetery on this sweltering May day, I visit my mom's grave. The lawn crew is weed-whacking, and I smile. So much for a relaxing, tranquil visit to my mother, I think. My father tells me they were not keeping up with the grounds, so he bought a battery-operated weedwhacker and cleared the entire area around my mom's grave. I chuckle when I think of him doing that.

Now the lawn crew is here, so they must have gotten the message. My dad and I visit my grandfather, Salvatore Michael Milanese, a U.S. Army War Veteran in WWII. His grave is about a quarter of a mile from my mom's and has an American Flag gently blowing in the slight almost-summer breeze.

At Dolores' funeral, I am crying. Yes, I'm sad for my mother's aunt (my mother's middle name was Dolores), but I feel more overwhelming sadness because I think of my mother. I can't keep it together. The tears are streaming down. I look down to see I'm standing on someone's grave, not on their gravestone, but their actual buried body. It's kind of hard not to do that, you see, considering many of the open spaces at a graveyard are basically on top of buried bodies.

I see the headstone in front of me. It says, *Vito and Catherine Moles*. My great-grandparents. I didn't even know I was standing there, on top of my great grandparents' bones. It feels weird but comforting also. It feels like synchronicity that I would be standing there unknowingly. Maybe they are just trying to get me to remember they're here with me. Perhaps I'm reaching. Either way, I think about how many family members I have buried in this graveyard, and I hope all their souls are together.

Just then, my cousin comes up to me.

"Do you want to hear a dream about your mother?"

"Yes. Absolutely," I say.

"She came to my house, walked right through the door, and she wanted to know where you were. We all knew she was dead, and she knew too. She was like, 'I'm fine; I'm fine, but where's Stef? I need to see her now. I know she's having a very difficult time, and I just need to make sure she's okay.'"

It comforts me to hear this dream because I *am* having a hard time.

"I feel like the dead never come to the person," my cousin says.

"I know. It's so rude."

We laugh.

Later, I meet a woman at the grocery store. She just kind of comes up to me and starts talking about deodorant. I usually buy a men's organic kind because, for some reason, the women's deodorants have ingredients that cause an allergic reaction in me. But I didn't tell her that. I didn't say anything. All I did was look in the deodorant aisle. I didn't even pick anything up or look at the men's deodorant when she says, "Are you looking for men's deodorant?"

Caught off guard, I reply, "Well, I mean, I usually buy the men's deodorant, but…"

"Here." She hands me a deodorant—she is a makeup consultant, and I guess men's deodorant just happens to be part of her product line. I take it, considering buying a new kind has been on my mind for some time.

As she speaks to me, she notices my jewelry.

"Yes, my mom always used to wear these," I say about my thick gold earrings.

"You said your mother wore this jewelry. What do you mean by that?"

"Well, she passed away a year ago."

"I knew it," she says. We talk about the loss of her mom, and she says she didn't deal with it well. "I'm still dealing with it now, all these years later," she continues. "And it gave me a bunch of health problems not dealing with it."

I tell her I'm doing the best I can, but it's hard for me.

"It is hard. As I said, I haven't dealt with it. Not really. You and your mother were very close. I know it. Listen, you have to keep doing everything you're doing. You have to keep your mom's business and make the jewelry and all the other things you're doing. I can't tell you more than that. I'm not allowed to. But I'll tell you this; God sure is looking out for you. He is taking care of you. So, thank him when you can because you are one lucky lady."

I didn't know how to respond except how to say thank you. When I tell Jon about this, he asks me if I asked her why she can't tell me more.

"I didn't," I tell him. "I just knew she was connected to something somehow, and I just trusted that."

fourteen

ONE MONTH UNTIL THE WEDDING

The wedding is coming fast and furious, and I'm still not all planned. I'm not the bride who has a perfect itinerary printed on her fridge about her wedding day and is eagerly counting down the days until she can show her perfect event planning skills to the world. I'm more the "what month is it? Holy shit!" bride. The "wait, I have to do that too?" Bride. If it weren't for my Aunt Diana, I don't think I would have any of it planned.

I didn't plan to be this bride, but here I am. And you know what? I am okay with it. I pat myself on the back for even being a half-there-mentally bride, given what I've gone through.

It's a warm day in early June when I have a complete meltdown. Talk about taking ten steps backward. It starts with anxiety. I have trouble concentrating. I cannot sit down at my computer to work. I'm irritable. When I have this kind of day, it sticks with me. It's kind of like a warning sign that I'm going to have a meltdown. I try to take the day to relax, but I'm so restless, I can't even do that. I feel this way on a Monday, and by Wednesday of that week, the anxiety attack comes.

I'm storming around the house, yelling at my mother like a crazy person.

I blame her for leaving me. I scream that it's her fault she won't be here for the wedding, that she's left me here all alone to suffer. I yell that she won't be here for my children, and they won't have her wisdom or love—that she ruined our plans for a happy life. After I stop yelling and crying, I realize how selfish I sound.

I look around my office, what used to be my mother's very tidy office—I am ashamed to say it's an absolute mess: half-opened books, half-filled coffee cups, notecards, papers everywhere, gemstones, pencils, loose change, my mom's old ledgers and bills, my paperwork, a plastic knife, a one-hole puncher, a popsicle stick, an electric pencil sharpener (on the floor), opened essential oils, and scraps of paper everywhere. I'm working in an absolute mess, and yet I cannot bring myself to clean this room even after a year and a month of my mom's passing. I want to gut the room, turn it into a quaint writing library with bookshelves, hardwood floors, and an electric fireplace. I want to turn its robin's egg-colored walls into a Crème Brule color and organize everything or completely Marie Kondo the place.

But I can't bring myself to clean it, even a little. I'm ashamed of how messy it is, yet I am fully aware it is equivalent to my mind. I am just trying to figure myself out, navigate these uncharted waters. I am no longer walking between two worlds; I am fully integrated into this new world. I'm not saying that I love it, only that I am completely in it. What choice do I have but to stop looking at this world as an unplanned "burden" and instead look upon it with wonder? It is full of mystery and uncertainty. My father always says, "life is an adventure." He's been saying this to me for so many years. I only now begin to understand what he means.

He was also thrown into a new world when his father died suddenly. My father was only twenty-eight when he lost his dad, and I was thirty-three when I lost my mother. I never really understood my father—it used to make me furious— why he would always have deep compassion for people that didn't deserve it, but now I understand. Tragedy can make us see the world and all its inhabitants from that more compassionate place. Each month that passes makes me feel more compassion for others.

If the seemingly *impossible* happens (for the worst), our understanding of what is *possible* must change. If the impossible bad things can happen, impossible good things can happen also. That's where the adventure begins. Life is like sailing through unchartered waters looking for an unclaimed island. Sometimes the seas are calm, the sun shines brightly, and the ride is quite peaceful, and other times the waters are treacherous, the waves are choppy and high, and the wind nearly knocks over your ship. And when all you see for miles and miles is water, it's easy to think there is nothing else out there. But when impossible things happen, especially if they're terrible, we have to remember remarkable things can happen also. Maybe that island we are on a quest for is only a day's sailing away.

But seriously, I have to do something with this room.*

---

*It is now December of 2020, and I am pleased to say I have accomplished my room transformation goal!

fifteen

TWO CATS AND A FLY

Today is my cousin's wedding. No matter how fun they are (and this one is fun), Sunday weddings are a bit off-centering. One is partying like the weekend, but halfway through the drinks and the dancing, realizes tomorrow is Monday. If that isn't the ultimate fun-sucker-outter, I don't know what is.

We dance and eat. I overeat—I probably should have slowed down on the fried shrimp. During the best man/maid-of-honor toasts, I am crying. They are talking about best friends—how much it means to have such a best friend who shaped their lives. I keep thinking, my best friend is dead. Then I start thinking about how in just a month, we'll be here, doing this all for Jon and me, but my mother won't be there to see any of it. After the toasts are over, I wipe my tears, and Jon and I decide to dance. But when the wedding ends, despite all the fun, knowing that it's Monday tomorrow, I am eager to get home and put my pajamas on. Now that the fun is over, I am back to pondering the serious things that help me understand my new world.

Mr. Bugatti and Veronica, two of my cats, stare at me as I write this, as though they're waiting for the teaser scene at the end of a great movie or for me to put on some entertaining show for them. Little do they know, the only excitement they're going to see is the green bookmark string of my journal, which is probably actually exciting to them, considering they keep pawing at it.

I've always considered myself an empath, but now I'm thinking about what that actually means. Merriam Webster defines an empath as "one who experiences the emotions of others: a person who has empathy for others." They define empathy as:

the action of understanding, being aware of, being sensitive to, and vicariously experiencing the feelings, thoughts, and experience of another of either the past or present without having the feelings, thoughts, and experience fully communicated in an objectively explicit manner

Before my tragedy, when something would happen to someone, I would feel their pain. When my mom was sick, I was suffering with her. Now, I'm carrying the empathic absorption of that suffering with me. I remember other times I've felt massive draws of empathy, absorbing other people's pain, but there was always a slight and purposeful separation in those instances. With my mom, it feels like I experienced everything and am carrying that experience with me, even now. There is no way to separate it because I lived it.

I think empathy increases to full capacity when you experience something someone else has. When someone else's parent, friend, lover, or sibling dies, I can feel what that person is going through on a whole other level. If someone is ill or someone that person cares about is sick, I can feel that energy. I feel complete compassion for those people and all people because anyone can be one of those people or me at any time.

As I write this, a fly that has been following me around the house follows me upstairs and into my bedroom. He's zipping around me like my puppy does when she wants attention. Meanwhile, my two cats are still staring at me, still waiting for something to happen, completely unnerved by the fly, and it's all very distracting. I want to tell the cats that of all the times they decide to ignore a fly in the house, this is the most inconvenient.

"Tinky would never stand for this," I say to them because, like most pet owners (especially cat owners), I talk to my animals as though they're proper little humans. Side note: I talk to my dog like she's a toddler. Anyway, Tinky is my other cat, a tall, muscular, white cat with orange spots. He is a professional fly-hunter. Not one has ever escaped his clutches. But tonight, he's not with the rest of the clan. He's curled in a ball in a bed in the other room, fast asleep.

Actual thoughts that go through my brain: *What if the fly is your mom and she's watching through the fly's eyes from some higher dimensional facility?*

Okay, the fly has stopped buzzing and is now sitting on a lightbulb. He and the two cats are all staring at me now. I'm not sure what they're all waiting for, but I'm glad "the human" can be of some amusement to them.

sixteen

A Sign from Catherine, Daisy, and Mom

There are days like today, a rainy Monday in mid-June when I feel out of sorts, like maybe I can't manage in this new world. It's one of those days where I need that second cup of coffee, even though I'm down to one cup a day (hey, that's a miracle for a writer). It's days like today, where a case of the Mondays means I feel like I'm a visitor in an alien world.

Today, I'm back to my normal worrying. It all begins with food. I want to eat healthily, but the cabinets are empty. So in between working, planning the wedding, and writing, I have to make time for the grocery store and cooking. The thought of not only getting the food but cooking it and making sure it's healthy overwhelms me.

I am incredibly irritable today for the main reason that my monthly friend hasn't arrived. She's supposed to be here, but she isn't, which means she might make me an unplanned visit on my wedding day. This depresses me.

I am thinking about God and the after-life today in a negative light—is there nothing beyond this world? It's funny how non-spiritual I am now compared to when everything was happening and even after. Now, I feel abandoned by my mother, like when I need her most, she is not there. I feel starved of feminine connection. I need the Mother energy now, that sacred female wisdom, more than ever.

We have a marble top table in our house that was my great-grandmother's—the same great-grandmother whose grave I was standing on just a couple of weeks ago. Every once and a while, I open the drawer attached to the table. Today, I am searching for a pin to stick into and open a particularly stubborn essential oil top.

In the drawer is a little box that was also my great-grandmother's, and it contains these items: a paperclip, three-button snaps, one large pearl earring, a long, folded piece of thick plastic, and a letter. The letter is from Daisy, my great-grandmother's family member. I have no idea if Daisy wrote the letter before or after my great-grandmother's death, but it goes like this:

Dear Catherine,

This is the letter I said I was going to send you. When I read it, I thought of you and all the laughter we shared over the phone. I miss it a lot. You were my teacher, my doctor, and my friend. Thank God for all the good memories we shared. Hope you enjoyed it as much as I did. Hope to see you sometime soon.

God be with you always,
Daisy

I've seen this letter before. My mom showed it to me many years ago. At the bottom of the letter is a poem called "Missing You." It's a beautiful poem that leads me to believe Daisy wrote this after my great-grandmother passed. But I can't find the author. Even when I search online, I find no information on this poem. It seems to only exist on this piece of paper. I fold the letter back up, put the box away, and see another notebook in the drawer. This one is a pink pad with flowers. On the bottom, it says, "Love Never Fails." 1st Corinthians 13:8. On this notepad is my mother's handwriting, and it says.

"Thoughts I wish I could eliminate."

1. I will never see my grandchild.

She continues to write:

"This is not what I wanted our days to be like. I thought I could walk and not get out of breath. I feel damaged. I feel like life is passing me by. I need some positive information—I need some **hope***. I should be living my life with my daughter and enjoying our time together."*

I don't know what to make of this letter. It's the only one I know of that my mom wrote during her illness. On this day, when I've given up all hope of her helping me from the afterlife, at least I have this. It's a reminder of how much my mom loved me—how much our friendship was a real bond. Even in her dying days, she thought of me. I'm feeling abandoned, lonely, left-out-in-the-dark. I'm depressed, angry, and tired of cryptic signs of help from the other side. I'm tired of seeing butterflies and of hearing the song "Rosanna."

Today is a bad day. Acknowledging this is all I can do.

At work, I have a breakdown. Luckily, Evelyn helps me. Maybe it's the wedding; perhaps it's the fact that my monthly visitor will be in town for my wedding that's really depressing me, or perhaps it's me just missing my mom, but this day is a colossal disaster mentally. I cannot keep my thoughts together. Eventually, I feel a little better and finish the workday.

Later that night, Jon, my aunt, and I work on wedding things. I am painting a welcome board sign (metallic gold paint on a chalkboard); I hand glue faux white roses on silver/light gold masks. Jon, my aunt, and I put together all the candelabra centerpieces and even start bedazzling the place cards. As we check off items for the wedding, my mood finally improves.

seventeen

TIM MCGRAW ON THE RADIO

I'm in my head a lot. I've isolated myself and spend most of my time thinking. It has to be my Pisces moon and rising doing this. I mean, is this normal? Without my mom, it feels like there's no one really to talk to. It's a funny feeling— to talk to yourself. I suppose that's why awareness and meditation are so important. It's so easy to get caught up in the constant thoughts of the brain, especially when you have no one to talk to. So, I'm sitting on my favorite chair in the living room on a particularly stormy Wednesday after work, gray daylight filtering through the window, and all I can think is this.

You know how people say, when you're sick of being sick, you will get well? Well, I'm sick of thinking and fearing food. I'm just sick of it. I realize this one day when I'm at the grocery store, pondering over what to buy. You would think it would be easy, but for me, it's torture. I am still worried that every food I buy will negatively affect my gut—from the much-beloved avocado to the cashews to the meats or the meatless meats, from the soy to the nuts.

Sometimes when I'm food shopping, I wish I never had to eat. If I didn't have to, then I wouldn't have to worry about eating. Mostly though, food makes me sad because some of my fondest family memories surround food and family recipes passed down from my grandparents. I feel that if my mother's death hadn't been from this disease—if she had died from a car accident or something like that, let's say—maybe this whole part of my suffering would be a joyous memory. Perhaps I would cook all the dishes my mom cooked, and I would remember her through those recipes instead of looking at the past as the good old days. Sometimes I want to throw it all to hell and just eat hot dogs every day. (Let's just slow down. I don't really like hots dogs that much to eat them every day.)

Here's the real problem. I didn't realize how much this fear has taken over my life. Honestly, it's been a year and two months, and this is the one thing that has stuck with me for that long. Every. Single. Day. And I'm so done with it. And yet, I'm not sure how to let it go. I have to rewire my brain somehow.

Suddenly, a memory pops into my mind. Several times during my mom's illness, I would hear Tim McGraw's "Live Like You're Dying" playing in my head. I would put it out of my mind when I would hear it and say, "No! I don't want to hear this" because it would make me think my mom was dying.

But it would pop back into my head and play on repeat like someone was trying to warn me of something. I remember being so frustrated. For some reason, as I am enjoying my cup of Green Tea on this gray Wednesday, the song pops back into my head, and I remember how it plagued my mind.

"That's it," I say out loud. The only person who hears this is Mr. Bugatti, who is always staring at me with "What's next, Master?" eyes.

I stomp downstairs and turn on my keyboard. I need to write how I feel, and when I'm really, really frustrated, the only way I can do it is through a song. The notes angrily fly out of my fingers, pushing the piano keys as the words erupt from my mind in a continuous stream *of thought*.

People ask me all the time,
how I'm doing, and I just tell them,
I'm fine, but they don't really know at all.
Soon people forget to ask,
'cause your death for them is in the past.
For me, it's just never gone.
But some things, you just can't shove
underneath your welcome rug.
And some things, you just can't stash,
throw in the corner and hide away from like...

Tim McGraw, on the radio
singing songs we know, like,
livin' like we're dying.
And I'm just, sitting here alone
wishing you were coming home.
Lord knows that I'm trying.
So, with the little chance that I've been given,
I better get to living.

Somewhere along the beaten path
I lost me and thought that
that was that
and succumbed to my woes.
Then I took a hard look in the mirror,
saw myself a little clearer,
and picked my broken self
up off the floor.
'Cause some things you just can't shove
underneath your welcome rug.
And some things, you just can't stash,
throw in the corner and hide away from like...

Tim McGraw, on the radio
singing songs we know, like,
livin' like we're dying.
And I'm here, sitting all alone
wishing you were coming home.
Lord knows that I'm trying.
And with the little chance that I've been given,
I better get to living.

eighteen

THE DEATH OF A DREAM

This June is an exceptionally rainy month. The skies are gray again today. I am having morning coffee in my sitting room, contemplating children. I think about a conversation I had with my mother when she was well. I would often talk to her about children. My mother and I had a great plan.

"I'll make sure we turn your room into a room for you and Raymond's children."

"Yeah, that would be so cool."

"We can put two beds in there, and any time they sleepover, they'll have so much fun."

My parent's house—well, I guess it's my house now—has a huge backyard. It's on an acre, to be exact (which is huge for where I live). At the time, I was having a conversation with my mom about my future. Jon and I had been looking for houses.

"Jon and I don't need a big backyard. Yours is big enough for both of us."

The plan was this: Jon and I would move into a house right by my parents. It would have a smaller backyard, naturally, because Jon and I would tend to my parent's backyard. Our children would grow up there, seeing their grandparents every day. My mom and I would plant a garden in the spring, take care of all the flowers, bushes, and trees. We'd have barbecues weekly, and our children would run and play in the backyard.

If they wanted to stay with their grandparents, it would be a treat—to stay in such a big house and spend time with their grandparents. My mother, a keeper of wisdom, would teach my children the most extraordinary things—especially, to express their artistic natures. If I had girls, they would grow up strong, with the confidence to do anything, just like I did. If they were boys, they would grow up with manners, talent, and kindness, as my brother did.

We were excited. My mom and I often talked about how fun it would be, how we would take the kids on lunch dates, and read to them.

But then that dream died.

Now, I'm contemplating if I even want to have children. I think about all the people who may have had a dream or plan, but a life event ripped that dream away from them. It's just another layer of loss for me to deal with on top of my mother's death. I think about parents who desperately want but can't have children, parents who lose a child, people who experience some unforgettable trauma, and people like me who have a plan for their life, but some unforeseen tragedy thwarts that plan. It's as though life stops us in the middle of everything and forces us to direct our attention elsewhere. Why?

I'm living in this strange world where I just want my freedom, and on the other hand, I know I'm meant to have children. I could spend the rest of my life traveling to distant countries and experiencing different places and cultures. After all, that's what my mom (before she died) made me promise I would do.

Or, I could settle down and have children (providing I can) and be the best mother I can be. Only, I feel like, to do that, I need my mom. With my mom alive, I was sure my children would turn out to be upstanding citizens. Without her—well, what if I'm a horrible parent? And there are other concerns too, about the dynamic between Jon and me once we have children, working, and following my dreams. I watch most people around me receiving help from their mothers with their children because it's too much to do it all. But I would be alone. Would I be expected to do all those women do without someone to help me? As I struggle with this idea, though, I understand that perhaps Jon and I are meant to have children because they will be lightworkers of the future. It isn't very in the now to worry about this right this moment anyway. Yet, I am.

nineteen

GRIEF IS MIGHTY FLIGHTY

Do people ever really talk about how flighty grief is? How one day you're just fine, and the next day you are two thoughts shy of needing to be institutionalized?

You just never know how you're going to feel on a given day. Like today, when I wake up, I'm exhausted, sad, and cranky. It's just two weeks before the wedding. I'm missing my mom. I'm feeling sad that she and I will never be on a family trip together.

One day I'm in work, which is on a set playlist that plays "Rosanna" almost every day. I remark to Evelyn that the song isn't special anymore because it's on a playlist.

The next day, as I'm driving to work, a red cardinal is in the middle of the road. It's standing there, a vibrant shade of red, and is staring at me. I've heard that a red cardinal is a representative of a loved one. I decide to turn on the radio as I pass the cardinal, and sure enough, "Rosanna" is on the radio.

Now, I'm laughing. Life makes sense. I feel connected. But a minute ago, I was so unhappy I could have skipped work, gone home, and hid under the covers the entire day. I feel crazy, but this is grief.

I can't forget that my mom is dead. I can't forget all the things I will miss out on with her because of that, but I can try to live my best life. I can try. I know how important being happy is to good health. I understand how the more I travel down the depression and anxiety pathway, the more cortisol and adrenaline will be released into my system, stealing all my essential nutrients and leaving me with more deficiencies than I already have. From a scientific standpoint, I have to create a happier, more harmonious life, or there is a chance I will be too ill one day ever to create one.

I understand that I am resisting this new life. Stuck in the past, I am playing a continuous loop of the good old days. Because of this, I'm missing out on the right now, which wouldn't be so bad if I weren't so stuck in my head.

The next day, I sit in our living room, the morning sunlight drifting through white lace curtains. I'm sipping a cup of coffee. Opening my journal, I write.

July 2nd. How am I going to live my best, happiest life today?

For several minutes I just stare at the page. I found the question, but did I have an answer?

Today I am going to live my best life by choosing to live in the moment.

What does this mean for me? I am going to try with all my might to stay as present as possible. That means staying out of the past and future and dealing with exactly where I am right now. It's not that I will forget what happened to me or forget who I am now because of what happened to me. I am just choosing to leave it in the past for a moment as I soak up all that's around me.

As I write this, I wonder if I can stick to it. Staying in the present moment is like staying on a diet. Thoughts about the past or future are like the most delicious chocolate cake you're trying to avoid. I have a hard road ahead, I know this, but I also know it's possible to re-wire my brain.

I think, even if I'm really good at sticking to the present, at any time, a memory or thought that slips through could derail me. That's grief, and I need to allow myself to be sad if I need to. So, I write this also:

I will let myself experience whatever I need to in order to deal with my grief. If I need to cry, I will. If I need to take a day for myself, I will. But all the while, I will stay committed to helping myself become a better version of the person I was the day before. I will not judge myself for getting upset. I will not judge myself for not being healed. I will just let what is be. I will not judge others for not checking up on me or helping me through this. But I will give myself all the compassion and self-love that I can. At the least, if I know that I've done my best for any given day, which may not feel like the best at that moment, I will be proud of myself and look forward to the next day to start over. I will be gentle and kind to myself. I will nurture myself however I need to. This is my path to healing.

twenty

THE WEDDING

On the day of my wedding, I wake up and decide, "Today, I'm going to be happy no matter what."

My bridesmaids arrive promptly and early at 7:45, and soon the house fills with chatter. My kitchen table has a spread of good food to start the morning—bagels and cream cheese, fruit, and, most importantly, mimosas.

We are giggling and excited as we get ready in my upstairs bathroom. My hair and makeup team make all the girls look excellent; everyone seems pleased with their hair and makeup. My niece is there too, wearing this adorable navy-blue dress that I bought her. Our colors are navy blue and gold.

I'm in my wedding day bridal robe that I ordered offline. My cousin, who is my Maid of Honor, snaps a photo of me sitting in my lounge chair on my balcony, a mimosa in my hand.

We are already having fun, and it's only 9:30 a.m.

My photographer for the wedding is one of my closest friends. And she's pregnant, so I am going at her speed. Jon and I do our first look in our backyard, take some photos, and now we are off to the venue.

As we are getting ready to go out there, I become nervous. Weddings are terrifying. To me, anyway. Not because of the actual vows or who I am marrying, but because I have to walk down the aisle with all these people staring at me. Did I really think this through? I'm scared to death. The weather is perfect—it's hot, but not as hot as I thought it would be. It's shady when the ceremony starts, and I'm still nervous. I peek my head around the corner to see if I can recognize anyone. Of course, I recognize everyone. The music starts, but I don't even hear it. My attention is in my head, thinking, *don't trip. Don't trip. Don't trip.*

I walk down the aisle on my dad's arm, although my heart is racing so fast it's likely unhealthy. But I do it because, well, I am marrying Jon today if it's the last thing I do.

I make it down the aisle in one piece, and the ceremony begins. Jon is looking handsome in his Navy suit with his glasses fixed perfectly on his face, and his brown hair slicked back to perfection.

One of my brother's closest friends is marrying us, so I feel safe. During our vows, though, something happens. As Jon is saying his vows, a dragonfly smacks him right in the head. He continues, not missing a beat. Then it's my turn for vows. I'm talking, but I hear a murmur in the crowd as I do. When it's all over, and we are married, I find out that during my vows, that same dragonfly landed on my dress and stayed there until I completed my vows.

I know it's my mother. So does everyone else. It's a magical moment in time, one that my photographer does capture, and one that everyone there was able to witness.

I don't know how many people come up to me to tell me my mother visited us to let us know she's at the wedding.

"There was not another dragonfly, insect, or bird around," someone says.

I don't want to cry, even though I'm feeling a little sad. I have to swallow the sadness because I promised myself that on this day, if only this one, I would be happy. My mother always told me she would come back to me as a blue butterfly, but I think she came back to me as a dragonfly. She let me know she was here with me on my wedding day and that her soul was free.*

Our wedding is fun. Everyone is dancing and seemingly having a good time. For all the planning we put into this wedding, it seems to fly by. By the end of the night, we are both exhausted.

But I feel happy. For the first time since my mother's death, I feel happy.

*See the *Symbolism of Dragonflies* at the end of this book for more information on the powerful meaning of the dragonfly.

Part Four

This Side of the Dream

"Your joy can fill you only as deeply as your sorrow has carved you."

Kahlil Gibran

one

INSIGHTS FROM ITALY

July 2019

JFK International is a crazy airport, just in case anyone wasn't sure. Jon and I get dropped off at the wrong terminal accidentally and need to go down the elevator, take a shuttle to the correct airport terminal, and check-in there. It's a painless check-in, but we are nervous, not knowing where we're supposed to go.

The plane ride to Italy is long. But I realize something as I gaze at glistening white powder clouds outside my window seat. These clouds are the same all over the earth. This Sun is the same, all over the planet. How often do we forget how connected we are to the rest of the world? If we never travel, it is easy to feel isolated and alone. Some of the greatest hatreds, judgments, and bigotry come from forgetting we are connected—that we all eat, drink, and breathe under the same sun, moon, and starry sky, that our clouds shift from one country to the next. What we do in one country or city truly does impact another. *It's only from the sky we see this*, I think. We realize it when we are out of our everyday life-bubble or high above the earth looking at the world from a different point of view.

But isn't that what higher-awareness is, I think? Looking at life from a higher, more expanded point of view? If we want to achieve higher-awareness, we must transcend limiting beliefs, step out of primal, animalistic mindsets, vibrate at a higher frequency, develop our spiritual awareness, and awaken to the eternal being inside us. Wouldn't we need to rise above all the human madness we suffer every day to do this? A preoccupation with the past and future keeps us in a madness that prevents us from seeing the truth. If we rise above that madness, we will look down at it from the present moment. And when we are present, we see the connection of all things, and we realize we are eternal beings connected to all other eternal beings. Sometimes we need to step out of the madness to see it. And high in the air, I finally see.

When Jon and I arrive, it's early morning in Italy. We have a layover in Rome and are in Florence by 10:45 a.m. We find a taxi at the Florence airport and arrive at our hotel a half-hour later.

"Wow!" we both exclaim as we walk into a cobblestone courtyard that has a large fountain in the middle of it. After checking in, we go straight to the pool.

Describing the beauty of lying by a crystal blue pool in the warm Tuscan countryside in mere words will never do it justice. It is peaceful, quiet—so quiet—one only hears the birds and insects going about their day. There are no lawnmowers and tree cutters, no honking or trucks unloading things and causing noise: just peace and quiet with the occasional sound of a Vespa passing by. I can finally hear myself think. I haven't had this feeling of peace in a very, very long time.

As I gaze around me, I see stone walls, an old water mill, and a beautiful river that is beyond the wall. A man canoes down the river, while other people sit beside it, dipping their feet in the water. One man is fishing. All the while, I am sitting by the pool, over-looking this beautiful scenery. The green Tuscan hills and a bright baby blue sky are my favorite backdrop.

Our room is beautiful and quaint. It has a large wardrobe, and I'm immediately excited. I practically run over to it and throw it open with the hopes of climbing on in just like in the *Chronicles of Narnia*. I am shamelessly geek-ing out. And while it turns out that, sadly, those wardrobes do not lead Narnia, and I will not receive wisdom from Aslan, it is charming and lovely all the same. After putting our stuff down, Jon and I decide we are hungry and head to the bar where we can also get lunch. As we sit there, tiny black and white birds fly over our heads, singing the prettiest songs. A cherub fountain is in front of us with soothing sounds of water.

After we eat, we walk through a large courtyard beside the old water mill and head to the pool. As I sit by the pool, staring at the green Tuscan hills, I feel happy for the first time. Florence is my happy place. I could stay here forever.

two

A WALK IN THE CITY

Why do they call Florence "Florence" in America when it's really just Firenze? Jon and I discuss it and learn from the internet that originally Firenze was Florentia in Latin, but we don't come to a conclusion before we both drift into a deep sleep, tired from the long day.

After a much needed, refreshing sleep, Jon and I head down two flights of stairs to breakfast, held in the same restaurant as dinner. As I walk down the stairs, I notice the hotel is like an art gallery, with beautiful dark paintings encased in gold frames. One portrait of an older woman in blue strikes me. She looks like the stepmother in Walt Disney's *Cinderella*, but a kinder, softer version. Yet another painting is of a woman, younger, more sexual in her appearance. She is voluptuous, with her dress falling off her shoulder and her hair pinned up messily. I wonder if these paintings are by the same artist or many different ones.

We walk into the restaurant, and the waitress sits us outside. The view is breathtaking. We sit at a table that overlooks the tranquil waters of the Florentine countryside. The temperature is just right, about sixty-nine degrees and sunny, without a cloud in the sky. Our waitress approaches us.

"Buon Giorno."

"Buon Giorno," we reply.

"Would you like…coffee? Cappuccino? Tea? Latte?"

"Coffee, please," I say.

"Coffee Americano. Okay. And for you?"

Jon replies coffee also, but he wants his with milk.

"Grazie," we respond.

"Prego," she says, and she heads off.

It's hard to feel any sadness at this moment. In fact, I feel a surge of excitement. I feel connected to this place, to this part of Italy. I feel at home here, relaxed, and comforted.

Jon and I make our way into the restaurant to get plates of food from the buffet. The spread is so different from American breakfast. They have scrambled eggs and sausage, yes, but they also have prosciutto, ham, turkey, mozzarella cheese, tomatoes, arugula, provolone cheese, and other cheese assortments, sweet croissants, little cakes, fresh-baked bread, fruits (grapefruit, pineapple, and cantaloupe), butter, jams, orange juice, and multi-vitamin juice.

I slice myself a piece of fresh bread, grab a couple of pieces of fresh provolone cheese, pour a tall glass of the multi-vitamin juice, and head back to the table.

There, the cutest little songbirds sit by us, hoping for a little bit of breakfast. I gaze out over the calm water. It is early, but Tuscany is alive. Across the river, men and women are jogging, walking their dogs, and fishing.

The Tuscan hills remind me of what an un-saturated Los Angeles might look like.

"Mi presta una penna," I say to the waiter. I've lost my pen. He smiles and gives me a new one.

"Grazie," I say.

"Prego."

"So, what is our plan for today?" Jon asks after we are full and relaxing at the table.

"I guess just walk around? We don't have anything to do, so it's a free day for us."

"That's fine with me."

"I don't remember Florence," I say. "I mean, I remember I love it, but I can't remember exactly what we should do or where to go."

"We'll just walk around. I'm sure we'll find some fun things to do."

After breakfast, Jon and I head back to the room. We take showers and get ready. By ten in the morning, we are ready and head down to the shuttle. By then, the weather has changed drastically.

It's so hot; the sweat is dripping off of us the minute we step outside. As we wait for the shuttle, we meet a woman from Chicago who congratulates us on our marriage and then tells us different places to go in the city.

"Our cousins live here," she tells us. "They tell us Venchi is the best gelato place, and you just have to commit to being hot because there's no way out of it."

The shuttle to the city is only mildly air-conditioned. It's one of those your-sweaty-knee-touches-his-sweaty-knee days, where you recoil in horror no matter how much you love him.

Soon the shuttle stops, and we step off at Plaza Lucchesi. It is hard not to be romanced by the rich culture and history of Florence. Several feet from us is the Biblioteca Nazionale Centrale di Firenze (The National Library of Florence). A few blocks down is the Galileo museum. I am like a kid in a candy store.

The Ponte Vecchio, which we learn is the last original bridge in Florence (World War II demolished the others), is filled with hundreds, maybe thousands of people. The city seems busier than I remember. Of course, that was twenty years ago. I grimace at the thought of twenty years passing since I was in high school. But I actually don't feel any older now. Not really. I still feel like the same young me who came here all those years ago.

I find it hard to relax in the actual city of Florence, even though I love it here. After all, it is a city brimming with tourists from across the globe. Maybe it's the summer, or perhaps it's because I haven't visited in so long, but the city seems so different to me.

I make small talk with some of the shopkeepers. My Italian is not as good as it once was, but I can still have a decent conversation.

We walk so much that there are painful cuts on my feet, and I already ran out of Band-Aids. Still, it's worth it.

At night, Jon and I eat pizza and go to bars. In Italy, a bar is not a place where people gather to drink alcohol only, but it is more of a café or eatery. Jon and I are Americans in Florence looking for a "bar only." We walk along warmly-lit, cobblestone streets, hand in hand, trying not to die by taxi or Vespa. The warm city is busy. Everyone is out eating, connecting, still sightseeing even after the last tour of the day. It's difficult for one not to feel the sensual sexiness of the city. It's a beautiful sight to see so many people from so many different parts of the world enjoying themselves together but separate. In America, walking down the streets of Philadelphia cannot compare. One has to worry or be afraid. Muggings, shootings, stabbings, and other attacks fill my mind, but Florence's life is safe, romantic, beautiful. Except sometimes it smells like pee for no random reason, maybe from a dog. When that happens, I wonder if all cities are the same after all.

Jon and I find a "bar" defined by American terms. It's called Grizzly. He orders an Italian beer as we listen to satisfying reggae music playing throughout the bar. The doors are open wide to embrace the hot steamy Italian summer night, and I order wine, better termed, Rosso Vino.

"This place is cool," I say. Jon and I are just making small talk. I think we're both exhausted but just want to enjoy this moment the best we can.

After a drink at Grizzly, Jon and I go on the hunt for another bar. We finally find one called Hair of the Dog. As we order (Jon a beer again and me another glass of wine), I start to realize I'm still sad.

"The wedding is wearing off," I say. "I'm coming back to reality." For the last nine months, I had thrown myself into work and planning this wedding as a way to escape. Now that the wedding planning is over, I am coming down off the high, and here I am, having to deal with my feelings again.

"Actually, I realize, I hate myself," I tell Jon. "I really don't like myself. My self-esteem tanked after I lost my mom, and I can't get it back."

"You'll get it back," Jon assures me.

"I don't know if I will, though."

"You have to give yourself time, Stef. You're trying so hard to be your normal, happy self, but you have to give yourself time."

Jon tries to give me words of wisdom, but my mindset is going downhill fast. I try to keep myself in the present moment. I am in Italy, for God's sake. Enjoy the moment, I think. Enjoy the fact that you're drinking wine in the most romantic city you've ever known. But I can't. No amount of world-traveling will take the pain from losing my mother, my best friend. Still, I try. I try to be present. I try to enjoy myself.

three

THE CHURCH OF SANTA CROCE

The next morning, I am feeling chipper. It's as if the release of emotion the night before leaves me in a place of light energy. I'm ready to take on the day. I enjoy a cappuccino this morning, a bit of cheese, fruit, and some bread. I sit watching the Tuscan hills and think, this truly is paradise. I could see myself living here with a beautiful garden in my backyard filled with fresh fruits and vegetables. I could see myself working in the city and spending time with friends drinking wine and eating fresh food. I envision myself writing books and jogging along this river in the mornings. *How amazing that would be*, I think. I don't know how Jon feels about this place, and I don't ask him. I know he is enjoying himself, that's for sure, but I don't know if he feels quite the same as I do.

Jon and I have a tour of Michelangelo's David at 11a.m, so we shower, dress, and are ready to leave by 10 a.m. Once we reach the city, we have to walk all the way to the tour, and it's already in the high eighties, so we know we're going to sweat, but we don't care.

I am feeling so happy today; I can appreciate the beautiful city. I realize, yes, there are a ton of people, but everyone appears to be in a good mood. People from all over the world are congregating in this one place, and they're all generally chipper. There's only one other place in the world like that that I know of, and it's Disney World.

Our tour of the David is as amazing as it was when I did it back in high school. Only this time, I appreciate the art. I love art, and I love art history, so I am genuinely enjoying the experience. I think Jon is also. He seems genuinely interested. Our tour guide tells us at the end of the tour that if we want to see the tomb of Michaelangelo, we should head over to the Chiesa di Santa Croce.

After the tour, Jon and I walk to the church, and when we enter, I feel a surge of excitement in me.

"This is Michaelangelo's actual tomb," I say to Jon. "And this is Dante Alighieri's actual tomb."

Jon doesn't know who he is, so I explain.

"This is Galileo's tomb!"

It's almost too much for me to take. Also, I'm a little concerned about how excited I am to see these men's tombs. But I know it's because these are a few of the greatest artists, writers, and scientists in the world's history, and I feel like for this small piece in time, I am part of their world.

"There's magic in this room," I say to Jon. "Pure magic. If you're an artist, you can feel it. You can feel the energy. You can feel it when you stand in front of the David, or I'm sure if you visit the Vatican. You can feel it if you see Da Vinci's *The Last Supper*. Because the energy of the artist always lives in the art he leaves behind. I can feel it affecting my energy. It only took a day to adjust. The pain is gone, and there's this free-flowing creative energy swirling around me. It tugs at my insides. It's calling me to do something great. Maybe it's because I've always been an artist and not just a writer, but a musician, and a painter, and a designer. Maybe because I have this Renaissance energy running through me. Perhaps because I am so intuitive and emotional, I don't know. I don't know what it is, but I can feel it. I am a hopelessly romantic artist, Jon. I've always been that person. I feel so deeply connected to these people; I'm almost freaking out at the feeling, but in a good way."

Once we exit that part of the church, we enter a courtyard. In a room off the side of the courtyard, a children's choir is singing. The sound is beautiful, and Jon and I sit in the room to watch the choir's performance. When we finally leave, I feel invigorated, expanded, and happy.

four

THE LAST NIGHT IN FLORENCE

Today is our last day in the magical city of Florence. Jon and I do not have to go to our Pizza and Gelato making class until 4:45 p.m., so we decide to lay by the pool. I am out there at 9:39 a.m., just after breakfast. It is already 85 degrees, so it's going to be a smoldering hot day. I don't mind, though. I love Florence.

I am sitting on a pool chair waiting for Jon. At 10:45 am, he sends me a text message saying he is on his way. At 11:30 a.m., Jon is still not at the pool. I wonder where he is, but I know him well enough now to know he often takes his time getting places (this is one hundred percent my way of saying he is usually late), and I think nothing of it. But something starts to happen to me at that pool. I look around at the people around me. I begin to envision that the guy with the royal blue swim trunks and the balding hair sitting alone, checking his phone, might be a detective. And the family of three next to me? The husband might be a spy. He walks with a limp and speaks a language I have never heard before. Suddenly, I'm wondering, what if Jon isn't okay? What if someone murdered him? These types of thoughts are typical for a fiction author. I am always thinking of a story, and if you have an imagination as I do you, you probably do the same thing.

A story begins in my mind. It's as if the creativity channels burst open. Anyone else would be running to check on their husband as fear takes over, but I'm pulling out my notebook. The man in the blue swim trunks *is* a detective. Yes, he is. And the story begins with the murder of a groom on his honeymoon. His new wife is bathing by the pool, but when the groom doesn't join her, she becomes worried and goes to check on him. That's when she discovers his cold, lifeless body.

Okay, I think. *Maybe I should check on Jon.* I'm not worried, per se, but then again, I wouldn't want to write this book and then find out my new husband is actually dead. I close my journal, walk through the courtyard, head up two flights of stairs, and eventually make it to our room. I knock on the door. Jon answers, sleepy-eyed.

"Sorry, I fell back asleep," he says.

"Okay. I just thought you were dead. But, the good news is, I feel a new novel coming on."*

"Glad I could help," he laughs.

Murder at Hotel Firenze is almost complete and will release in 2021!

We meet at Via Vinegia, right behind the Palazzo Vecchio, for our pizza and gelato class on time. It's hot and very humid. I feel ugly and sweaty today. We take cabs up to a Tuscan Farmhouse, way in the hills. At first, we are all a bit shy, but our guides, Matteo, Luigi, and Christone, are fantastic.

Within a half-hour, we are bonding with people in the class. The camaraderie between all of us is lovely. We meet two girls from Norway who are traveling with their families. We meet a couple from New York and a Filipino family from California.

Matteo helps me twirl the pizza with my fists. I can't believe I'm doing this.

One of our new friends from Norway takes a video of Matteo helping me. She airdrops the video to me. I watch it and giggle, then show Jon.

He shakes his head and playfully remarks, "It's like I'm not even here."

By the way, Italian mosquitoes are no joke. They love to bite and are out in full force. But for some odd reason, they are not biting me. Almost everyone else except for one of our new friends from Norway and me is slapping and scratching, and I'm just sitting here sipping my red wine like I don't see what the problem is.

"How come you're not getting bit?" Jerry, one of our new friends from New York, asks.

"Maybe it's the red wine," I say off the fly. "Maybe the red wine is actually a mosquito repellent."

"You may actually be right. Red Wine Mosquito Spray."

"Alright, keep it down," I say, "Don't say it too loud. We have a new business venture here. It's a good idea, and a hell of a lot safer than some of the sprays out there now."

I look around. Leia from Norway (who is also not getting bit) and I are the only ones drinking wine. Jon and Jerry are drinking beer, and Jerry's wife and Leia's sister are drinking water.

We are all shocked at how this is possible.

"It *is* the red wine!" We keep exclaiming. "It's the best repellent!"

"How are we going to market this?" we all joke as we eat our delicious pizzas.

"Give the gift of Red Wine Spray this summer. Stains your clothes but keeps you mosquito-free!"

We all share many more laughs and talk about life. I find out that the sisters from Norway are encouraged to take a gap year before deciding to continue school so they can travel.

"I wish America was like that," I say. "We're overworked and underpaid, and never encouraged to step out of the box unless it benefits the person telling us to step outside of it."

After the class is over, we meet up with our new friends from Iceland for a drink. They've just eaten at Locale Firenze, and when we arrive, they are just finishing up dinner.

"We're going on a tour," they tell us.

"Okay," Jon and I say. We are very, and I mean very, underdressed for this place. Here we are, having just come from cooking outside in the heat, sweaty, and probably smelly as anything. I'm wearing sneakers, and I know I smell like pizza and a wood-fired oven, but I don't care. We are having fun. At least I remembered to take my apron off.

The waitress at Locale Firenze corrals us to the top of a set of stairs on the ground floor, which leads to the basement of the Concini Palace.

As we follow the waitress down the stairs, she explains about the palace. We learn that the first owners built the place as a dwelling in the 1200s. The ground floor was built in the 1500s, and the basement was turned into the servants' quarters. There were two kitchens because the palace accommodated both guests and residents. With old stone arches and floors, the place is stunning.

Florence carries an incredible historical and creative energy of some of the most famous artists and ancient people who lived long ago. I feel this energy so strongly. It tugs at me, opening a part of myself that I've longed to feel.

To relate it to a chakra or energy center in the body, it's full-force Sacral energy, a sexual, sensual feminine creative power. I am feeling it—it's as if my sacral chakra that has been closed for quite some time has burst open. I only realize it just now. If you're present, really present, you can almost feel it coursing through your veins.

"We better get home," we say after we share some drinks and good conversation with our Icelandic friends.

The next morning, I wake with full-body hives. I'm not surprised that they're back. The last time I had them was in Sedona. We pack and head for the train station. We take a cab to the station, S.M. Novella, which is very crowded. I realize I don't know how to catch a train in Italy. Jon and I ask employees at the station, and they answer us in broken English.

"You just go in there," they say.

Jon and I are two hours early for the train. This is a mistake on my part. I am always worried about being on time. My Italian teacher in high school always impressed upon us that *to be early was to be on time, to be on time was to be late, and to be late was to be left.* So, I was usually early. But occasionally, being too early was a mistake. This is one of those times. There's nowhere to stand at the station. Jon and I are bored. We could have spent extra time at breakfast this morning, soaking up the Tuscan Hills. If I didn't stress out so much worrying about the train, I probably wouldn't have woken up with hives. I needed to learn to relax and be mindful of time but not defined by it.

By the time we get on the train, we are just happy we know which train to get on. Jon is tired and falls asleep almost instantly. I stare out the large train window, watching the green Italian hills, quaint little villages, farms, and occasionally a city pass us.

When we finally reach Napoli a few hours later, it feels like we are in a different country. The moment we step off the train in Napoli, I know I'm in a whole other world. The magical Tuscan hills have turned into the citiest of cities. The first thing I notice is how fast people are moving. Although many people crowded Florence, everyone was moving at a relaxed pace. In Naples, people are practically running everywhere, moving at a much quicker pace. Naples reminds me of New York or Philadelphia. I instantly feel the energy change, from light and magical to dense.

Our driver is waiting for us when we arrive. He doesn't appear to speak English, and he doesn't seem happy. He neither smiles at us nor tries to engage us in conversation. If he had, I would have spoken what little Italian I know to him, but he doesn't. He doesn't want to talk to us or even try—he is all business.

I stare out the window as we drive. Seeing Mount Vesuvius is a marvel to me. I can't help but think about Pompeii. We don't have enough time to go there on this trip, but I am lucky to have gone there before and learn about the ruins.

"This is completely different from the last few days," I say.

"Yeah, it is," Jon agrees.

The Tuscan magic is gone, the sensualness-gone, and we don't know what we've walked into. It's not bad, per se, just different.

five

THE AMALFI COAST

Everyone raves about the Amalfi coast, but I'm over here still pining for Florence. I miss it already. Sure, the coast is beautiful, but it has much less magic than the Renaissance city of Romance and History.

We head into the mountains through twists and turns that tie my stomach in knots. I don't want to say anything, but eventually, I can't hold it anymore.

"I am getting so sick," I say in a low voice. To be fair, I can't even ride the teacup at an amusement park, and here I am, whipping around the mountainside on a never-ending wild teacup ride.

"Me too," Jon says.

If *he's* getting sick, then I don't feel so bad.

About forty-five minutes of twists later, we arrive in Amalfi. We climb out of the car. It's extremely hot. The beach, what little they have of one, is so crowded it looks like a street corner in New York City.

Our hotel is located right on the water. It's a nice hotel, with friendly staff, but I don't care for the location. It's too busy, too loud. And it's totally my fault. I picked to stay there. The advantage is, Jon and I can walk out of the hotel and be right in the heart of the town of Amalfi.

One thing I will say is that the town has beauty and charm. We walk to the Piazza Del Duomo and see the tall medieval Amalfi Cathedral. The first day we are there, a wedding is happening. We observe the bride and groom on the stairs, one set of their parents on either side of them as a photographer snaps a picture. The woman standing next to the bride is wearing a crimson red dress. The man standing beside the groom is wearing a black tux with a red flower peeking out of his pocket. They look magnificent. As we walk uphill through town, I observe the people. On more than one occasion, I see a young woman escorting a little old woman up the hill. Vespas pass us frequently, and we see small Italian trucks with open back hatches filled with fresh produce. That night, we eat at a restaurant under the lemon trees.

Amalfi certainly has its charm, but still, it isn't Florence.

I try to work on the book I started in Florence. My mind is still creative with ideas, and I wonder if my characters can travel here for some part of the book. I certainly have the details. Because it's so busy, I find it hard to put my thoughts onto paper. I write down an idea here and there, imagining how we might have felt if we had stayed just a few more days in Florence.

One night, we walk around town and see they've set up a concert. The man who sings sounds like Michael Bublé. He sounds incredible as he performs on the stairs to the Amalfi Cathedral. Hundreds of people are gathered in the piazza to watch him sing. Someone has set up lighting, and the colors of the cathedral change from red to blue. It looks like a magic show. Directly next to the cathedral, a woman sits half out of her apartment window, watching the performance below. In Italy, even little things like this look magical. Back at home, if I were sitting half-outside my window, people would question my sanity.

"Who is performing?" I ask the hotel clerk.

"His name is Walter Ricci."

We watch Walter sing the most beautiful songs. Then I visit my favorite bakery in Italy—one reason I would stay in Amalfi again. The bakery is called Pasticceria. Their Occhi di Bue Italian cookies are my favorite cookie in the world, and I can say that because they're half-way around the world. I can't wait to get one, even though I had one earlier that morning.

"Seriously, I could just eat these cookies for the rest of my life."

"That's kind of how I feel about gelato," Jon says.

"My biggest regret is that one day, we're going to leave, and I'm never going to eat this cookie again. It'll be an awesome thing for my waist, but not for my heart."

"Priorities," Jon says.

"Yes, one should always follow their heart."

We laugh.

At night we eat at Il Teatro. I love the restaurant. It's tucked away in an alley off the main street in Amalfi.

"The food is amazing," I tell Jon as I munch on an arugula, fennel, and olive salad with a hint of olive oil.

"Everything in Italy is so fresh. Still, I miss Florence. I felt so alive there. I felt like a part of me that has been closed for so long just popped open. I felt everything for the first time in a year."

"That's good."

"It is, but I miss it. I need that feeling again. That magical high is something I haven't felt in a long time. I wonder if it's because of all the energy of the great artists like Michelangelo, Donatello..."

"You mean the Ninja Turtles."

"Yes," I reply, knowing I set myself up for that one. "But you know what I mean. Dante Alighieri, Botticelli. And what about Galileo? These were amazing people who did incredible works of art or made incredible strides in science. Being around their energy, which is still around in their work, opens my creativity channels without me even trying. I feel a high there that I don't feel anywhere else. Plus, there's the clean food and wine. And very friendly people."

"You'll get it again," Jon reassures me. "You'll feel that again."

Despite his positivity, I'm feeling more skeptical. Being in that space healed me in ways I couldn't imagine. I didn't want to lose that. I wanted more of it.

six

THERE'S MAGIC IN RAVELLO

The next day, Jon and I take a bus ride up to Ravello, known on the Amalfi coast as the Music City. We have no idea what we're doing or where we're going. All we know, courtesy of the front desk, is we have to catch a bus to get there.

I only know of the city because my co-worker had gone to Italy a few weeks before Jon and me and mentioned how beautiful it is. Still, Jon and I are blindly traveling up there. When we get off the bus, there is a line of vendors with jewelry, toys, purses, and other items. We continue walking along a cobblestone road through a tunnel of vendors and hear intense orchestra music coming from beyond the tunnel.

"Welcome to Disneyworld," I say. "What did we just enter?"

Just hearing the orchestra playing is stirring something in my heart.

I definitely feel connected to this place: the villas, the gardens, the music, the shops. I think about the DNA test I took and how it said part of my Italian heritage is from Salerno, Italy. Perhaps I was connected to this area more than I realized.

We visit the Villa Rufolo, a breathtaking structure with incredible architecture. Soft music plays throughout the villa. It's scorching hot, almost unbearable, but sometimes a gentle breeze sweeps through, and we feel okay. We can't drink enough water to feel comfortable. But the villa sure is beautiful.

With tall castle towers and pointed archways, courtyards, and incredible amounts of gorgeous plants, including thick ivy that crawls up the stone walls, hydrangeas, colorful flowers, and palm trees, this villa makes me feel as though I'm in a fairytale. It's tropical and historical at the same time. The view of this colorful, classic villa against the Tyrrhenian Sea is unique and spectacular. We visit the stage of Ravello next. It also overlooks the sea.

"How amazing would it be to listen to music here?" I ask Jon.

"It definitely would," he agrees.

After the villa, we head into the town, which is full of small shops. First, I notice the stray cats, who are extremely friendly, by the way. I want to take all of them home with me. Then I think about where they live and where I live, and I realize these cats are one hundred percent living the life. I'm not going to downgrade their living experience. I mean, if I were a cat, and I had the choice between living on the tropical Amalfi Coast in a small, safe town or in New Jersey, I think the answer would undoubtedly be Amalfi.

I want to buy one thing in Ravello to remind me of it. We are walking down a long narrow, cobblestone street full of tiny shops when suddenly I stop in my tracks.

"Jon, look!" I exclaim.

"What?"

"Up there. Look."

Ahead of us is a store. The sign says, Rosanna.

"Woah," Jon replies when he sees the sign.

"If that isn't my mom, I don't know what is."

We walk up to the store. Out front are a bunch of items hanging on a metal lattice structure. They're for another store but are right under the Rosanna sign.

"Now, I know it's my mom," I say, pointing to one of the objects hanging on the metal lattice. There, under the sign, is a big butterfly.

seven

SORRENTO

From Amalfi, Jon and I head to Sorrento. I haven't been here since I was sixteen. Like Florence, I have bits of memories of this city, but I don't recognize anything when we arrive. One thing I do notice is our hotel's gardens. Tall sticks and wire hold up old grapevines. Netting covers the lemon, lime, and olive trees that make up much of the inside of the gardens. I want to look up why they might do this, wondering if it is to filter the rainwater or sunlight, but we have no cell phone service in our part of the building. I don't even mind. It's just nice to be somewhere with all the plants, clean air, and no cell service. Lavender and sage bushes and a ton of beautiful wildflowers also adorn the gardens.

When we wake, a rooster crows on the Sorrentino hillside. We can see Mount Vesuvius from our hotel room, which is in an annex part of the hotel, away from the main building. Rain clouds cover the mountains—this is the first rain we've seen since we've been to Italy, and as a result, the weather has cooled slightly. We plan to go to our Capri excursion today, but when we reach the hotel's front desk, we find out it's canceled because of the rain.

"The waters will be too choppy," our front desk attendant, a tall, thin Italian woman with dark hair in a bun, confirms with the tour company. "Can you go on Wednesday?"

"We're leaving Wednesday, unfortunately," I say.

"Perhaps you can visit Pompeii," she says.

We contemplate visiting Pompeii. Clouds have completely covered Mount Vesuvius. If I didn't know better, I would think the mountain had vanished.

This morning my stomach feels sick, and I'm confident it's from all the cheese I've eaten. It's near impossible to visit Italy and not eat cheese. I had my DNA tested months ago and learned I scored highly likely to have lactose intolerance. Because of that, and the discomfort I get after eating ice cream and too much dairy, I decided to cut it out a little. But not on this trip. This trip has been cheese and dairy everything.

Jon and I settle on going into the town of Sorrento for the day to walk around. As we wait for the shuttle to pick us up (there's a pick-up spot right outside our hotel), a man on a Vespa whips around the corner.

"If we were standing out in the street...death by Vespa."

"Yep," Jon agrees.

Vespas are everything in Italy, and if they're coming your way, all I can say is...MOVE.

It's still raining when we get to town. We hope it passes quickly. After the shuttle drops us off, we head right to a small store and buy umbrellas. We walk around for a while, and soon the clouds pass, and the sun is out again.

"You know what?"

"What?"

"I never thought I would be able to say this, but I cannot eat another pasta dish or another pizza, or another bit of cheese. All I want is some Standard American Food. The good old SAD diet. I want the *most* American food we can find."

"I agree, actually. Let's see what they have."

Sorrento has a lot of Irish Pubs and a place that has food from Amsterdam, but we are going to Dublin tomorrow and don't want to spoil any authentic Irish Pub experiences. We find an English Bar filled with English food. Jon and I both get burgers and fries, and they are delicious.

After we eat, Jon and I walk to the water's edge. We are overlooking the Gulf of Naples.

"I still miss Florence," I say.

"Yeah," Jon replies. "It's just a different vibe here. It's all pretty amazing. But it is different."

"I'm also ready to go home," I reply. "I can't keep eating pasta, and most of the places down here are pizza and pasta, whereas Florence has more vegetables and fresh food, organic pizza, gluten-free stuff."

"I'm ready to go home also, but I'm pretty excited for Dublin."

"Me too," I reply.

On the shuttle ride home, we sit next to a man who ends up being from Dublin. When we tell him we're going there the next day, he tells us where to eat and where to visit.

He also tells us a wild, fascinating story about his son-in-law, who went to Africa for work, had an encounter with rebels, and who almost did not make it back to England for his wedding, but I digress.

"When you get off the airplane, you need to take the Airlink to Jury's Inn Christchurch," the man says in his thick Irish accent. "You just get on the Airlink, and you'll go right to your stop, get off, and walk up the hill. You'll see the church right there. It's right across the way."

We thank him as the shuttle arrives at our hotel.

Jon and I shower, dress, and head to the hotel restaurant for dinner. Our Irish friend and his family are there too. The hotel is expensive, but Jon and I decide to splurge. Then we sit outside by the pool bar and enjoy a drink on two large white lounge chairs. I can't see the stars as well as I'd like, but I love looking at the night sky, enjoying the mild night.

"Breathe in the last of Italy," I say. "Tomorrow, we're off to Ireland."

eight

JUST ONE NIGHT IN DUBLIN

Dublin is a whole other world. As we fly into gray skies and rain, I see a misty coastline covered in green. Jon and I step off the plane into cool, rainy weather. We collect our bags and grab the Airlink to Jury's Inn- Christchurch. The Airlink driver is bubbly and funny. He cracks jokes as we step on board, telling us that honeymooner seats are in the back. As we ride along, we notice Dublin looks a lot like any other city (at least from our view at this point). The Airlink stops at a few stops, and we keep looking at the map to know where we get off. Our stop is Essex. But, the Airlink never announces our stop. When it announces the stop after, Jon and I panic, push the stop button, and head down the stairs (we were sitting at the top of the Airlink) to grab our bags and exit. Oddly, the driver is not the same when we get downstairs.

305

Jon asks the driver why it didn't announce Essex. He definitely isn't the same guy we saw when we got on. This guy isn't the happiest, and just says, "You'll need to get off here if you're going to Christchurch. You should have gotten off at the last one."

"Do they change drivers half-way or something?" Jon asks me once we step off the Airlink and are standing on the street corner by the river.

"I have no idea. Maybe. Either that or we traveled into another reality."

Jon shrugs. He's used to me by now. I'm only half-kidding with my remark.

"Well, regardless, the other driver was a lot nicer."

"He was a jolly guy. Okay, so, let's figure out where we are."

Jon and I trek up an up-hill side-walk with our luggage and eventually make it to Christchurch. I notice that everyone drives all over in Italy, and people just cross the street without much direction or rules. But in Dublin, everyone crosses only when the little walking man on the light is green. Cars abide by the rules too. It's very much like the U.S. in that way.

In Ireland, at least at Jury's Inn-Christchurch, we are told there is no air conditioning. It's relatively cool outside, so I don't think we need it, but our room is a little warm regardless.

Jon and I shower and get ready. We are excited to walk about the city, and when we're ready, we leave and walk toward Temple Bar. We decide to eat at a pub called The Old Storehouse. It's lovely inside—very pub-like—wood everything, old photos on the walls, a man playing guitar in the corner of the pub. We sit upstairs to eat, and I order fish and chips and a Guinness. This is very unlike me. I do not drink beer (it doesn't agree with me), but I've been waiting for this moment for ten years—a true dream-come-true.

The fish and chips are so delicious; I'm still thinking about them when we leave the pub and head to the crowded Temple bars. It's still raining, but we don't care. The magic in Ireland is quite different from Italy, but it's magic, none-the-less. You can feel the energy of Ireland in that bar—when everyone joins in on a song. We're all united in that bar. We're all Irish. I actually am Irish, but *everyone* is Irish in that bar when the music starts. At this moment, I'm free. I'm happy.

In the morning, Jon and I walk around a little before we catch the Airlink back to the airport. We go to a little place called Queen's Tart to have a pastry.

I order a Guinness Cupcake.

"Next time we come back, we're going to the countryside."

Jon nods in agreement as he eats a blueberry scone.

"For just one night, I think we did a lot."

"I think so too. I-rish we were staying longer."

Jon laughs.

"I-rish we were too."

nine

THE CROSSROADS OF LIFE

In late August, a year and four months after my mother's death, something strange happens. I realize I am at another crossroads in my life. Everything that happened to me brought me to this moment. Yes, I lost the life I thought I would have. Yes, my dreams of living near my parents, raising my children with my mother's powerful influence, and keeping a life full of family and tradition were cut short. I could never have that life, not in the way I had always envisioned it. But I could still write my books and could still fulfill my passions.

When I lost my mother, I realized I had no more reason to be tethered to certain traditions. I could replace the idea of a family and children with endless travel and a life of freedom. Perhaps when my mom begged me to see the world and travel, she felt she hadn't made the most of her life, although I know she did not regret having children. What was the point in tethering to one place and playing life "safe?" Then again, there were positives and negatives to every choice. Perhaps I could commit to living fully but keep the traditions I loved. They wouldn't be the same, but they could be a new creation in this new world in which I was living.

Right now, though, my current lack of creativity and apathy to pursue my passions unnerves me. I wonder if these feelings are all part of the process of healing. I'm not certain of my future, but I know this point in my life is very important. I can no longer work a job with half-hearted ambition and write on the side. I need to decide who I am going to be.

Who do I want to be?

If I am a writer, I need to discipline myself, finish my work, and get it out there as quickly as I can. I will do that. But I am not *just* a writer. I am passionate about it, yes, but my creativity expresses itself in many other ways too. One of those ways is in the gemstone jewelry I create through *Rosanna Gemstone Creations,* which also helps me feel connected to my mom. So, I will continue to run my store. Sometimes my creativity leads me to write music, while at other times, I find great solace in painting. I enjoy acting and creating movies, also.*

I believe many artists express their creativity in a multitude of forms. Even as a writer, I find myself expressing creativity in numerous genres. The world tries to fit people into

*I can't forget my big acting debut—two lines in the cult film, *Return to Sleepaway Camp.*

just one hat, but so many of us wear more than one hat. And while today we say, "you should pick mystery fiction or children's fiction but don't dare attempt both," some of the greatest historical and successful figures of our time did the complete opposite. Benjamin Franklin, for example, wore many hats. He was a publisher, a printer, an inventor, an author, and a diplomat. Every part of my expression, no matter what type, is an essential part of me as I am sure his many "hats" were important expressions of him.

In addition, I have a continued thirst for higher-consciousness, a quest for truth, and a love for science. I root myself in studying and figuring out the mysteries of life. So, not only must my life revolve around my creative endeavors, but also around my studies. All I know is I cannot continue on the path I have been on because I have outgrown it. It no longer serves me.

In Italy, for a brief moment, I reawakened my creativity. But now that I have opened it again and returned home only to feel my creative doors shut once more, I am more determined than ever to reopen those doors. There are so many stories inside me that want to emerge, just like this one.

I realize now that authenticity is important to me. Perhaps that's an effect of such a great trauma. I am no longer willing to compromise my authenticity to please the people around me. I no longer care if people like me or if they support me. I do not mean this condescendingly, but in this way: I only have to love and support myself if I am going to be happy. I *have* to love myself and my life. And I have a long road ahead of me to get there.

I also dream of being able to help others manifest the things they desire in their lives. So, with all of this desire, I have to ask myself, when do I think I'm going to do all this? The answer is undoubtedly *now*.

This crossroads is the most important one in my life, and I know it. It is a life or death situation. I want to do all that I can to live a full and happy life with the cards life dealt me, and for me, that means following my dreams and stepping out of my comfort zone.

ten

RELEASING TRAPPED EMOTIONS

During one of my therapy sessions, I express to Anna Marie that I'd like to find an Emotion Code Practitioner. This desire comes after finishing Bradley Nelson's *The Emotion Code*, where he discusses how trapped emotions can cause issues in our bodies and explains how to release those trapped emotions. For a few months, I've been having debilitating pain in my shoulder. The first time I felt this pain was when my mom got sick. Now it is back, and even more debilitating than it was then. My physical issues are not limited to my shoulder. Back pain, pains in my ovaries, and inter-menstrual bleeding lead me to realize, I am storing a lot of emotional energy in my body. I do not want to carry those emotions around with me forever. I do not want them to lodge in my body like they appear to be doing and then produce some terrible disease nine months from now or ten years from now. So, I begin to study trapped emotions and what they do to the body. I need to understand more about how emotions affect the body, mostly because of all the known emotions running through my mind daily.

"I know it's a trapped emotion," I tell Anna Marie. "If I'm certain of anything, I am certain of this. I can almost feel its density. I know it surrounds my mom getting sick and her death. Loss of my relationship with her, maybe?"

Anna Marie doesn't respond about the trapped emotion but says, "You know that Marie is one, right?"

"An Emotion Code Practitioner?"

Anna Marie nods.

Marie is part of our higher-consciousness book club. She is 90 years old and a nun, and is the most progressive nun I know.

"I did not know that, but I am definitely going to go to her for a session."

This happen-chance is synchronicity I cannot ignore. I make an appointment with Marie that night and see her regularly for the next three weeks.

After one of our sessions, Marie uses a pendulum to determine if I have any chakra imbalances. She discovers my Throat Chakra, the energy center located around the throat known as the communication center, is blocked. She suggests I do a meditation to unblock it. I usually wear my Turquoise bracelet. Turquoise is a stone associated with the fifth energy center. It is a communication stone that I find keeps my throat chakra open. But I am not wearing it now, and I haven't for many months. My truth, my word, is stifled, and I don't feel I can express myself. I have felt this way for some time. I completely understand why this chakra is blocked for me, and I know I must use meditation to focus on this fifth energy center. I also meditate and focus on all my other energy centers to keep them all open.

When I see Marie next, she checks my chakras and finds they are all open and balanced. In our sessions, I realize that I am holding onto much more than my mom's death. Her death is just a catalyst that pushes me to open these doors of understanding myself more deeply than I already do. If I'm on a quest to know myself truly, I must do the work to bring to light that which may be causing me to live a certain way. And then I can work on re-wiring those parts of my life.

Spending time with Marie enlightens me in other ways. She knows everything I know. She's read everything I have and has studied everything I have. Even though I do not consider myself a Catholic anymore, here I am sitting with a very Catholic nun regularly. I am really listening to her. She understands me. When she delivers a message to me, it's as if she can translate it into what I need to hear to get the message but not get caught up in the dogma. She teaches me how to be grateful and live in a place of love.

At the same time that I am doing the emotion code work, our book club begins reading and studying Joe Dispenza's, *Becoming Supernatural.* We are also doing the meditations daily. Marie has studied this also, and she frequently talks to me about the power of meditation, prayer, and rewiring the mind.

I look back, only briefly, where I was a year ago, two years ago, and I realize how much my life trajectory has changed. I am at the beginning of a powerful transformation, and I am excited to take the next step in my life adventure.

eleven

THE POWER OF MEDITATION

In October, I completely immerse myself in studying the brain, quantum physics, energy, and the body. I take Dr. Joe Dispenza's Progressive and Intensive workshops online and use his meditations regularly. Now, I am meditating in a new way, finally understanding how our brains, bodies, and frequencies affect our realities. After a week of studying a couple of his intensive workshop videos, I decide I need to take a short sabbatical from work. I realize my body and mind have been running since my mother's death, never taking the time to stop, relax, and recoup. I had even packed my trips with activities. I don't think I've stopped and just relaxed, and my mind is overwhelmed with anxiety. The pain in my shoulder is unbearable at this point. My other physical symptoms have not subsided. So, I take a leave of absence for two weeks. During this time, I plan to give my mind and body the rest it needs. I am going to change my life by eating well, exercising, writing, and relaxing. I am happy to be nurturing myself in this way. I have put too much pressure on myself to continue life normally and be "healed" from my grief without realizing my body and mind need some extra love during this painful time.

One night, I'm in my bedroom. I finish meditating and feel quite content and peaceful. What begins to make sense to me is that my mother's death may have had roots in the chronic stress she experienced. She hurt her neck on a ride in 1994, and her body never really recovered. The immense stress on her body from the accident, her financial hardships, and not feeling supported by certain people in her life contributed to years of chronic stress. I have been studying—for quite some time—that chronic stress makes the body malfunction. And while my mother's stresses were seemingly normal, she put her body in a chronic state of stress as many people do. I was doing it at this moment.

I think about how many of us try to take on too many tasks and worry too much. We are in a constant state of anxiety from trying to stay afloat financially while mastering everything else in our lives. We are moving too fast and forget how to live and how to love.

By November, I am meditating in a new way every day. Something amazing happens after those few weeks of disciplining myself to meditate. My anxiety disappears. My physical ailments disappear. Even normal ailments, as simple as menstrual cramps, disappear. I have two months of complete bliss as far as my body and mind. Everything in my life is going well also, including my business and writing. I've even found meaning and joy at my work.

If only I can keep doing this, maybe I can achieve the lasting peace and happiness I know I deserve.

twelve

Two Steps Forward, Three Steps Back

It's December, and I am so busy, I stop meditating. The anxiety returns shortly after I stop, and it's three-fold. The physical ailments also return with a vengeance. I have hives, abnormal bleeding, and dizziness. I get a terrible cold that I have for weeks, which is immediately followed by food poisoning. My body's immune system has tanked. When the clock strikes midnight and the new year, 2020, begins, I make myself a promise to dedicate myself to wellness again.

Why did I stop when everything was working so well? Why did I stop? I don't have an answer. All I know is that I must get back into that space. I know change does not happen overnight, but I also know that I will feel wholeness and happiness again if I re-start and stick to meditating.

One Sunday morning in January of 2020, Jon and I enjoy coffee and talk about the book I am writing. At this point, he hasn't read any of the book, not because he doesn't want to, but because I want it to be complete before he does. Even though I have made incredible strides on my journey, my mother's death is still so present in our lives. I find it strange that when one loses someone that she loves so much, death has no time. No matter how many years go by, the death of a loved one feels like just yesterday.

Jon and I are discussing this when he says, "You know the one thing I regret is I didn't go to the hospital more with you."

"You would have understood how I feel more," I say, "But then again, you would have been affected much more. Maybe it would have been a bad thing. I re-listened to the mediums the other day," I tell him. "And you know what's so crazy? Everything Jonas said about the book about what happened to me, the spiritual business, it all came true. I think I need to see him again. And, I realize that his words are such a source of comfort to me. I sometimes forget that my mom and I are so psychically connected. I forget that she's with me. And I think I've closed myself off a little because I'm so busy being sad. But I have to remember that we are connected. It changes the way I look at the world when I remember that."

Jon just listens.

"And I really need to get back to my meditations. I remember how I felt when I was doing it regularly, like I was on a high I never needed to come back down from. It took a few weeks, but it was amazing. For the first time, I didn't worry about food or my body. I didn't worry about money or work. I just knew everything was going to be fine and that I could create the reality I wanted. I was drawn to the things that made my life better. And I felt better. For the first time, my body wasn't falling apart. I need to return to that."

Jon doesn't understand this concept, but he doesn't reject it either. He just doesn't study what I do, so he isn't really aware of its power. I realize that he is on his own path, and I can't make him choose to study this stuff with me or meditate.

My mom had always been my partner, the one who held me accountable for continuing on my path of self-discovery and higher awareness. Now I was doing it on my own, or at least I thought I was. I deeply crave connection with people who are on the same path as me and who are as dedicated as I am to higher awareness. But maybe I am meant to make this journey alone. Perhaps we all are. And maybe my mom is still holding me accountable. Perhaps her death prompts me to dive even deeper into uncovering my true self and is helping me soar even higher in my awareness.

thirteen

A MESSAGE FOR A NEW YEAR

In January of 2020, Jon's work has a kick-off event that significant others can attend. Their guest is Kevin Hart, and everyone is excited to hear what he has to say. Jon's company's CEO has many questions for the famous actor, some surrounding Kevin's documentary on Netflix. Kevin Hart shares how he rose to stardom and what it is like getting to the top. He even talks about where he's going from there. But then he says something that speaks to me on a whole other level.

I hear Kevin Hart say (I'm paraphrasing) that we are all writing the book of our lives. He asks what the takeaway is of who we are. He also asks what we want people to take away from our "life book" when it's said and done.

He's speaking mostly metaphorically, but the message cannot resonate with me more. I am in the middle of writing my story, my journey, and I'm not sure where this book is truly taking me. So, I think about what my takeaway is. What do I want people to remember about this book? About me? I know I want people to know that grief, tragedy, or any hardship is an ugly, messy, complicated process. There is no rule book, no linear route to overcoming adversity. One day you're happy. One day you're miserable. Possibly for the rest of your life. One moment you're joyous, and another moment pain wells up inside your chest, and you're not okay—not by a long shot.

But I want people to know that everyone has a choice—to face life's challenges and to move through them to become the best version of themselves or to shrink and surrender. I want people to know I chose to persevere and that if I can do it, they can too. I want people to walk away feeling hopeful and more willing to pursue their dreams, whether it's writing a book or changing the world in some positive way.

Most importantly, I want people to know that they can be happy again, despite their pain.

If my experience has taught me anything, it is this; to pursue my dreams with relentless determination, enjoy the life I am currently in, and make the most difference in the world with my time.

In my heart, I know a tragedy is a teacher. It shows us how very little control we sometimes have over our lives. This prospect can keep us awake at night. It can grip us with fear and keep us stuck in a particular job, relationship, or a certain behavior or temperament. While those who have not experienced significant suffering might see it as extremely frightening, the experience can be liberating for those who have suffered. Tragedy and trauma can mean that we lose the need to control. We realize that life is unpredictable, and actually, that is what makes life so *exciting*.

People talk about the mystery of life, the excitement of unknown possibilities. I never truly understood that concept until now. When the worst happens, all of life feels unsafe, unpredictable, and uncomfortable. In the unknown, what other things could go wrong? We like familiarity, security, and safety. But are we looking at the unknown all wrong? Because on the other side of those frightening feelings is excitement for the positive, incredible things that can or may happen.

Now I understand that the crossroads we face in our lives are the most important points in our lives. These are the points in life where one experience can literally change our destiny. It's important to our evolution if we allow it to be. Will we embrace the experience, tragedy, or trauma and allow it to shape our destiny into the person we are meant to become? Or will we shrink from it, define ourselves by the pain it causes us, and never rise above it? Of course, it is easier said than done, but the choice is still there, and it's one many of us must make. I know I am hardwired to overcome, to shift, and to evolve. I am willing to let what happened to me positively shape the person I am going to become.

Becoming the best version of ourselves means being vulnerable and being willing to change. I finally understand that suffering can be the greatest gift from our Divine Creator.

We are often so immersed in our everyday problems— our jobs, our relationships with loved ones, neighbors, and co-workers, our health—that we don't realize that we have it so much better than we know. It only takes a tragic death to forget all the problems of the world. Our pain and suffering make us aware of a whole other existence that we knew nothing about just seconds before. And we are never the same because of it. If we choose to overcome what we've experienced, then the small, ego-based issues that plague others mean nothing to us.

We can see past illusions and become more humble. We become more grateful, more compassionate, and forever changed.

What matters now is life. What matters is enjoying the world around us—partaking in life's smallest pleasures like breathing, enjoying a glass of wine with friends, and sharing love with those around us. All the other issues seem trivial. And yet, we watch as those around us are still so immersed in a mind-made movie that they cannot see how beautiful life is. And that is the gift of suffering and tragedy. It has the capability to shift us. We can become the best versions of humanity through our experience—full of real love, genuine compassion, and wisdom. We can develop more meaningful relationships and friendships. We can forgive the wrongs of the past because they have no place in our future. Once the trivial is out of the way, the real meaning of life reveals itself to us. Now we understand, we are meant to enjoy and love life. And every bit of it, from breathing to sleeping, is a chance for us to truly live.

fourteen

A QUICK GETAWAY

On Saturday morning, in early February of 2020, I re-read the first part of my memoir. It's hard to read it even now. I don't want to remember the pain. But I realize something about the time I spend with my mother during her illness. Because of our close friendship, I realize I made an important choice when my mother fell ill. I did not run from her condition. I did not shy away from my mother because the pain was too much then. Instead, I immersed myself in the experience with her every step of the way. Yes, it was hard, but I have no regrets. I do not wish I spent more time with her in her final days. I spent every minute I could with her during the ugliest and darkest of times, during the scariest moments of her life. I never left her alone. Because of this, I don't feel any guilt at all. I know I did the very best I could. Knowing that is a comfort to me. I realize I did this because of how connected we were. I never once thought about leaving her side.

Jon and I are both anxious—he's having trouble at work, and I have heightened anxiety. I can barely concentrate. We are both on edge. We decide we need to get away, and we book a three-day trip to Florida to do nothing.

Right now, there is a threat of the Coronavirus, but New Jersey, Pennsylvania, and Florida have no cases yet, so we decide it's okay for us to travel. My cousin has anti-viral masks, so we decide to bring them just in case someone looks suspicious on the plane and is coughing like crazy. Not that they are going to help, but just having them comforts us.

Florida is amazing. It's warm, sunny, and relaxing, and our hotel is perfect. We are on the beachside of the resort in Lauderdale by the Sea. I'm so grateful to be here, and I can't wait to relax.

"I need a new life plan," I tell Jon as we sip on our morning Cappuccinos from a little coffee shop inside the hotel.

I have been listening to Suzanne Somers' audiobook version of *A New Way to Age*. It's one of the best books I've ever read.

"Yeah? What do you want to do?"

"First, I need to stick with meditation. Consistent meditation. I know how I feel when I'm not meditating, and when I am, and the anxiety I feel when I'm not is three-fold. Secondly, I need yoga or some regular physical exercise. I need to get back into it and make sure I do it at least four times a week, even if it's a two-mile walk. I also think I want to be Certified in Nutrition. I mean, I'm already obsessed with studying food anyway. Maybe I can help other people. Maybe it can help me overcome my fears about food."

Jon nods.

"If that's what you want to do."

"Yeah, and lastly, I need to see a doctor who is on the same page as me. I'm done going to doctors who aren't. I may have to pay out of pocket, but my health is worth it to me."

"Okay," Jon says.

"So, that's my plan. It may take a while to implement. But I have one. Do *you* have a plan?"

"Not really," he replies. "I'm just here to relax and not think about anything."

"Fair enough," I tell him.

For the next few days, we relax, but there is a collective feeling brewing in the country. Everyone is still out and about enjoying themselves. I tell Jon if either of us is single in our sixties, the place to find a new lover would be Fort Lauderdale by the Sea—especially the strip of bars and restaurants at the end of Commercial Boulevard. But even though baby boomers pack the bars, the threat of the Coronavirus is growing.

The next morning as we casually walk to the Publix across from our hotel, we see a man in a blacked-out van stacking packs of waters into it. He is telling another man to hurry up and get his goods because the "end is near." Jon and I raise our eyebrows and laugh. To us, this man is completely crazy. But neither of us can deny that some uncomfortable energy is brewing.

When we leave Florida, the experience is very different than when we were traveling there. People are wearing masks on the airplane and in Philly at the airport. No one wants to get near one another.

One guy coughs at the baggage claim in Philly, and nearly everyone moves quickly away from him.

"A huge energy shift is taking place," I tell Jon. "I can feel it. It's so uncomfortable."

Jon nods.

"I don't think this is the end either. I think we are at the beginning of the shift."

"I'm just glad we went now. Who knows what's going to happen in the upcoming weeks."

fifteen

FEAR, THE REAL DEVIL

When I re-read the chapter in my memoir about God, about how angry I was, I realize how my mindset has changed. Before my experience, I thought I had transcended religion. I hadn't. What really happened was that another side of my ego emerged. Before, when people would talk to me about religion, I would become angry. I preached oneness and unity, but I didn't really believe it. I mean, I thought I did, but if someone would tell me I was going to hell, I would still get offended. I still needed to break down religion and point out its flaws. I was just a frustrated Christian, angry with the shortcomings of the religion. I was attached to how religion made me feel.

But my tragedy helps me understand my truth. I say *my* truth because I don't expect others to believe what I believe. Who am I to judge someone based on their beliefs? If that belief brings them comfort and brings out the most loving, compassionate version of that person, then who am I to challenge that?

The lie isn't the religion or belief, whether it's Wiccan, Christianity, Muslim, or Judaism. The lie is *fear*. If there is a devil, then he or she is **fear and manipulation**. *Fear* drives most religions, belief systems, and businesses in the world. *Fear* drives the media. *Fear* turns us away from connecting with ourselves and those around us. *Fear* divides us and breeds hatred for ourselves and those around us. *Fear* even drives our healthcare system.

When we buy into *fear*, the world becomes a scary place, both outwardly and inwardly. Instead of being honest about a product or service, we manipulate others for profits. Instead of being in tune with our bodies, we are afraid of them. Instead of being one with God, we fear him/her/it. Instead of loving our neighbors and friends, we judge them. Instead of having honest conversations about difficult topics, we hide behind social media platforms and berate our friends or people we don't even know. Then we spend our time trying to convince them that *our* beliefs about religion, politics, healthcare, and science are *right* and *their* beliefs are *wrong*. We use facts, evidence, statistics, and even examples in the Bible to show people they are *wrong* and we are *right*. And while we say we do it in the name of God or Science, we actually do it in the name of fear, control, and manipulation. But this is not the truth. What I learned is that there is only *one* truth. And we can only live in that truth when we live in the absence of fear.

Call it God, Goddess, the Universal Creator, Source, Intelligence, or Energy, whatever you'd like to call the power that runs through us and every living thing. This Divine Intelligence is pure Love. It is not fear. It doesn't matter what faith people believe because every religion and way of life, from Catholic to Buddhist, leads to Love. Any parts of those religions or beliefs that are rooted in fear create separation. And separation is so far from the Divine. The vibrations of Love and Gratitude are our only truths. There is no separation in love. Only fear separates us, and manipulation drives that fear. It spreads like cancer, infects, and brainwashes us, our family, friends, and neighbors. We are left uncertain about life and afraid of each other.

Living in a state of fear, we become disconnected from our bodies and each other. Our body stays in a state of stress. In this place, we are not in tune with our bodies. We cannot listen to our bodies and know what they need to be well or how to strengthen our immune systems. We are too fixed on listening to others outside of our bodies telling us we need this test, this supplement, this food, or this drug instead of genuinely listening to what *our* body needs. What I understand now is how powerful and intelligent our bodies are. And while we should always make choices that are best for us, which may mean getting a particular test, having surgery, or taking a medication, we must also make more of a conscious effort to be in harmony with our bodies.

In a state of fear, we also feel separate from one another. We feel alone, like no one understands us. We feel the world is unsafe and that people different from us are frightening, unkind, or unsafe. We constantly fear illness, loneliness, and death. But this is all an illusion. Fear is an illusion. Sometimes fear is warranted, needed even, but not to the degree to which humans take it. Survival mode is meant to come and go once the threat is gone. But we fixate on the possibility of some impending doom; we spend hours worrying about what may happen. And we are all in constant states of paralyzing fear because of it. Anxiety plagues many of us. We don't follow our dreams because of it. But if we can disengage from fear and live our lives in emotional states of Love and Gratitude, we will be in a place of peace and harmony.

I finally look at the world the way I thought I did before, only now it is authentic. I finally understand. And I credit my suffering for that. It is because of my experience that I see the connection in all things. When my father says he's going to church on Sunday, I understand that it is *his* sanctuary. I do not judge him, do not bother examining flaws within the religion. It is easy to do that when we lose sight of truth. And when someone preaches to me, I see they are viewing the situation from their truth. I try not to judge them. Some people say hurtful, even wildly crazy things because they've interpreted something a certain way, but I still try to overlook that. However, if a person condemns someone, hates a group of people, or tries to control and convert people to his beliefs using fear, manipulation, and hatred, he has turned away from Love. He is likely missing the point, regardless of what religion, belief system, or political affiliation he holds. People who resonate in the vibration of Love make choices that protect, help, and lift others.

I translate, just like Marie did for me, to the bigger picture. Because behind individual beliefs, which are so often rooted in fear and manipulation, is Love. And all the parts that are fear, I simply filter them out of my mind. In this way, I can have a conversation with anyone from any religion or way of life. Instead of noticing the differences between that person and me, I recognize the connections. I know they are connected to me when they speak from Love. And because of my experience, this connection is more authentic, empathetic, and compassionate than I could have imagined.

sixteen

THE FLOWER SHOW

On March 8, I go to the Flower Show in Philadelphia with my co-workers. One of my co-workers, Lindsey, who is my age, brings her mom. They are laughing and giggling together, and naturally, I feel sad.

I wish I were here with my mom, I think. It's still difficult to see girls my age having fun with their mom. It's gut-wrenching. I try to pull myself into the present and access the "wise" me. *I'm so happy Lindsey has this kind of relationship with her mom,* I think. *It's so special, and I'm so lucky to have had that relationship with my mom.*

I'm still sad as we walk around the show, but I truly am happy that Lindsey and her mom can bond similarly to how my mom and I used to.

The Flower Show is eerily empty, and we attribute it to the Coronavirus. The energy shift that I felt just a couple of weeks before was growing. It feels like a dark cloud covering the state, or one of those Stephen King novels where an ominous, evil fog covers the city. Just hearing a person cough made one want to run and hide.

The show has a butterfly garden with beautiful blue and black butterflies flying around everywhere. I think of my mom telling me she would return as a blue butterfly. It's hard for me to associate this as something she orchestrated because these butterflies were already here. But maybe me purchasing a Flower Show ticket and forcing myself to go, despite everything going on, was a nudge from the spirit world to see those butterflies and remember she *is* with me.

seventeen

LIFE IN QUARANTINE

When we finally go into "quarantine," something happens to me. I should preface what happens with this— I want the virus to go away. I want quarantine to end.

However, for the first time in almost two years, I feel genuine happiness. Every day, I get up, go for a walk outside, and connect with Nature. I hear the birds singing. I notice the buds on the trees. I breathe in fresh, clean air. Forced to slow down and cease my regular busy go-go-go routine, I can actually stop and smell the roses. (Literally, I smelled them.)

My anxiety disappears. I take photos of Nature— Cherry Blossom buds, Violets, and Apple Blossoms. I capture the tiny upside-down hearts of the Purple Dead Nettle, the patches of dandelions nestled in a stretch of wild purple flowers, and the bright yellow Forsythias. I even find a four-leaf clover patch. I notice how perfectly designed each part of Nature is. Each flower, each leaf is perfectly geometrically designed with the most intricate details. I wonder how this is so. *These creations must be the work of some Divine Intelligence,* I think.

It's April. My mother's birthday is approaching quickly. We are also nearing the second anniversary of her death. I post the yellow Forsythia photo on Facebook with a message that I am going to post one picture of Nature a day as a tribute to my mom. When I walk outside a few hours later, I see someone has cut a bunch of them and put them in a jar of water. They've done this for me as a reminder of my mom, and I am so thankful. I don't know who has put them out there, and even though I have asked who left such a lovely gift, I don't expect I will ever know.

In the next days, I begin to write, compose music, and cook wholesome, homemade foods. I decide I am ready to become certified in Nutrition and chose Cornell as my school. They let me start earlier than usual for my first class. Within a week of studying these amazing foods that keep the body in complete homeostasis, my fear of food is gone.

I have never felt happier.

I'm amazed at how happy I am during the worst week of my life: my mother's birthday, the anniversary of her death, the threat of COVID19. How is this possible? I am in the most creative, free, grateful, connected place I have ever been.

I am finally living life from a place of peace, happiness, and authenticity. Each time I spend creating, meditating, cooking, and reveling in Nature's simplicity and beauty, I feel grounded and connected to everything. And while I feel this way, some of my friends don't feel the same, understandably. They are miserable in quarantine. They cannot wait to go back to the way their lives were before. But here I am in complete bliss. The more time I have to connect, the more grateful I feel. I find an incredible high in the most natural, simple ways, and I do not want the blissful feeling to end. This experience is so profound to me. I want to be in this place of expansive, connected creativity forever. I can only hope that the virus will go away soon, but my joy and love for life will not.

Of course, the feeling does not last forever. Soon I realize how others are suffering during this time, and I feel such compassion for them. Those who are losing loved ones to this virus and other conditions are suffering the most. Not being able to see those loved ones and be with them during their final hours makes me cry for them. I think about my grandmother, who is in a nursing home with dementia. We cannot visit her. I think about my mother. Even though we were at the hospital as much as possible, I wonder if she felt alone in her final days. When I remember her talking to someone on the other side, it gives me hope that all those who pass during this time have angels and guardians guiding them to the next realm.

We are in quarantine for many months. I look at the world differently than many other people. For them, the world is unfamiliar now. So many people ask themselves, "How did the world get to this place? Is this for real? Is this the apocalypse? What's next?" For me, this abrupt change in life happened two years ago. I never returned to the old world I knew. The new world is this one, and it is a strange world indeed. So, with this coronavirus and a host of other issues going on in the world, I feel flowing *with* the river is more beneficial than pushing against it. And even though the moment seems uncomfortable or unsafe, there is something inside me that knows going against the current will only make life more difficult. So, I act like water and allow myself to flow with it. Even though it's difficult, and even though there are days when I can't take it, I meditate, and I remember to flow with the river of life and change.

eighteen

ON A QUEST TO FIND MOM

One night I have a dream about my mom. When I wake, I think about it all day, wondering what it means.

THE DREAM

I am standing by a tall stone wall. It is about thirty feet high. I know if I want to see my mom, I must climb over it. I use all my might to climb, digging my feet into the tiny grooves of the wall. Eventually, I reach the top, exhausted, and I hurdle myself over the wall. I know I am in a dream, and I drop to the ground, landing perfectly on my feet. When I look up, I am standing in my backyard, looking at my house. I smile. It feels so familiar. Suddenly, I see a golden retriever bounding toward me. It is my dog, Jingles, who passed away when I was fourteen. She is so happy to see me. She jumps on me and licks me as I pet her, happy to see her too.

"If you're here, is Bella here?" I ask. Bella is my other dog who passed away just a couple of years ago.

Jingles doesn't answer. She is just wagging her tail. She runs inside the house, and I follow her.

This house's setup is different than mine. It is mostly made of stone caverns inside with all kinds of hallways leading to other parts of the house. I look around for Bella, but I don't see her.

"Mom?" I call out. I don't hear a reply. I walk through one of the tall stone archways into another room. It is empty except for lit candlesticks.

Strange, I think. What is this place?

I walk back the way from which I came and see a stone archway that leads upstairs.

I decide to use the stairs and follow it up. The upper part of the house looks more like a house, but not mine. There is a master bedroom and a bathroom at the least. I hear movement and wonder if it's my mom. I walk into the room and see that it looks familiar, but there is a long tunnel attached to the room. A woman is guarding the tunnel. She is alien-like, all blue with jet black hair. She has a gold emblem on her forehead, and I sense she is of Egyptian descent.

"You can't be here," she says.

"I'm looking for my mom."

"She's not here."

"But this is our house. Can I at least look around for her?"

"No, I'm sorry. You have to leave."

Disappointed, I walk out of the room, but I have no intention of leaving. I wait until the alien woman goes to the bathroom, and as soon as she disappears, I sneak back into the room and run down the hallway as fast as I can. The hallway spirals downward, lit by a host of torches. When I reach the end of it, I enter a large convention hall filled with people.

This place feels familiar, I think. *Have I been here before?*

I start walking around the convention hall and notice people shuffling into an auditorium. I ask one of the people,

"If I were looking for my mom, do you know where I would go?"

The person shrugs.

I follow the group into the auditorium and watch as they take seats on either side of the main hall. The auditorium has a glass ceiling, and sunlight cascades into the room, making it bright. Outside are the most beautiful gardens.

I don't sit, but I stand near the front.

"Excuse me!" I shout. The people in the auditorium talk loudly to one another. They are a mix of all ages, races, and ethnicities, although I do not see any children.

"Excuse me!" I cry out again. They finally quiet down. "How many of you are here because of COVID?"

Most people raise their hands. Suddenly a man and woman appear at the front of the auditorium.

"You aren't supposed to be here," the man says. He is about 5' 8, with salt-and-pepper gray hair. He seems annoyed I am there.

"Did all these people die?" I ask.

"You're ruining orientation. You need to leave."

"But I need to find my mom."

"I'm sorry. You'll have to wait to see her. Now go back before we force you to."

"But can't you just tell me where she is?"

"No." The man sighs. "I'm really sorry, but we can't."

"Okay," I say, feeling defeated. The man and woman proceed with their orientation then, expecting me to leave. I notice all the people in the auditorium have pamphlets and are flipping through them as the man and woman speak.

I see a door on the side of the auditorium that leads to the gardens. Without looking behind me, I burst through it. Outside, I am standing on the porch of the auditorium. It has large white marble columns. I run down the porch steps and

341

into the gardens, which have many brick roads running through them. I just keep running and running, looking for any signs of my mom. *She has to be in this place*, I think. Is this Heaven? I wonder. It is beautiful enough to be. With the brightest greens and the most vibrant magentas and blues, the entire place looks like *The Wizard of Oz* once Dorothy arrives in Oz. Suddenly, I see my friend Brian who passed away when I was younger. He is walking hand-in-hand with a blonde girl.

"Brian!" I call to him. "Brian!"

He finally turns around to me.

"Stef?" He smiles and gives me a big hug. Then he frowns. "What are you doing here?"

"I need to find my mom. Will you help me?"

"I can't. I'm sorry."

"Please," I start to cry. "No one will help me find her. I thought maybe you would."

"I wish I could. I don't have any way of knowing where she is. She could be anywhere."

"Well, maybe we could narrow it down."

"Stef, you have to run. They're coming for you."

Sure enough, the man and woman from the auditorium are chasing me.

"What can I do?" I plead with him.

"Here," he says, handing me a pair of skates. "These will get you to the top of that hill, but you should just go back. They will get you."

I put the skates on as quickly as I can and use the railing to hurl myself up a set of wide steps. But the woman gains on me, and eventually, she catches me at the top.

"Let's go," she demands.

"No, please. I have to find my mom."

"No. You're going back. Now."

"Please," I start sobbing. "I've been looking for her for so long, and I know she's here."

The woman purses her lips and frowns, but she seems to take pity on me.

"All right. I'll distract him," she says, pointing to the salt-and-pepper haired man. "You hurry off. I'll say you got away."

"I...I don't know where to go, though. Are there butterfly gardens here?"

"Yes," the woman nods. "Down there."

"Okay, thank you so much. Thank you. You have no idea."

"Just go," she urges. And I take off. In the distance, I can see more beautiful gardens at the bottom of a large cliff—the butterfly gardens. My mother has to be there, and I am finally going to see her.

Then, I wake up.

nineteen

LIKE WATER FLOWS, LIFE CHANGES

June 2020

I find out I am pregnant. I am happy, sad, afraid, and excited. I don't know what to expect. I don't have my mom to ask questions. Pregnancy isn't easy for me. I am having complications from the beginning, but at seven weeks pregnant, I hope to experience better days. I can't help but think about the state of the world, where we are now, and the world my baby will be born into.

When I reflect on this experience, I realize that this life is a gift; we are lucky to be here in this time, right now, experiencing this transformational shift in humanity. As I write these words, I think about where I am now and where I will be in a few years. I am not perfect. Some days, I feel depressed and sad; some days, I feel euphoric. But I love more. I feel more compassion. I am more aware and more open than I ever was before my suffering. Who will I be in another year, five years, ten years? I know that the next chapters of my life are sure to be exciting, and each of our evolutions in this lifetime is an ongoing journey. It is for me, and it is for you too. This journey is one that connects us. Perhaps I will write another book, detailing more of my journey. If all of this can happen in just two years, what growth can I experience in the next decade?

twenty

REFLECTIONS ON TIME

September 2020

It is September, and I am four months pregnant with a baby boy. Looking at the world, I see history unfolding: the pandemic, the election, the wild-fires, the riots. Usually, changes happen slowly over time, but 2020 is a year of constant change. Sometimes I feel I am living in a dystopian science-fiction world. A.I. is only one step away from taking complete control of our brains. If my mom came back, just for one day, and I explained everything that is going on, I don't even think she'd believe me. She'd probably think I was telling her the storyline of my newest fiction novel.

And while the world is experiencing this tremendous change, I realize I don't feel alone. I think we are all living in a different world. This experience is making history. And one day, I will look back on this moment and say, "What an incredible period of change we lived through!"

But not now. Now, I worry about what kind of world my baby is being born into. I worry about the coronavirus. I feel unsafe again, just as I did when I lost my mom, but the feeling is different because many other people in the world feel the same as me.

After a meditation one day, I contemplate time. We humans define our lives in time, especially now. The concept of it is a mystery, but I often wonder, what if time is just a human creation?

What if there is only one moment, and our brains are recording those moments, making it appear as though we are experiencing linear time when we are only experiencing one moment our entire lives? What does this mean for us if this is true?

It means, for me, that I am the same person I was when I was sixteen. Have I aged because I believe in time? What happens if I believe in only one moment? What if I stop putting so much emphasis on linear time—on days, weeks, months, and years? What if I stop thinking that every year I'm getting older, I'm acquiring more wrinkles, and I'm growing weaker? What if I believe I'm the same as I always was? Yes, I have grown, and I will continue to grow until I no longer need to. Yes, my body will age, but is my belief in linear time accelerating this process? Is rooting myself too much in time hurting me? If I believe in just one moment being my entire life, then each moment is special. Each moment in my life is the only moment I will ever have like that. My past is just a recording now. And worrying about my future seems silly as it has not happened yet. And when it does, it will also be the present moment, another special moment to cherish on the adventure of life.

Without time, I am *free*. I don't have to worry about ten years from now. I can focus on right now.

twenty-one

Is Life Just a Dream?

Today I listen to the soft leaves of the still green October trees rustling in a cool breeze. A dog barks in the distance, and my neighbor's wind chimes play soothing bell sounds. I feel an overwhelming sense of peace.

I ponder an idea; what if life is only a dream? I've heard life described this way before from countless people: life as a dream, a matrix, and an illusion. This dream has rules and boundaries, so it is not exactly like the ones we have when we sleep, but what if, from the moment we are born until the moment we die, we live in a dream world—a world where we have choices and consequences. In this dream world, we use our senses to experience. And like our nighttime dreams, we

THIS SIDE OF THE DREAM

don't realize we are in a dream as we experience life. We are entirely rooted in the dream, believing life is harsh and cruel to us; we stay rooted in our physicalness. We fear death, thinking that it is the end. But what if it isn't?

And what if we become lucid in this dream of life just like we can in the dreams we have when we're sleeping? What if we unplug from the illusion like Neo in the movie, *The Matrix*? What if we suddenly know we're dreaming? How does that change how we live life? How does it change how we spend our time? And if we're dreaming, then there must be an us outside of this dream doing the dreaming. Like all dreams, there will come a time to wake up from this one. What is on the other side of the dream? I don't know.

What I do know is that if life is just a dream, then being in this dream is a special privilege. The ability to experience this life must mean there is significant meaning for each of us in our short time in the dream. Those who dream with us are here, for a short time like we are, experiencing life and all it offers. So how do we live our lives knowing we are only in a dream? Do we cherish those in our lives more? Do we fulfill our goals and ambitions with more courage? Do we love and forgive more? Do we let go more? Do we worry less? Do we understand the lessons others present to us through our interactions with them? Do we see those interactions as experience to better ourselves here so that when we wake up from this dream, we are better versions of ourselves?

If this dream is ours, do we want the best for ourselves and those around us? I've thought about this many times before. If I'm dreaming, then I'm no longer afraid of failure, no longer slighted by a critical comment, no longer defined by my circumstances, and no longer fearful of death. If we are in a dream, we know we can let go of all our pain and fear because life is just an experience.

I like the idea of life as a dream. I imagine a conversation where I discuss this with someone.

"But wouldn't people just be bad then?" I imagine someone saying. "Wouldn't they do terrible things because they would think there is no consequence for their actions?"

"No, I don't believe so," I would reply. "To understand life as a dream, one must detach from the illusion. The illusion is what causes pain in the first place. Pain and fear are what cause people to hurt people. And for the most part, when you dream while you sleep, are you often the aggressor? Are you often doing bad things? Or are you the one who is running from the bad things? Also, there are still consequences in this reality, even if it is a dream. But if people knew this place was only a moment in time for them, that they would wake up one day possibly in some other form but still existing, they wouldn't have to be victims of their circumstances here. If they understood life exists beyond this dream, this moment in time, they could create happy, wholesome lives for themselves and their families. If they weren't taught that fear and manipulation would get them further in life than love for themselves and those around them, then perhaps the need for consequences would be much less."

I suddenly feel the joy of being alive, feeling that this experience is temporary, and we are the lucky ones to be here. Perhaps hundreds of souls are waiting to come into this dream, and here I am fortunate enough to be experiencing it right now. I feel pure gratitude for life, genuine happiness that I have never felt before. All I know right now is this: I never want to leave this side of the dream.

The End.

Advice from the Heart

I think about what I have learned on my journey so far about suffering and pain. I have compiled some advice for those who may have a friend or family member going through what I'm going through.

1. **Healing from suffering and pain is not a linear process.** I know for sure that suffering and pain are a series of random ups and downs as one's body and mind figure out how to cope with what's happened. Two years after my mom's death, I still had several bad days. Sometimes we think it'll never end. But the bad days do subside. They do not go away completely, and I find myself, even now, two and a half years later, still experiencing longing and a tough day. But the more you choose to rise, the easier it becomes to deal with your new life.

2. **Grief hurts more in the second year.** People tend to "be there" for those who are grieving within the first six months but slowly because of a misconceived notion that "time" is what heals wounds, people stop checking in on their friends, stop bringing them food, or stop helping them get back on their feet. But grief hits more after the shock wears off after survival mode is over. When we are no longer in survival mode, we start to process what has actually happened. That didn't happen for me until well after my mother's death. And when that happens, that's when we need people most. But because we are all misguided that time heals wounds, people don't understand why we feel so much depression and anxiety a year and a half after our loss compared to, let's say, eight months prior.

Our loved ones and friends want us to be happy. They want our pain to go away, and they don't understand why the passing of time did not do this. So, they don't reach out to us as much or talk about what happened for fear that their doing so will cause us more pain. They do not understand how we need them most at this time.

3. **While time does not heal our wounds, we *can* heal. It is our acceptance of what *is* that truly heals us.** While time healing wounds may be a falsely circulated idea, we *can* heal. That I could heal, and how I was able to, is perhaps my greatest piece of wisdom. I learned that what heals us is our willingness to embrace the new world we find ourselves in and our decision to make the best of this new life. Despite the gaping hole that loss has left in our lives, when we decide we will take on this different world and make a wonderful experience of it, we begin to look at life in a new light. We categorize our lives into two parts: our old life and the new one. Sometimes we still long for the old one, but we know we are no longer in that one. Whenever we look at our life as a continuation of our old one, we feel the pain again. But if we are able to look at it as a completely new life, we can start to mend the pain. Acceptance is key.

4. **External things, situations, and experiences will never help us heal.** No drug, no vacation, no material item, no substance, and no relationship will heal the pain inside us. The more we focus on external methods of healing, the less happy we will feel. Healing is an internal job, and we are the boss. Focusing on our external reality gives us the kind of anxiety that causes us to seek more outside stimuli to help ourselves. But despite how much we fill up our lives with these external methods, they just don't work. They just don't get rid of the anxiety or pain permanently. The only

thing that can do that is by healing from within. We must realize the wealth of happiness, rooted in love and gratitude, that rests just under our pain. Sitting quietly in meditation and connecting with Nature are two ways to access our reservoirs of happiness. Science is beginning to show us that feeling love and gratitude while meditating and going about our day can help us experience joy and healing.

5. **Unconditional Love is the only truth and the greatest feeling in the universe.** The unconditional, expanded love that I felt, which came to me in a dream, was the most incredible feeling I could ever feel. I consider myself extremely grateful to have felt this, but I also understand that not everyone has. Everyone in the world deserves this feeling, especially those who are suffering. The greatest gift we can give to one another is true, unconditional love, but how can we when we don't know what it truly feels like? We can start by having compassion and empathy for ourselves, other people, and animals. Those feelings can change a relationship in an instant.

I try to imagine the feeling from that dream again and again, but it only exists as a faint memory now. I wish for myself to feel it again and for the world to feel it also. Forgiveness, to me, is the ability to look at those who have wronged us with complete compassion and empathy and hope that they experience unconditional love. Once a person feels it, he understands how everyone would be changed by it.

The incredible feeling that comes from a connection rooted in love surpasses any feeling in the world. It is a small glimpse of the unconditional love from above, and it comes from connecting on a soul level with others. It is not rooted in gossip, pain, judgment, or anger. It is not rooted in political or social issues. It does not allow energy vampires or negativity into its circle. It is a bond much higher in frequency than that. It is light, happy, and carefree. It is infectious happiness. It is the power that human beings have and are completely unaware of. It is something we feel when we are with our people, our tribe. And the more of that we have, the easier it is to heal from our pain because when we are with those people, the pain dissipates. The more people we connect to on this level, of soul connection, compassion, fun, and happiness, the more love we feel, and the happier we feel.

6. **Stress causes physical pain.** One thing I know for sure is that emotional stress can cause physical issues. I know this because of the physical problems I suffered and occasionally continue to suffer from dealing with loss. It is up to us to find ways to de-stress our bodies and keep ourselves well. I have learned that breathing correctly, exercise, meditation, or stillness of mind, eating well, and finding joy in whatever capacity is possible will help assuage the mental stress of suffering. As a result, many of our physical issues will dissipate.

7. **Find happiness in the simplest of ways.** Be creative. Write music. Write books. Paint. Garden. Dance. Sing. Spend time noticing the perfect and incredibly detailed geometric designs of Nature. Breathe in the fresh air. Watch plants grow. Cook your own food and enjoy the variety of colors, tastes, and aromas that food brings. Look at your family members, friends, neighbors, and colleagues as though they're children, like you, on their individual journeys but on a larger global one as well. Meditate and fill your mind with thoughts of wellness, happiness, gratitude, and love. Stop the worry of the future or the pain of the

past in its tracks. *Wrap yourself in love. See the magic in everything. This way leads to real happiness.*

Symbolism of Dragonflies

Represented in a host of cultures and belief systems, the dragonfly is a highly spiritual creature full of deep, insightful symbolism. Known as one of the first winged insects to evolve over 300 million years ago, the dragonfly is an impressive ancient insect that has roamed the earth well before our human beginnings. Dragonflies are a symbol of change and transformation, wisdom, and adaptability.

According to J.C. Cooper, in his book, *An Illustrated Encyclopaedia of Traditional Symbols*, dragonflies also share the meaning of immortality and regeneration with the butterfly (Cooper 56). But dragonflies hold even more powerful symbolism as one researches the meaning of these majestic creatures in several cultures and belief systems around the world. Here are a few symbolic meanings of dragonflies from those cultures or belief systems.

General: Dragonflies symbolize good luck, transformation, change, personal growth, and wisdom. They are tied to the subconscious, allowing us to bring what is hidden in dreams to the light. To many, the dragonfly is a powerful spirit guide, preparing a person for a powerful transformation. Known in some cultures as the "souls of the dead," the dragonfly is a powerful message to those it appears to. When a dragonfly appears after a loved one's death, it is said that it is the deceased loved one's soul taking form as the dragonfly. This experience is to let the grieving one know that their loved one is free.

359

Native American: The spiritual meaning of the dragonfly differs from Native American tribe to tribe. Some tribes believe the dragonfly represents swiftness and activity because of the dragonfly's ability to dart quickly in different directions (Cooper 56). Other tribes believe dragonflies are powerful symbols in dreams and are associated with shamanistic powers (O'Connell 196). To many tribes, the dragonfly represents change and enlightenment. Considered by some tribes to be a medicine animal, the dragonfly often is associated with healing and transformation. To other tribes, dragonflies symbolize pure water, purity, and renewal of life after tremendous hardship.

Christianity: While no passages in the Bible specifically mention dragonflies (to my knowledge a least), the dragonfly is nonetheless a power symbol in the Christian culture. Perhaps the most significant meaning is the transformation from darkness to light, as represented by the dragonfly. Dragonflies are born into darkness and are initially transparent and colorless beings, but when light shines upon them, they become beautiful colorful undergoing a transformation that is similar to the human who is transformed by the light of Jesus Christ.

Chinese: In Chinese culture, the dragonfly represents summer, instability, unreliability, and weakness. However, in Feng Shui, the dragonfly seems to have a more uplifting and powerful meaning. The dragonfly is said to mean "The Soul of the Dragon." Because the dragon means ultimate happiness in Chinese culture, the dragonfly is a powerful symbol of happiness, wisdom, and harmony.

Swedish Folklore: The dragonfly flies around the neck as a way to measure the value of the soul.

There are other cultures, including the Celtic and Japanese, that revere the dragonfly as a positive, powerful ancient being.

References

Breeze, Sunny. "Feng Shui Symbols And Their Meanings | Feng Shui Articles." *Sunnyray.Org*, 2020, https://www.sunnyray.org/Feng-shui-symbols-and-their-meanings.htm.

Buettner, Dan. *The Blue Zones Solution: Eating and Living Like the World's Healthiest People*. National Geographic Books, 2015.

Campbell, Joseph. *The Hero With a Thousand Faces*. Princeton, N.J.: Princeton University Press, 1972.

Clifford, Garth. "Dragonfly Symbolism & Meaning (+Totem, Spirit & Omens) | World Birds." *World Birds*, https://www.worldbirds.org/dragonfly-symbolism/.

Cooper, J. C. *An Illustrated Encyclopaedia Of Traditional Symbols*. 1st ed., Thames & Hudson, 1978, p. 56.

Dispenza, Joe. *Becoming Supernatural: How Common People Are Doing the Uncommon*. 1st edition. Carlsbad, California: Hay House, Inc., 2017.

"Empathy." *Merriam-Webster.com* Dictionary, Merriam-Webster, https://www.merriam-webster.com/dictionary/empathy. Accessed 21 Dec. 2020.

Insidetrackalmanac.Com, https://www.insidetrackalmanac.com/post/2019/08/23/thank-a-dragonfly-today

Nelson, Bradley. *The Emotion Code: How to Release Your Trapped Emotions for Abundant Health, Love, and Happiness*. Vermilion, 2019.

O'Connell, Mark et al. *The Illustrated Encyclopedia Of Symbols, Signs, & Dream Interpretation.* 2nd ed., Fall River Press, 2009, p. 196.

Red Dragonflies | Maple Hill Chapels/Talarski Funeral Home | West Hartford CT Funeral Home And Cremation, https://www.maplehillchapels-talarskifuneralhome.com/red-dragonflies

Redish, Laura. "Native American Indian Dragonfly Legends, Meaning And Symbolism From The Myths Of Many Tribes." *Native-Languages.Org,* http://www.native-languages.org/legends-dragonfly.htm.

Tolle, Eckhart. *The Power of Now.* 1997. Preface to the Paperback. California: New World Library, 2004.

Zielinski, Sarah. "14 Fun Facts About Dragonflies". Smithsonian Magazine, https://www.smithsonianmag.com/science-nature/14-fun-facts-about-dragonflies-96882693/.

About the Author

Stefani Milan has published seven other books across multiple genres, including Children's Fiction, Self-help, and adult fiction (under the pen name R.A. Milan). She graduated from Rutgers University Camden with high honors, an English Degree, and the Betty Harris Jones English Department Award. Her search for spiritual truth began in 2010 when she immersed herself in a host of spiritual teachings. The tragic loss of her mother forced her to create a new version of herself, but she is always evolving, as is her writing. When she is not writing or traveling, her free time is spent studying books about metaphysics, psychology, neuroscience, nutrition, alternative healing, and spirituality. She tries to bring an element of all she has learned into her writing. She resides in New Jersey, where she lives with her husband, her rescued-cats, and her dog.